FOOD AND FAITH

FOOD AND FAITH

A Pilgrim's Journey through India

SHOBA NARAYAN

HarperCollins *Publishers* India

First published in India in 2020 by
HarperCollins *Publishers*
A-75, Sector 57, Noida, Uttar Pradesh 201301, India
www.harpercollins.co.in

2 4 6 8 10 9 7 5 3 1

P-ISBN: 978-93-5357-903-6
E-ISBN: 978-93-5357-904-3

Typeset in 11.5/16.2 Adobe Garamond Pro at
Manipal Technologies Limited, Manipal

Printed and bound at
Thomson Press (India) Ltd

Dedicated to Lakshmi, Krishnan, Arvind, Nithya and Ryan,
fellow travellers on countless pilgrimages all over India,
and most especially to
Siddhartha Yarine Rodriguez-Krishnan—welcome to the world!

Contents

Introduction

THIS BOOK BEGAN AS a food book before it morphed into one on faith. Two decades ago, editor Kamini Mahadevan approached me to write a book called 'Sacred Food'. The idea, she said, would be to link food and faith. I would visit Hindu pilgrim sites and write about the sacred food or 'prasadam'.

We made a list of temples with signature foods and then chose amongst them. Tirupati laddu, for example, was nixed because it was overexposed. The whole world knew about Tirumala Tirupati temple and its prasadam. Instead, we decided to choose lesser known temples, trying to balance regions and tastes.

The original list only had Hindu temples, because the idea of prasadam was specific to Hinduism.

I started with a simple calculation. I would visit those temples that had good prasadam or sacred food offerings. These are, literally, foods for the gods, which belong to a time, place and a specific deity. After offering it to God, the devotees partake of this 'gracious gift of God'. I had routinely visited temples all my life and partaken of the prasadam. My ancestors originated in Palghat and so Kerala temples and their thick fragrant ghee (nei) payasams were practically a summer's rite of passage, year after year. I grew up in Chennai, so Tamil temples with their rice and lentil prasadam (*chitra anna*, or rice varieties, and *chundal* or chickpeas seasoned with coconut, raw mango and lemon) were part of our family's beat.

Using food as an anchor and guide seemed like a good way to parse the hundreds of thousands of Hindu temples in India, each with specific creation-myths, rituals and, yes, recipes. If nothing else, I would eat well.

(Let me just add here that although in North India, words are shortened of their ending, I have chosen to go the South Indian route here so prasad becomes prasadam and ganga-jal becomes ganga-jalam.)

An interesting thing happened as I traversed the world of Hindu temple prasadams. I discovered that while the food was interesting, my journey also prompted larger questions about faith and its place in our lives and society. And that is what this book eventually became: a pilgrim's quest into the world of faith told through food.

When I began writing the book, it was mostly about Hindu temples and their prasadams. And so it has remained, with a few exceptions. There is a saying in Hinduism that applies to pilgrimages: You can only go to a temple when the god 'calls' you. In that same spirit, some of the other faiths that make up India 'called' me through a series of fortunate incidents that resulted in chapters of this book.

Jainism and Zoroastrianism haven't made it to the book for a variety of reasons. I have visited their shrines and interviewed experts, and I am in the process of compiling these into chapters. I will have to wait to send them out to the world: perhaps as a sequel.

In the end, this is a book largely about Hinduism written by a (sceptical) Hindu who seeks to answer larger questions about faith. Like the below.

What is the role of religion in your life today? Do you pray? How do you pray? Do you commune with the divine through rituals? Is it through chanting verses in Aramaic, Arabic or Sanskrit? Or is it a comforting routine—going to the mosque, church or temple once a week or month? Is religion part of your identity? Or is it something that you seek to distance yourself from? Is it an occasional activity that you do out of habit or because your parents ask you to? Or is it simply a connection with your heritage, home and ancestors? Do you think religion is a private act or can it be part of the public discourse? Are these questions making you uncomfortable?

These are the questions that came up during the many pilgrimages that I undertook. These are the questions that I sought to answer in my writing.

As it turns out, the religion that I was born into, Hinduism, has answers for many of the above questions. It is also an imaginative faith, full of myth and folklore, rituals that incorporate lights, lamps, flowers, music, dance and sacred food.

All religions share broad strokes. They talk about developing courage, character and tenacity to cope with the ups and downs of life. Faith, at its best, is about giving strength and succour.

I am a Hindu. It defines who I am, perhaps not as much as feminism, and certainly not as much as being a writer or a mother. But if I had to list out the top five things that are part of my identity, it would be part of the list.

Around the time I began visiting temples to write about their sacred food, I decided to figure out my faith. I wanted to figure out how I felt about the Hindu rituals and practices that I had dismissed as being patriarchal. I re-read the marvellous and imaginative Hindu myths that I had heard from my grandmother as a child. And I talked to many experts about my religion.

After being an atheist as a teenager, agnostic in my twenties and thirties, I turned to religion late in life. As the mother of two young daughters, the daughter of fairly religious, traditional, South Indian parents and in-laws, I had to come to terms with my religion, and indeed, all religions. Instead of avoiding and disdaining faith, I had to find a way to include it in my life. For my children's sake. For my parents' sake.

Food seemed like an innocuous way to do this. Sacred food as a way of fusing a secular identity with spirituality in some form: that was my plan. What I didn't know, what I didn't anticipate, is that once you step into the realm of faith, your heart and emotions open in ways that you cannot predict or control. You'll see.

There is one caveat that I would like to make here: As a deeply secular person, I find caste mentions abhorrent. But it is hard to get away from that in certain areas—crafts and textiles, for instance, are linked so much to caste. As is faith/religion. It is hard not to talk about caste when you write about religion.

Let me tell you what this book is not. It is not a scholar's guide to religion or food. Rather it is a *sceptical seeker's pilgrimage* to understand her faith. *And like I said, while a few other faiths make cameo appearances, this is largely a book on Hinduism.*

I hope that you, dear reader, will accompany me on this journey. Your questions may be different than mine, but together we will discover food, faith and, through them, India. Or our version of India anyway.

1

Udupi: The Boy Who Stole Butter

I AM IN THE sanctum sanctorum of the Krishna temple in Udupi. My mother holds my hand, leading me towards God, as she has done since childhood. I purse my lips and sigh, an irritated child led by an enthusiastic, itinerant mother on pointless pilgrimages. Now, as an adult, I am irritated with my irritation. I should be over this.

I do the next best thing. I inflict the same thing on my protesting children. I drag them on periodic pilgrimages to temples in hot, humid, Indian towns with multiple-consonant names (Thiruvudaimarudhur—try saying *that*). Names that make the tongue contort itself into yoga poses.

I belong to a traditional Hindu family where visiting temples occurred with boring frequency. As children, my brother and I had no choice but to participate.

There were the annual visits to the Bhagavathi (or goddess) temple where my ancestors came from, or rather 'hailed from', as we say in India. We went, first as mewling infants, to have our heads shaved by the village barber. There were pilgrimages to specific temples upon the advice of our family astrologer. Whenever there was a malefic planet, casting aspersions on some aspect of my horoscope—the ability to get married, for instance—my parents would drag me to a temple to light ghee lamps in a hollowed-out half-cut lemon. There were other things a believer could do: circumnavigate the temple 101 times or climb a sacred hill as a kind of cure or compensation. By torturing ourselves, we told the planet to lay off torturing us.

The last type of pilgrimage was to visit *ishta devata*s or favoured deities, not for any particular reason but simply to add good karma to the proverbial coffer. It was for this reason that my mother and I were in Udupi. My brother was to have come with us, but he suddenly developed flu symptoms and begged off the trip.

'There is a limit to the number of temples you can visit in a lifetime,' my brother and I would mutter to each other as teenagers.

In India though, there isn't. There are millions of temples in India, with new ones springing up with astonishing frequency. Down the road from where I live in Bengaluru is a new temple, built beside a garbage dump. Its construction has my cousin in Silicon Valley hopping mad.

'Why do they spend thousands of dollars on building yet another new temple when they could just as well use the money to clean up the garbage?' he asks when he visits us. 'How will India ever improve if God is prioritized above garbage? If temples are prioritized over trash cans?'

Such a question doesn't make sense to the faithful. Garbage in India is a fact of life. God, however, is a pathway to the divine. Why mix up one with the other?

'Will you stop eating because you have constipation?' asked an uncle. 'If one side is clogged with garbage, that does not mean that you cannot partake of the other.'

So how many temples are there in India?

An estimate of the total number of temples in India varies widely. Some say that India has 1,08,000 temples, which seems like an understatement given that my street in Bengaluru has five temples within a stone's throw. Multiply a temple per street with India's 400 large cities, 5,000 towns, and 6,40,000 villages, and the total number of temples in India runs into millions. For Indians, every place along the Ganga river is considered sacred, as is pretty much the entire Himalayan mountain range. Add to that, sacred groves, sacred street corners, sacred trees—you get the picture.

Given this abundance of temples, most families end up having a beat. Just like you choose certain travel destinations to suit your lifestyle, Hindu families choose certain temples to visit on a regular basis.

Udupi is part of my mother's regular beat. She has visited the temple twice annually for the past twenty years.

Keeper of cows, the cloud-skinned god

So here I am, staring at Krishna, the dark-skinned one whom some call Shyam (after whom my brother is named), the multifaceted god who stole butter, danced with milkmaids and yet rendered one of Hindu philosophy's most profound texts, the Bhagavad Gita.

Krishna is one of the most compelling gods in Hinduism, but here in Udupi, he stands as Bala Krishna, young and innocent, holding churned butter in one hand.

Sandalwood and the sea

Udupi is a small, dusty town, no different from those dotting interior India. Its temple and cuisine, however, hold an outsize place in the local, regional, national and even international imagination. Situated between the Arabian Sea and the Western Ghats, Udupi was founded in the thirteenth century by the Hindu saint-philosopher Madhavacharya.

The Krishna temple here has many legends associated with it. One begins in Dwaraka at the time of a great flood. The temple is submerged. Along with it, the Krishna idol falls into the ocean. It is by then covered by the sandalwood used for the daily *abhisheka* or ritual bath and floats away. Many decades pass. A ship discovers the sandalwood-laiden structure on a beach, not knowing that there is a Krishna idol inside it. The captain decides to use it as a ballast and sails south. He encounters a storm. Enter the saint, Madhavacharya, who senses something important in the ship. He waves his yellow robe and guides the ship to safety. The grateful captain gives Madhava the sandalwood ballast. Over days and months, Madhava chips away at the sandalwood, discovers the infant Krishna idol inside and installs it at the Udupi temple. Therefore, the idol is also referred to as Gopi Chandan.

The other story has to do with Kanakadasa, a famous bhakti composer, whose songs are still sung in the state. He was a Kuruba shepherd and was denied entry into the temple. He would stand behind the temple and sing songs. One day, *while Kanakadasa was singing praises of the lord*, the rear wall collapsed and the Krishna idol turned 180 degrees to face *the devotee*—the cavity in the wall is still there and is referred to as Kanakadasa's window or Kanakana-kindi.

'Look, how the Lord turned to yield to the prayers of a simple devotee,' says my mother as she peers through the window.

Probably an earthquake that caused the wall to collapse and the idol to turn, the sceptic in me thinks as I peer through the window.

What makes you a believer, one of the faithful? Some of it has to do with age, I think. When you are young, you have boundless confidence and believe yourself to be infallible, unconquerable. It is only when life gives you some hard knocks, when events happen that are beyond your control, when health takes a beating, or when you have, in some cases, an accident or near-death experience, that you begin to question your assumptions. Some people turn to God at this stage; some are born again, as Christians say. I am not there yet.

The link between food and faith

So we go, my family and I, year after year, to say hello to Krishna, but really to scarf down the masala dosas, which originated in this picturesque strip of land between the Arabian Sea and the Western Ghats. With its fame, the dosa carried the Udupi prefix to restaurants across the globe. There are Udupi cafés all over the world. All serve vegetarian Indian food, including masala dosas, which began as a sly filling to stymy orthodox Brahmin priests.

According to the book *The Udupi Kitchen* by Malati Srinivasan and Geetha Rao, the masala filling that is hidden within the fold of the dosa came about because the sautéed onions that complement the potato filling were considered taboo by orthodox Brahmins.

Previously, the dosas were served with chutney and plain potato palya, as it is called here in Karnataka. With changing food tastes, the people wanted to eat their cake, or in this case onions, but had to hide it within the dosa.

Today, the masala dosa routinely makes it to buckets lists such as the 'top ten foods to eat before you die'. Rightfully so, in my opinion, as an avid masala dosa eater and self-described dosa connoisseur. Magazines anoint it as one of the world's most delicious foods.

A rockstar temple?

As temples go, Udupi is both important and innocuous. It isn't a rockstar temple like Tirupati or Badrinath. Udupi is important because it is here that an important branch of Indian philosophy originated.

In the thirteenth century, after the advent of advaita and vishishtadvaita, came the third big school of Hindu philosophy called dvaita—and this is where the Udupi connection comes in. Dvaita is often explained as dualism. It says that humans are different from God and the human spirit yearns to reach God.

It was formulated by Madhavacharya who was born in Udupi. Madhava is huge in Udupi. Wherever you go, people talk about him, almost as if he were alive. 'He was such a great debater,' says an elderly pilgrim I meet while standing in the queue. 'Went all over India and defeated the Advaita philosophers.' He glanced around as if Madhava would materialize next to us any minute.

Madhava doesn't materialize, but many of the faithful walk in with folded hands, worry and hope writ large on their face. They don't care about Madhava and his philosophy about how to reach God. They merely want their problems solved, so they come with sincere faith, with wholehearted bhakti, in the hope that this infant god will make their problems go away. As intermediaries, there are the numerous temple priests, who just happen to be Madhava's successors.

Madhava had a smart succession plan. After his time, he said, worship at the Udupi temple would be taken over by not one, but eight students, who would all take turns doing priestly duties for the lord. This tradition continues with the *ashta-matha*s (*ashta* means eight; the word *matha* translates to monastery, but also means a spiritual gathering or community) that administer the temple by rotation.

Never go hungry, O faithful devotee

These eight spiritual centres take over the administration of the temple for a defined period—typically, two years. The handover of the administration happens with great pomp and circumstance, and involves feeding some 15,000 people every day during the handover. For this reason, this temple's god is called Anna Brahma or the creator of rice/food. As grand as that sounds, there is perhaps a more prosaic reason for the focus on food. Here, the lord is an infant, and the best way to make a child stick around is to offer him great food at all times of day. The temple makes a variety of prasadams to satiate this flighty child god.

The rules of cooking the Lord's food are clear, if constrained by rules of tradition and consistency of recipes. Udupi cuisine is robustly vegetarian. It forgoes meat and fish, and even onion and garlic, focusing instead on whole grains and vegetables that are hyperlocal and seasonal. No foreign vegetable is allowed. This means no carrot, cauliflower, beetroot, radish or tomato. Everything has to be indigenous.

One specialty is the round, green eggplant or brinjal (called mattu gulla) that grows only in a nearby hamlet. This brinjal is sliced, soaked in salt water (brine) to preserve its colour and prevent it from oxidizing and becoming dark, then stuffed with a mixture of fenugreek, cumin seeds, red chillies, tamarind, salt and grated coconut. The stuffed brinjal is then fried in coconut oil—the oil that is now the darling of the beauty world. Gwyneth Paltrow says that she douses her hair and skin with coconut oil to soften and nourish. Well, the people of Udupi cook with copious amounts of coconut oil, which is perhaps why their skin is radiant and their hair long and lustrous.

A variety of lentils are used for protein. These are typically mixed with gourd or pumpkin, with green chillies, asafoetida and curry leaves added for flavour. The seeds and skin of the white pumpkin are ground with buttermilk and served as a summer drink. When pineapples are in season, they too are cooked with black sesame seeds, red chillies, lentils and fenugreek seeds to make a flavourful, aromatic relish.

Udupi cuisine is famous for its chutneys, including one using yams, colocasia leaves and the skin of ridge gourd. Served on a banana leaf, poured over hot white rice with a dollop of ghee, it tastes divine. Udupi vegetable curries are made from jackfruit, plantain, colocasia and other unusual root vegetables. The sauces are spicy from the local Byadgi red chillies, sour from the tamarind and sweet from the pinch of jaggery that is almost always added to the dishes. Most distinctive of all, however, is the gojju: a spicy, sweet—sour gravy that contains ground sesame seeds, coconut, jaggery and a local spice mix the base ingredient of which could be vegetables such as pumpkin and bitter gourd or fruits such as pineapple.

Monsoon Moorings

The faithful in Udupi eat locally and seasonally for religious and regional reasons. Rains lash this fertile strip of land during four months from late July to early November, cutting it off from the rest of the world. This has led to a cuisine that is almost macrobiotic in its adherence to local, seasonal foods.

Traditional Hindus in Udupi don't eat certain foods during these four monsoon months, a tradition of abstinence that seems at odds in this age when New Zealand apples and Malta oranges are airlifted to every region of India. They call this the 'chatur-masya vratha'. The phrase means four-month austerities, and perhaps began out of necessity. You have to hunker down in one place during the monsoon, and certain foods would have simply not been available. The protocol itself seems rather strict and forbidding, but intuitive once you get used to it. It is as rigid as those keto or paleo diets that many of us have experimented with.

Some say that the practice began with Lord Buddha, who observed these four-month austerities some 3,860 years ago and set the tone for the sanyasis who followed. The logic was this. During the rainy season, a large number of insects breed on earth. If you happen to be a wandering monk, chances are that you are going to stomp on these insects, which goes against the code of nonviolence held dear by the Buddha and other ascetics. Hindu monks therefore decided to stay in one ashram during these four months and read religious texts or hold satsangs.

Feasting and fasting per the Hindu calendar

The Hindu lunar calendar overlaps the Gregorian one at about the halfway point, by which I mean, for example, that the lunar month of Pausa/Paush/or Thai in Tamil starts around 15 January give or take a day. Each Hindu month straddles two 'English' or Gregorian months.

Fasting or even giving up certain food items has a lot of merit in Hinduism. The monsoon heralds both the feasting and fasting months.

July–August (the month of Shravana): No shak, leafy greens and other vegetables.

August–September (Hindu month of Bhadrapada, also known as Bhado): No curds.

September–October (Aswayuja): No milk products.

October–November (Karthika): No lentils or pulses.

These four months also mark India's festive calendar. So there is literally feasting by one section of the population and fasting by another. The feasting and fasting involve certain prescribed foods. In the first month, which happens to be when Krishna's birthday falls, devotees make a lot of milk-based sweets. Leafy greens don't fare well in the rainy season anyway, so no one really misses eating them. Similarly, in the last month of Karthika, which happens to be when the famous Navratri (the Nine Nights of the Goddess) worship happens, people offer a variety of rice dishes each day: lemon rice, coconut rice, curd rice, tamarind rice, sesame rice, jaggery rice and so on. None requires lentils.

A naturopath once told me that a good way to get rid of toxins was to give up certain types of foods for a while to see what impact it had on your body. So you give up gluten one month, dairy the next, meat in the third month and fish in the fourth. The Hindu monsoon diet is broadly akin to this.

Why this vratha, this restriction? The story from the Skanda Purana: Brahma Khanda, goes thus:

Narada asked Brahma, the creator, about the importance of the chaturmasya vratha. Brahma said, 'Chaturmasya is the period of four months during which Lord Vishnu is believed to take rest in the *ksheer sagar* or milky ocean. So quite naturally, all the oceans, rivers and ponds are believed to attain divinity due to the presence of Lord Vishnu during this period.'

More practically, as I said, the monsoon rains cause perambulating brahmins to stay put in one place and perform austerities.

Seeking and finding comfort in the cocoon that is a Hindu temple

It is 11 a.m., and the granite floors and pillars offer cool respite from the heat outside. Devotees line up quietly, muttering prayers, hands clasped together fervently. It is a scene familiar to anyone who has visited a temple in India. Swishing saris, the smell of sandal and incense, topless Brahmin priests hurrying between idol and devotee, clanging bells, chanting men and women. For the faithful, Hindu temples inspire devotion, hope and a preternatural peace that descends in spite of the surrounding chaos, as if generations of muttered prayers have muted the soul into peaceful surrender.

The Krishna temple in Udupi is no different. It isn't very crowded on that June morning. My mother and I are pretty much left alone to pray in peace. We walk around the sanctum sanctorum many times and peer at the idol. No hustling priests, no crushing crowds, no furtive glances suggesting a small donation for closer access to the deity. It is just us in quiet communion with the lord.

In one corner, a group of ladies sit in a circle, singing Krishna songs and stringing garlands with lightning fingers. They have separated yellow marigolds from green tulsi leaves, jasmine from tuberose and each woman takes a flower or leaf to string together or alternately. Several string fragrant jasmine flowers—Jasminum sambac or what we call gundu-malli in South India—in garlands. In the opposite corner, a visiting group spreads out their tanpuras and dholaks before commencing a spirited Krishna bhajan.

Near the temple tank, one of the hubs of activity, there are men in dhotis bathing, praying and performing rituals. One monk, clad in saffron robes, sits by himself, singing a bhajan that is remarkably soothing.

My mother and I sit leaning against the pillars, listening to bhajan mixing with folk song, breathing in incense mixing with the smells of jasmine and coconut, watching idly the run-off stream of milk and honey and holy water that is used to bathe the idol every morning. After a while, my mother repeats the phrase that countless others say after their communion with God.

'Let's go eat.'

Udupi's prasadam

Hinduism, like many great religions, is about feasting and fasting, praying and, it must be said, eating prasadam. The Udupi temple is part of the famed pilgrim's triumvirate of Udupi-Sringeri-Dharmasthala, all of which serve very good food to thronging devotees. Udupi's temple food is the best, the faithful tell me. We walk out and turn left to the feeding halls, my mother leading me with the expertise of having spent a lifetime visiting temples.

Indians are funny that way. The elderly in China play mah-jong. American senior citizens go on cruises and play golf. Europeans visit museums, tour wineries and dine at Michelin-star restaurants. Indian elders visit temples. Pilgrimages are a big part of their lives, as I see daily with my septuagenarian aunts and uncles, not to mention my mother. For her latest birthday, I offered my mother the choice between a two-week trip through Europe or a week through interior

Maharashtra to visit one of the twelve jyotirlingam shrines to Lord Shiva. She chose Shiva over the Sistine Chapel.

Udupi is part of my mother's regular beat since the Mookambika Temple of Kollur (which happens to be our family deity) is in the same area. She has been visiting the temple twice annually for the past twenty years. En route to her devi, she usually stops to see Krishna.

So we hurry, mom and I, down the corridor, to the feeding area.

'The Brahmins are fed separately. Upstairs,' my mother says.

I wince.

Guilt and solace

Let me just come right out and say it. Although I grew up in a devout Hindu family, I am uneasy about my religion—about all religions for that matter—for all the usual reasons. Faith gives solace, for sure, but it also inspires guilt. Religion brings people together, but also divides them. It gives peace and causes war; it hurts and heals. Since I come from a fairly traditional, devout, Tamil Brahmin family, I don't express my antipathy very much. Instead I disengage, to the extent that it is possible, in a religious family such as mine.

I follow my mother up the stairs to the separate area where we, as Brahmins, will be fed. 'What about "in the eyes of God, all are equal"?,' I feel like asking my mother, but she is racing up the stairs.

The hall is huge, and people are sitting cross-legged on the floor. Young, good-looking boys exuding what my mother calls *tejas*, or radiance, stride through the hall carrying giant containers holding rice, rasam, vegetables, sweets and ghee. We take our places. Banana leaves are placed before us. Then a veritable feast with all the regional delicacies appears. There are spicy pakoras, sweet payasams, brinjal gojjus, jackfruit curry, several chutneys, kosambari salads and a mound of rice in the centre.

A priest walks down the corridor. With his fair skin and a bright red vermilion dot in the centre of his forehead, he looks resplendent in a purple silk dhoti. Behind him are a line of young ascetics. I stretch my upturned palm like the rest of the congregation. The chief priest pours a little holy water into my palm, which I assume is to wash my hand.

'Drink it,' my mother hisses.

So I do, wondering if the water is safe.

'Govinda,' says my neighbour, uttering one of the many names of Krishna, this one meaning 'the one who protects cows'.

'Govinda,' I repeat obediently.

Govinda is one of the names of Vishnu. The Vishnu names I know by heart are the twelve that my grandfather used to recite while doing his sandhya vandanam or evening prayer. They are:

1. Keshava: The one with long, matted locks.
2. Narayana: The one who gives refuge.
3. Madhava: The one who gives knowledge.
4. Govinda: The one who knows and cares for cows.
5. Vishnave: The protector in the Divine Trinity.
6. Madhusudhana: The killer of the demon Madhu.
7. Trivikrama: The one who lifted his legs so he could conquer the three worlds—heaven, earth and the underworld.
8. Vamana: An avatar of Vishnu.
9. Shridhara: The beautiful lord of love.
10. Rishikesha: The master of senses.
11. Padmanabha: The one whose navel is shaped like a lotus.
12. Damodhara: The one who had a cord tied around his waist as a child.

Each name has a story behind it—of battles fought, demons subdued, benediction given, wisdom dispensed, compassion offered and devotees charmed.

The food is delicious. Barring the jackfruit curry, which must be an acquired taste, I polish it all up. Udupi is justly famous for its rasam, and this one doesn't disappoint—piquant with a lovely spicy, lemony flavour. I take a second serving of the rasam, then a third.

A young boy comes and distributes ₹10 bills to all of us as *dakshina* or fee for eating the meal.

We end the meal as we began it: with holy water poured on our upturned palms.

Takeaway

After I returned from Udupi, I decided to do two things. Both involved denial. Once a fortnight, on Ekadashi (the eleventh day of the waxing and waning fortnight), I would fast. This meant not eating anything and drinking just water through the day. Oh, and napping a lot. I did this for a year regularly, and continue to do it intermittently.

The trick is to make religion an ally instead of rebelling against it. If fasting on Ekadashi gave me good karma, fine. But shedding a few pounds was a more immediate goal.

The second was to eat seasonally, which in today's world meant *not* eating certain foods, even though they were available in the supermarket because they were wrapped in polythene and were clearly imported from Thailand. Frankly, I am not sure of the benefits of seasonal eating. I am not even sure that the seasonal fruits and vegetables that I consciously choose taste better than the dragon fruit imported from Thailand, the New Zealand apples, Malta oranges or Washington cherries. But if such a practice is good enough for a community that gave rise to one of Hinduism's greatest philosophers and the creators of the iconic masala dosa, it is good enough for me.

So I persisted—and still do—with my banana stems, young jackfruit, seasonal greens and tender peas, but only when they are in season, cheaply and abundantly available.

Let me see if this turns me into an enlightened soul. For now, I'll simply settle for a lightened body.

2

Kashi: Living and Dying in the Centre of the Hindu Universe

A DEAD COW IS floating down the river Ganga. She is a black and white Holstein Friesian cow, like the one I own in Bengaluru. She floats sideways, legs spreadeagled. Half of her face is visible, even though it is dark—7 p.m. I wish I could say that she looks peaceful, but her teeth are bared as if hurt.

Some 100 boats filled with Indian and foreign tourists are converging on the Dasha Ashwamedha Ghat for the evening Ganga aarti, the spectacle that is the culmination of daily religious life in most of North India. The cow floats amidst the boats, forcing embarrassed guides into stuttering, apologetic explanations in Spanish, French, Russian, Hebrew and English.

'Sometimes when people have a pet cow that died and they cannot afford to bury or cremate her, they simply throw her into the Ganga,' says our guide. He stares at our horrified faces and shrugs. 'Ganga is the mother. She accepts everything.'

Would the Ganga river have been better served had we imagined her to be our child rather than mother? What if our ancients imagined the Ganga to be a daughter, or better yet, given the Indian preference for male heirs, a son? Would we have taken better care of Ganga, our child, than we do of Mother Ganga? Too late. Rationality cannot alter lore. Myths are carved in stone, and certainly one that is so braided into the Indian psyche cannot be morphed so easily, even if it might potentially help the river.

The revealed texts: The Vedas

These are moot questions, whispers into the mists of time that date back to 1500 BC when the Vedas were 'revealed'—not written or composed, but revealed—to Hindu rishis (more on that later). The first Veda, the Rig Veda, mentions the Ganga, but only a few times. The most famous reference to the Ganga in the Rig Veda comes from the 'Nadistuti Sukta', or the 'hymn in praise of the rivers'. Even that mentions the Ganga somewhere in the middle, along with nineteen other rivers—including the Saraswati, Yamuna, Purushni, Asikni and Gomati.

The hymn is predominantly in praise of the river Sindhu or Indus, described as the mightiest of all rivers into which other roaring rivers run 'like mothers to their calves', not calves to their mothers as I first mistakenly thought. The Sindhu—which flows flashing and white, with ample volume, whose roar can be heard to the heavens, which bellows like a bull, and which is beautiful like a steed. Ganga is just part of a list in these early days of Hinduism.

Unlike other ancient literature like the Egyptian *Book of the Dead*, recorded on papyrus, or the Sumerian tale, *Epic of Gilgamesh*, often called the first story in the world, recorded on carved tablets, the Vedas were not written down until much later. They were not even believed to be composed by humans. They were heard, rather seen, as visions, by Hindu sages, who were therefore called seers. For this reason, the Vedas are apaurasya or authorless—revealed texts that were grasped by Hindu seers as fully formed philosophies or insights about the world. The Vedas have been preserved as shruti or listened literature in exactly the same form—unchanged words, the exact same metre and intonation—for millennia.

He who lifts one foot to the sky

It is only later, when stories and myths were compiled into the Puranas, that the Ganga gains importance. Her creation myth, depicted in the Bhagavatha Purana, is spectacular and goes thus: To teach a lesson to an arrogant king called Mahabali, Lord Vishnu lifts one of his feet heavenward in the trivikrama pose, and pierces the sky with his toenail. Like piercing an egg, this causes the milk of human creation—the Ganga—to flow downwards from the upper reaches of the cosmos into Brahma Loka—the heavens, where Brahma, the creator, resides. (In some versions, the Ganga is imagined as the Milky Way. The gods enjoy her fertile waters, and she enjoys her stay and status in heaven.)

Several millennia later, on earth, a dutiful son, King Bhagiratha, is in a quandary. He has discovered that 60,000 of his ancestors are trapped in the netherworld because of a sage's curse. They cannot even attempt reaching heaven. The dutiful son performs a lot of austerities, which please Brahma. Brahma tells him that the only way his ancestors can ascend to heaven is if the purifying waters of the Ganga touch them. Bhagiratha begs Brahma for help, who in turn orders Ganga to fall to earth. Ganga is reluctant to leave the heavens, but cannot refuse. Brahma is, after all, the creator, her father. The problem is that the impact of her descent will smash the earth to smithereens—wash it away in a great cascade of water. So Bhagiratha prays again, this time to Shiva, begging him to cushion Ganga's fall by absorbing her into his long, matted locks. This scene is seen in a wonderful painting by Raja Ravi Varma; there stands Shiva with the six-pack abs that have been imitated by Bollywood since. His long, matted locks flow out; a leopard skin is wrapped around his waist, a snake curls around his neck. Shiva gazes upwards as the Ganga rushes down. He wraps her in his hair, allowing only a small trickle to fall to earth.

Man subduing woman—is that the message here? I feel like asking. Then again, ancient mythology in most cultures was written by men. Women play secondary roles that we only now are viewing as misguided stereotypes.

Hindu myths are a little more inclusive. There are enough Durgas and Yoginis who will ruthlessly kill the bad guy and swallow his blood if they need to, like Kali did with Raktabeeja, the demon.

So Ganga hits the earth. With folded hands, Bhagiratha leads her to the netherworld where she purifies the souls of all 60,000 of his ancestors, allowing them to make their journey upwards to the heavens. No wonder all Hindus want to have a dip in this holy water—touched by Vishnu's feet, Shiva's hair and Brahma's command, she is the liquid goddess linked to the divine trinity in Hindu mythology.

As far as legends go, the story of how Ganga came to be is hard to beat or duplicate. The sad thing is that her story is so removed from her current state.

Cows in a river

The dead cow irritates me on many levels. Cleaning the Ganga is a Gargi Vachnavian or Greta Thunbergian task! Or should I choose from Indian myths instead of Greek and say Bhagirathan task? This dead cow with her wide-open eyes symbolizes everything that is impossible about this venture. Why couldn't this cow have been given to a slaughterhouse? Did the poor farmer who owned it live in a state that banned the killing of the cow? Why couldn't he have cremated the cow instead? Did he love the animal so much that he wanted it to attain salvation through the holy waters of this river? Or was it simple economics? He didn't have the money to deal with her death. Tossing her into the Ganga was an easy option: faith and desperation leading him to throw the dead animal into the waters, polluting them further.

The place where horses were sacrificed

At the Dasha Ashwamedha (Ten Horse Sacrifice) Ghat, the Ganga aarti is about to begin. The boats are fitted against each other like a jigsaw puzzle, to form an arc that faces the bank. In the next boat, two young women—American by the sound of their accent—sit cross-legged on the wooden boat, chatting with their guide. Ahead of us, on the steps of the ghat, a huge crowd of people has gathered. In the buildings behind them are billboards with photographs: actor Sunny Deol posing, as if in a Calvin Klein ad, selling 'Cozy' underwear to religious tourists who want to elevate their minds.

Those of us on the boats are a captive audience, or, as it turns out to be, customers. Within a few minutes, an energetic group of children balance their way across the boats, carrying bamboo baskets filled with ice water, candles to float on the Ganga, matchboxes, incense and photographs of gods.

One young boy, who looks about seven years old, entreats the two American women near me to buy his wares, in broken English.

'This candy (he means candle) very nice,' he says, holding up a leaf cup inside which nestles a small tea candle amidst a bed of yellow marigolds.

It is a beautiful arrangement, Balinese in its simplicity, handmade and tenuous—a floating candle, carrying wishes and hopes into the Ganga.

'You buy? Good price,' the boy says.

The two American women shake their heads even though he is charging them the same price that he charges everyone: ₹10. Hardened by beggars and touts who swarm around them, warned by guides about bargaining for anything sold to foreigners in India, they fail to recognize a good deal. I feel sorry for the kid and buy six candles, even though I don't intend to float them on the already overburdened Ganga.

Seven men, seven fires

A male voice begins singing over the loudspeaker. Seven priests, all male, take their positions at different points on the broad ghat. They depict the Sapta Rishis, or seven primordial sages. They follow the protocol of a puja, beginning with flowers, then incense, then a lamp with a single wick, then a beautiful multilayered lamp with a tiered pyramid of wicks, all shining in the darkness. In synchronized movements, the seven priests lift the shining pyramids of flickering lamps, face the river and move their arms round and round in a clockwise circle. A group of men paying homage to a woman goddess.

All religions are male-dominated. Hinduism is no different. I have never seen a woman priest in any Hindu temple. I resent the fact that the Ganga aarti does not even have a token woman as participant—a woman singer at least?

'Here, have a peda,' says our guide, opening a box. 'It is from the Hanuman temple.'

In Kashi, sacred food is everywhere. The peda (a type of sweetmeat) is delicious, and we chew it contentedly while watching the priests do their synchronized movements—like chewing popcorn at a movie. The aarti lasts about half an hour. At the end, I search for the cow, wishing I had photographed it.

'*Gaay? Woh chali gayi,*' says the boatman casually. The cow? It has gone.

'At least it is better than those corpses we used to see floating in the Ganga,' says our guide soothingly.

We take the motor boat upstream to Assi Ghat where my hotel is. Along the way, we see a dead buffalo right by the bank of Harishchandra Ghat, which, along with Manikarnika Ghat, comprises the two crematoriums on the Ganga. Somehow, this doesn't horrify as much, perhaps because it is at the banks of a crematorium. A remnant corpse, even if it happens to be an animal, left behind, perhaps by a poor farmer, who couldn't pay for its funeral.

A few yards upstream, a couple is immersing themselves into the river. Like most devotees, the man is bare-torsoed, with a cloth wrapped around his midriff. The woman is fully clothed in a maroon sari and mustard-yellow blouse. She wades into the water and dunks her head in. The man does this three times. Can't they see the dead buffalo to their left?

'So many people take a bath every day in the Ganga. They don't fall sick. It is the power of belief,' says our guide in explanation.

The zig-zagging path to belief

Ah, belief. The great divide between the rational and the spiritual. The problem with religion is that it is predicated on tenets that are hard to measure, understand, explain or duplicate. Like reiki healing, noticing auras, or anything to do with intuition, religious belief has to be experienced. That is the problem.

The path to belief can be zig-zagging and precarious, full of questions and second-guessing, like mine is. Sometimes, belief builds up gradually, over the course of a lifetime, through a guru—although that too is a circular, chicken-and-egg situation. They say that a guru will come when you are ready to accept the lessons he/she has to offer, but how can you evolve to the stage when you are ready for mysticism, faith and spirituality without a guru? Faith can also happen in an instant, like a lightning stroke, through divine grace, although that is rare and requires miracles.

'Look at me through the corner of your eye, your *kadai-kann*,' go the lyrics of a Tamil song.

Just a glance from the goddess—not even a full one, just from the corner of her eye—can elevate a moron into a mystic, as the goddess of learning, Saraswati, is supposed to have done to the poet, Kalidasa, by drawing on his tongue.

Faith is about feeling good

As nebulous as faith is, numerous studies point to its benefits. Faith is in vogue—on the cover of publications worldwide. It confers self-control, peace of mind, fosters relationships, increases happiness and nurtures community. Faith is the ultimate feel-good pill on this rocky road that we call life; it heals and empowers. I get all that. I would like to embrace my faith. I would like to be a better Hindu.

Religion, however, poses a perplexing paradox. Only if I have faith will I experience the benefits of faith. But how to embrace faith without some sort of proof? Not scientific proof necessarily but even some sort of inner awakening, some sign from the cosmos? 'Anything?' as George Constanza said in *Seinfeld*. How do I get on the religious bandwagon?

Where do I jump in?

The Ganga would be a good place to jump in. The question that looms before me is whether to jump into the Ganga in Kashi: the holiest of rivers in the holiest of cities, according to Hindus. I ask friends and family. My French friend, Pasquale, jumped into the Ganga in Kashi. 'See, nothing happened,' he says. Then again, he is a war photographer who thinks riding a motorbike through the Swat Valley is normal. Another friend, Ashok, recently returned from Varanasi, and said no, he didn't even dip his feet in.

An older uncle says to go deep into the Ganga and jump in. 'In the middle, there is flowing water, so even the pollutants will be washed away,' he says.

'To be in Kashi and not immerse yourself in the Ganga is a waste of a trip,' pronounces an aunt.

It is this unshakeable faith in the Ganga that causes millions of Hindus to plunge in even though they see sewage flowing into it. This type of faith ignores rationality, data about faecal matter, coliform bacteria counts, contamination, or even their own eyes—which is probably why it is called blind faith. It is a mind game, really. You may see dirt; you may even see the dead buffalo a few yards downstream. But because you believe that the Ganga is holy, you don't really care. She will purify your mind, heart and soul. The body doesn't even enter this equation. It is superfluous to this worldview—a mere carapace to be shed en route to liberation or moksha.

'*Ganga mata pavitra hai!*' they chant. Mother Ganga is sacred and pure.

Dirty doesn't mean impure

The problem is the semantics—the difference between pollution and purity. Indians know that the Ganga is dirty. They also believe that she is sacred and pure. After all, that is why she descended from the heavens and came to earth: to wash away sins. It is the reason for her existence. Her power originates in her creation myth. She is liquid Shakti, a tangible reality of divine power. She connects the heavens to earth, washes away the sins of us mere mortals. This is why she is a great tirtha or pilgrimage site: because of what she takes from us (our sins) and what she gives to us (moksha or liberation from death). This is why the Ganga is pure even though she is dirty.

When former Prime Minister Rajiv Gandhi launched the Ganga Action Plan in 1986, he alluded to this distinction. Standing on the steps leading to the Ganga, Gandhi said, 'The purity of the Ganga was never in question.' The problem was that a river 'that was a symbol of India's spirituality was being allowed to get dirty.'

Pavitrata versus *gandagi*: purity versus dirtiness. The Indian mind has no problem in perceiving the Ganga as both pure and dirty. It accepts both ideas, without really wanting to do much about it.

People bathe, wash their laundry and defecate all along the 2,510 km long river that serves a staggering one-third of the Indian population. Faecal coliform bacteria levels are off the charts. Chromium levels are at least ten times the permissible amount. Untreated sewage flows directly into the waters. Add to it industries that feed their waste into the river, such as the leather tanneries along its banks in Kanpur, carpet factories in Mirzapur, paper factories, distilleries and dyeing units, and you have the makings of an environmental disaster. The Ganga is choked by sewage and pollution, state reports from bodies that analyse her water quality based on dissolved oxygen (DO), biological oxygen demand (BOD) and total coliform matter (TCM). Her vaunted oxygen levels and ability to regenerate are being choked by the sheer amount of garbage being thrown into her, ranging from corpses to contaminants.

A Kanpur-based uncle of mine, whom I will call Mahen, said that when he was young, crocodiles and tortoises were teeming in the Ganga, eating up corpses. 'Within Modi's term, the Ganga will get salvation,' he says. 'It has to because it is a huge part of his promise to India.'

The Ganga's pollution is linked to India's population. Sometime in the sixteenth century lived a Bengali scholar named Raghunandana, who wrote twenty-eight books on *tattva*s or elements, which could be viewed as 'how to' books. *Vivaha Tattva*: How to get married; *Daya Tattva*: How to show compassion; *Grihastashrama Tattva*: How to live as a good householder; *Durgopujo Tattva*: How to celebrate Durga Puja are some of the books. One of the books is called *Prayaschitta Tattva*, and it means how to make amends or how to expiate sin. This section contains a verse about how to treat the Ganga.

Ganga punyajalan prapya caturdasa vivarjayet
Saucamacamanam kesam nirmalya madyamarsanam
Gatrasamvahanam kridam pratigrahamatho ratim
Anyatirtharatim caive anyatirthaprasansanam
vastratyagamapaghatam santaram ca visesatah

It lists, or rather prohibits in some detail, fourteen acts. Comments in parentheses are by me. The prohibited actions are: excretion, bathing, brushing teeth or spitting out gargling water (only holy dip permitted), cleaning of the ear and throwing earwax into the river (seriously, people did that?), shampooing of hair, throwing of used garlands (done all the time these days as a commercial activity—the Ganga is full of leaf candles and marigold garlands), frolicking or playing in the water (come on—not even frolicking?!), no obscene acts, no attachment or praise of other sacred places (meaning that they viewed the Ganga as a goddess who could get jealous?), no washing clothes and throwing garments (we discharge corpses instead of dirty laundry water these days) and, in particular, no swimming across the river (wonder why—because the river is so broad that people could urinate en route?).

Not a single one of these dictums has been followed.

Instead people believe that the Ganga will self-rejuvenate, that her waters, considered healing and self-perpetuating since the dawn of Hindu civilization, will simply continue to do so.

This is alluded to in a type of literature called Nighantu literature: a Sanskrit materia medica of sorts, a glossary of words and objects that delineated the characteristics of herbs, trees, forests, water bodies, minerals, rocks, humans, animals—well, pretty much everything that was available at that time. Some thirty works were written in this manner, empirically classifying, amongst other things, water. Nighantu is a hard word and concept to translate. It alludes to the secret meaning inherent in objects.

Madanapala Nighantu, for instance, says that coconut water is an aphrodisiac, digestive stimulant and a cardiac tonic. How would the ancients know this? By making thousands of people drink gallons of coconut water and seeing the effect it had?

Water that is exposed to the sun's rays in the morning and the moon's rays at night is considered rejuvenating, strength and intellect promoting, and balancing to all the body humours. My mother does this. She places water in a copper pot, throws in some tulsi leaves, along with some cardamom and cinnamon, leaves it out in the sun in the morning and makes it 'absorb the moon's rays' through the night and then drinks it on an empty stomach the next morning. All good things; all prescribed in Ayurveda. But how did my mother know? Through word of mouth and homespun wisdom that she heard from her parents perhaps, or through the all-encompassing word that we call tradition.

That which has been passed down through the ages

The Sanskrit word for tradition is *agama*, or 'that which has come'. The word *gam*, meaning 'to go', and the prefix *a*, which means 'towards'. Agama means 'to come towards' us. The word, Ganga, flips this around. *Gam-ga*, or 'because she goes, she is Ganga'.

River waters too are classified in the Nighantu literature. In an English translation titled *Materia Medica of Ayurveda: Based on: Madanapala's Nighantu* by Vaidya Bhagwan Dash (Health Harmony, 2008), the rivers Ganga, Yamuna, Sarayu and Satadru (or Sutlej) are considered to have healing properties—because they have fast-flowing water that originated in the Himalayas and flows through rocks. In contrast, rivers that flow out of the Sahayadris, the Sahya mountains, like the Godavari, cause *kustha* or obstinate skin diseases like leprosy. Rivers like the Shipra and Reva, which originate in the Vindhyas, causes anaemia and skin diseases. If I were a non-Himalayan river (and I know I am anthropomorphizing here), I would be really annoyed that bad things were attributed to me.

Enter Narahari Panditha, a Kashmiri polymath who lived in the seventeenth century (although some say fourteenth century), knew eighteen languages, and wrote the magisterial *Raja Nighantu*. He took this riverine water analysis to the next level in his book, with chapter headings such as the following:

1. 47 types of forests with details of names, properties, actions and uses
2. 40 types of fragrances
3. 154 types of human beings with age, qualities, character and ailments.

One of the twenty-four chapters talks about the Ganga's waters, which have the following properties: coolness, sweetness, transparency, high tonic property, wholesomeness, potability, ability to remove evils, ability to resuscitate from swoon caused by dehydration, digestive property and ability to sustain wisdom.

The river that removes evils and sustains wisdom

Consider this. Ancient Indians believed that the Ganga gives you the ability to sustain wisdom. That belief has percolated down the centuries. For a Hindu, wisdom is the highest of aspirations on the evolution ladder, falling just below liberation or moksha. If Indians believe that the Ganga can give you wisdom, the highest of all human desires, then pollution and defecation are trivial hindrances. If faith can heal the planet, then the Ganga doesn't need human intervention.

The reason why cleaning the Ganga is so complicated is because it requires behavioural modification—or brainwashing—on a scale that is staggering. You cannot even point fingers and say that it is the peasants, the illiterate, the great unwashed hordes who are causing this contamination. It is People Like Us (PLU).

My cousin, Vikram, studied economics at Oxford, went on to Harvard Business School, and now works in public policy in Geneva. When his father died, he acceded to his mother's wishes and brought his father's ashes to immerse into the Ganga. He knew that this act only increased the amount of anthropogenic waste (or waste from human activity) that went into the already burdened Ganga.

'As a climate change activist and someone who believes in sustainable living, what I did to the Ganga was abhorrent to me,' says Vikram. 'But, as a son, it was the least I could do for my grieving mother, who firmly and fervently believed that throwing my father's ashes into the Ganga would take his soul to heaven.'

There are tens of millions of Vikrams in India who do this every single day. Eighty million of them converge during the Kumbh Mela to bathe in this holy river at a holy moment. This happens all along the course of the river: across some twenty-nine cities and ten states: Uttarakhand, Uttar Pradesh, Bihar, Jharkhand, Madhya Pradesh, Himachal Pradesh, Haryana, Rajasthan, Chhattisgarh and West Bengal.

What's in a name?

Kashi, as it turns out, is one of the worst offenders. And while we're at it, I might as well tell you that I am going to refer to the city by its ancient, intimate name: one that is used by locals, and all over South India. Not Banaras, the name given by invaders beginning with the Sultans, the British and even Mark Twain who famously observed that 'Banaras is older than history, older than tradition, older even than legend, and looks twice as old as all of them put together.' Not Varanasi, the city's official name, denoting the stretch of land between where the Varuna river and the now-dry Assi river join the Ganga. The name I love is Kashi, from the Sanskrit root *kash*, which means shining, as in *prakash* (light), as in '*moksha prakashi kashi*', the effulgent city that offers the path to moksha or enlightenment. Kashi, the city of light, the luminous one.

In South India, wedding rituals include the Kashi Yatra, where the bridegroom mock-threatens to walk out of the wedding and head to Kashi to become a sanyasin, an ascetic scholar. My husband did this. With a great deal of merriment, all my relatives charged after him to ask him to stay back.

'Please don't leave for Kashi!' my father repeated after the priest. 'I will give you the hand of my daughter, a good woman who will stand beside you for the rest of your life.'

After that, the South Indian wedding rituals took over with a lot of flower-throwing and drum-beating so that the poor bridegroom or bride could barely think—which perhaps is the point of these rituals: to literally beat the young people into thoughtless submission.

My husband didn't leave—not then, not now. Although both of us have threatened the proverbial walkout, not necessarily to Kashi, to each other many times.

The oldest city in the world

Kashi was not just the place where eligible young men went off to escape getting hitched. At one time, it was a centre of learning where young ascetics and students flocked to study with scholars, formulate their beliefs and search for the divine. Like Greece in the time of Socrates and Plato, Sanskrit scholars used to stand in the street corners of Kashi and invite other philosophers to debate with them. Anyone who came up with a new theory or a new philosophy had to road-test it first in Kashi. The famous grammarian, Patanjali, who wrote the yoga sutras, taught here in the second century. Vatsyayana lived in Kashi in the third century and wrote the *Kamasutra*, the treatise on sensual and sexual pleasures and positions. The three great Hindu philosophers, Adi Shankara in the eighth century, Ramanuja in the eleventh century and Madhva in the thirteenth century, all spent time here.

It wasn't just the Hindus. At least two Jain *tirthankaras* (sages and teachers) spent chunks of time in this city. An entire sect of people who believe that Jesus was buried in Kashmir also believe that he spent time in Kashi. The Buddha spent his summers in Kashi. Many of the Jataka tales about the previous births of the Buddha (he was called Bodhisattva before he became the Buddha, the enlightened one) were based in Kashi.

Several stories begin with the sentence, 'Once upon a time, when Brahmadatta ruled Kashi ...'. The Jataka tales are dated between 300 BC and AD 400, and they refer to events that happened a few hundred years ago, all of which lends weight to the Hindu claim that Kashi is the oldest continually occupied city in the world.

Kashi was to Indian philosophy what Florence was to Renaissance artists, what Paris was to the Impressionist painters, and what

Silicon Valley is to today's entrepreneur: an intellectual hub where ideas could cross-pollinate. It was the place to be—to learn from other scholars engaged in the same pursuit, be it philosophy, logic, metaphysics, spirituality or poetry.

'There is hardly any city that can claim greater antiquity, greater continuity and greater popular veneration than Banaras. Banaras has been a holy city for at least thirty centuries,' said the great Indologist and Sanskrit scholar and Bharat Ratna P.V. Kane, in his book, *The History of Dharmashastra* (Chapter 13, Vol. IV, published by Bhandarkar Oriental Research Institute). 'No other city in India arouses the religious emotions of Hindus as much as Kashi does.'

Communing with a goddess

As I stand in front of the idol of Goddess Annapurna, I am trying to feel aroused—religiously, I mean. All around me are men and women, palms together in supplication, muttering appeals, lost in hope and prayer, their gaze unwavering, staring at the goddess with her large black eyes.

I envy their transcendence, their engagement with divinity. I want to feel it. If Kashi doesn't do it for me, I am a lost cause. 'Please,' I mutter, 'let me experience transcendence.' Instead, my mind remains stubbornly observant, questioning and judgemental.

Faith requires suspension of belief—or is it the opposite? Faith requires belief? Visiting temples is an exercise in watching countless fellow humans commune with the gods and goddesses—devotees with the unshakeable belief that the goddess will change their lives. How? How can they surrender free will, ego, pride and sense of self to a nebulous higher power? The goddess gazes back at me passively. Don't tempt fate, I think to myself, a little fearfully. I remember the Tamil movies I watched as a child in which a wrathful God decided to teach a disbeliever a lesson by throwing hardships and life lessons her way. Those movies showed a beautifully simple cause-and-effect relationship between humans and God. You go to this temple and *voila*, your blind son gets his eyesight back. Sudama offered Krishna some beaten rice. When he returned home, his hut had become a mansion.

Letting go of attachments

Having grown up in a religious family, I am not an atheist. I am not even agnostic. I am a Hindu. A questioning one perhaps—one who is hypersensitive to petty religious hypocrisies for sure, but I have long lost the boundless self-confidence with which I could dismiss the divine. The school of hard knocks has made me a little more humble, has taught me that everything in my life is not in my control, that there is such a thing called luck—or the divine hand if you will, that random acts can change the course of a life.

A priest stands in front of the idol, chanting Sanskrit mantras, some of which I recognize.

Annapurne sada purne Shankara prana vallabhe
Jnana vairagya siddhyartham bhiksham dehi cha Parvati

Oh Annapurna, always whole, the one who gives Shiva his life force. Please give me the boons of wisdom and detachment.

My grandmother used to say these verses to Annapurna, which is why I know this bit by heart.

Indian ancients were obsessed with detachment as a path to wisdom. Yoga says the same thing. It says that Vairagya is letting go of attachments, of fears, of sins, of false identities. Put that way, it is uplifting. You fly free of all these illusions or delusions of grandeur and remove yourselves from the shackles of fear. If a goddess can do that, I will stand in line.

The goddess of grains, the giver of sustenance

Above the stove in my home is a tiny bronze image of Annapurna, given to me by my grandmother after she visited Kashi. My cook, a devout Hindu, places steaming hot rice in front of this tiny idol and allows the steam to envelop the goddess, offering the cooked food to her first before setting it on the dining table.

In Kashi, I view first hand the goddess who has been part of my family for three generations. Two (human) women stand on either side of the idol. They are folding saris into long strips and placing them on top of the idol. Stalks of yellow wheat are placed next to the idol. Annapurna is the goddess of grains. She epitomizes sacred food, holding in her hands a vessel and a large ladle to dole out an unending supply of nourishing food to her people. She is the queen of Kashi. The story of how she came here is one that I relish: as a spouse and as a feminist.

Turns out that Shiva and his consort, Shakti as she is called in this story, were having a philosophical discussion in their Himalayan mountain abode. Shiva grandly pronounced that the whole world was maya, an illusion. Only he (or the realization of him) was the true reality.

'Is that so?' asked his wife. As Shakti, she was the material half of the world, present in all things. Stung by her husband's dismissal of her role in creation, she vanished. The world came to a standstill. Time stopped. The earth became barren, devoid of sustenance. All of creation suffered. Seeing this, the compassionate goddess, Shakti, appeared in Kashi as Goddess Annapurna. She set up a kitchen and began feeding the world again. Her husband,

Shiva, did something that all men ought to do when they are
proved wrong in a spousal quarrel. He showed up at his wife's
door and made amends. The mythological version of an apology is
that Shiva appeared with a begging bowl in hand, shamefaced and
sheepish at his grandiosity.

'Say it,' the wife must have said.

'I realize that the material world is as important as the spiritual,'
Shiva must have mumbled. 'I shouldn't have dismissed it. Your role
is as important as mine. More important.'

The smiling wife fed her husband. All was forgiven.

The husband and wife made a deal. In Kashi, Shakti would take
care of the people during their lives. Shiva would help them after
they died. Living and dying: a good division of duties. Both are
important in Kashi.

The more-is-more aesthetic

Annapurna is a beautiful goddess. In paintings and photos, she is
beautifully proportioned, lean for a Hindu goddess, with four hands
and three eyes: one in the middle of the forehead and two in the
usual place.

That day, the goddess is wearing a green silk sari and is
covered with jewels and garlands. Not a single spot is free of
human ministrations. This is *alamkara*, the Hindu notion of
ornamentation, to decorate the goddess till not a speck of space
is left. Indians aren't much for the 'less is more' aesthetic written
about by Robert Browning in his poem 'Andrea del Sarto', and
adopted by Ludwig Mies van der Rohe, the architect, as his design
philosophy. India has a more-is-more aesthetic that bombards the
senses with fragrant flowers, sandalwood paste, jasmine incense,

silks, ringing bells, fresh fruits, vermilion powder, grey sacred ash, betel leaves, nuts and sacred food offering.

Sensual pleasure and deprivation

Hinduism is at once about self-denial and sensual pleasure, alternating with each other: sensory overload followed by asceticism or deprivation. Hindu rituals are full of sensual pleasures ranging from the rangoli drawings on the floor to the flavourful food that is offered to the gods. We have the whole nine yards: lights, music, action, incense, flowers, bells and chanting. After the action comes the withdrawal: fasting on Ekadashi, staying awake all night on Shivaratri, sitting in meditation, not speaking, withdrawing the senses—colour, chaos, noise and community followed by silence, calm and withdrawal.

Kashi epitomizes both ends of the Hindu spectrum. You come here to enjoy the pleasures of this world, ranging from music, art, food and love. You also come here to renounce the world and be an ascetic subsisting on alms collected in a begging bowl—like Shiva did.

India's genius, in comparison with most other cultures, is that it preserves and values that archaic element that continues to live in mythical time, the time before mundane time. It is as if Kashi's citizens are acting in a sacred play that spans time.

Where gods roamed the earth

The Romanian religious historian Mircea Eliade calls this hierophany, or manifestation of the sacred (he found theophany too constrictive). Eliade divides experience into the sacred and the profane. Myths, he says, are where the world of the gods breaks through the clouds and mixes with the world of humans. In Hinduism, we call these avatars, where the gods literally walk amongst us and teach us lessons, show us how to live. Most modern societies have moved beyond myths into the worlds of science and rationality. Their creation myths, the way their ancestors made sense of the world, have been relegated to museums, theatre, storytelling and history textbooks. Today's Rome with its Prada and Bottega Veneta stores is a far cry from the time when Roman gods walked the earth. The same goes for other ancient cultures such as Greece or Egypt. In Cairo today you don't see Egyptian gods like Ra and Anubis on street corners in temples.

India is an exception to this trend. Here, gods routinely intrude into daily life. On my street is a small Ganesh placed at the location where three streets join. There is also a Mother Mary figurine, actually two; and a mosque that attracts hundreds of Muslim men who come on Friday, clad in white kurtas and matching skullcaps. A large chunk of our population carries on conversations with their gods—at temples, rivers, at home and through rituals. When we buy a new car, we place lemons in front of the four wheels and do a little puja. When a lift was installed at my parents' apartment building, a priest came and did a ritual for this yantra or device that may well have been done 2,000 years ago. We build images of gods like Durga and Ganesha during Durga puja and Ganesh puja, sing and dance with them, and immerse them into water during festivals. We communicate with our gods regularly. Our daily routines and reality include a healthy mix of myth and legend. To paraphrase what Jawaharlal Nehru, our first prime minister, said about the Ganga, we Indians have not cut ourselves off completely from the past. Consciously or unconsciously, our lives reflect the fact that we are links in an unbroken chain that goes back 'to the dawn of history in the immemorial past of India'. The sacred and the profane are meshed together in India, and nowhere more so than in Kashi.

'I want to die in Kashi.'

Hindus come to Kashi to die. It is as simple as that. One of its names is Mahasmashanam (or Mahasmashan in North India) or the great cremation ground, where Shiva, ever quixotic, roams at night, surrounded by ghouls, ghosts and other dregs of society.

The devout go to extraordinary lengths to bring the dead bodies of their parents, siblings, or relatives here, by bullock cart or horse carriage, slung over and tied to the top of a bicycle, by car, truck, or plane. They want to cremate their loved ones in the two famous burial ghats: Harishchandra and Manikarnika. The former is older and named after a king who never uttered a lie. The latter is where Goddess Shakti's earring fell—or Shiva's, depending on who is telling the story.

Manikarnika Ghat holds a fire that has never been extinguished since the first century, say the locals, pointing to a fire that is burning under an alcove, protected from the elements. The Hindu belief is that fire and water are bridges between the spiritual and protean worlds. They are both purifiers and symbols of fertility. 'Kashya maranam muktihih,' goes the Sanskirt phrase. Dying in Kashi offers mukti: absolution, deliverance, freedom, liberation, escape from the endless cycle of birth and rebirth. No wonder countless Hindus tell their relatives: 'I want to die in Kashi.'

Frankly, I am not sure why my people think of birth and rebirth as torture, unless you are born as a stray dog or a cockroach perhaps, although cockroaches are the only creatures that will survive apocalypse, so maybe there is some virtue to being a cockroach. But the desire to prevent rebirth, so all-pervasive amongst Hindus, doesn't really resonate with me, perhaps because I am having quite a decent life in this birth. I wouldn't mind coming back again.

The concept of a good death, though, is something I can wrap my head around. The Hindu worldview considers dying as important as living. The way you die is important. '*Anayaasa maranam*', they say. A good death. Just as people in the West plot where and how they are to be buried, Hindus plot and fantasize about how they will die. Dying on Ekadashi and being cremated on Dwadasi, the next day—the eleventh day and twelfth day of the lunar fortnight—is one way to achieve a good death. Sipping the waters of the Ganga or chanting the Lord's name:—'Ram Ram', as Gandhiji said in his last moments—is another. Dying in Kashi is the third, for a very mystical reason.

Whispering in a dying soul's ears

In Kashi, it is said, Lord Shiva breathes the sacred Taraka mantra into a dying person's ears. The Bengali saint Ramakrishna, it is said, went into a trance while boating along the Manikarnika Ghat because he got a vision of Lord Shiva moving around the cremation pyres, breathing this sacred mantra into the souls that had been released from their human cages, sending them on their way to heaven.

There is some debate about what this Taraka or 'crossing over' mantra is. Some say that it is 'Ram Ram'. The *Tarasara Upanishad* says that it is 'Om Namo Narayanaya', but this Upanishad is biased towards the Vaishnavite tradition. Others say that it is simply the Om mantra. In a sense, the actual mantra itself seems irrelevant. The important thing is to have Shiva himself, as guru, whispering something into your ears. If the Hindu god of destruction comes to your deathbed and whispers the secret code to immortality, I would say that it is a pretty good guarantee of safe passage, sort of like diplomatic immunity. No matter what sins you have committed, this singular act of received wisdom from Shiva can change your destiny; which is probably why Hindus, to this day, make plans to spend their golden years in Kashi. There are hospices like Kashi Labh Mukti Bhavan where people at death's door can come and stay for a maximum of fifteen days. If they don't die after fifteen days, they have to move out and make way for the next person on the waiting list. Such people are called *mumukshus* or people who yearn to die and find liberation through death.

When my beautiful great-grand-aunt was widowed, family legend went, she shaved her head and discarded every feminine adornment. No more jewellery, silk saris or even the bindi. No more chewing the betel leaves that she loved. No more sitting in the front row at family weddings. Widows were consigned to the back. She wore a simple beige sari without a blouse and spent her days plotting how to get to Kashi in order to die. That was her life goal from age fifty-six to age eighty-six, when she eventually died—not in Kashi, because her family couldn't figure out how to send and maintain a frail eighty-year-old woman in Kashi endlessly. Her son had a business to run and children to send to school. This aunt died in Chennai. In partial fulfilment of her wishes, her son took her ashes to sprinkle into the river Ganga.

A parade of corpses

One morning, I asked the boatman to take me close to Manikarnika Ghat. Traditionally and typically, women are not allowed inside a Hindu cremation ground. They grieve so much, they cry so much, that the departed soul does not want to leave, is the reason given.

'With women, there is always the risk that they will jump into the funeral pyre,' said a man from the Dom community that controls the burial ghats.

I stare at him and think: *Really? In this day?*

Not being allowed into the ghat, I have to stand on the boat and peer at it. From my vantage point, I can see a parade of corpses. There are approximately 250 corpses for cremation per day, with an average cost of cremation being ₹7,000 per corpse. The corpse is wrapped in colourful cloths, carried down the steps of the ghat and dipped into the Ganga before being placed on a pile of wood with sandalwood shavings. The eldest son lights the fire. It is a solemn ceremony. Not much is said from what I can see. On average, it takes about three hours for a human body to burn. Someone from the Dom community helps out by prodding stubborn body parts that don't burn, usually the fatty middle section. At the end, a handful of ashes is put in a terracotta pot and handed to the family to throw into the Ganga. The soul is released. The family has to walk out without looking back. Hinduism is a forward-looking religion.

What is your attitude towards death and dying? For people of a certain age, who are sandwiched between ageing parents and young children, this is an engrossing topic. Just before I came to Kashi, I had a discussion with my parents and in-laws, all octogenarians, about living wills. There was this idea in the US, I told them, about writing a living will, or 'advance directives', through which a person could specify how they wanted to die.

'Do not put me on a ventilator, no matter what,' could be one directive.

'Do not resuscitate (DNR),' could be another.

I have dozens of uncles and aunts in their eighties. Most of the elderly Indians with whom I have spoken about living wills look utterly confused. Medical directives—DNR, DNI—are not part of their worldview. They want to achieve a good death, without suffering, without troubling others. They want their souls to achieve moksha. They want to die in Kashi.

Removing the soul from the dying process

As I sit in the morning cold near Manikarnika Ghat, watching the final rites of strangers, I wonder if modern discussions have taken the sacredness and profundity out of death. Using medical jargon ('he died of cardiac arrest') and writing living wills may be necessary, but it somehow trivializes death. It removes the soul from dying. For Hindus, dying is not a merely physical act—it is almost entirely about the soul.

My mother, who was present during both her parents' deaths, told me that her father's soul 'went out through his eyes', and her mother's soul 'went out through her tongue'. How did she know? 'I could see it,' she replied.

Dying is as natural as being born, or should be. Watching the funerals that are going on in Manikarnika Ghat is weirdly calming—as if the stillness and inevitability of this most final of passages has permeated the air. Death is profound. Reducing it to medical parlance: 'his vitals are okay; his numbers are good; he passed urine and tolerated a feed,' is a grotesque modern version of what Hindus consider a sacred act.

As Caitlin Doughty, a funeral director who was profiled in the 30 November 2015 issue of the *New Yorker*, says, 'Death is not an emergency. Death is the opposite of an emergency. Look at the person who died—all that stress and pain is gone from them. And now that stress and pain can be gone from you.'

I watched a family walk down the steps, holding aloft a terracotta pot. A man clad in a dhoti, presumably the son, lifted the pot and poured the ashes into the river. It was oddly touching, even for me, who sat far away. Death was not something to feel queasy about. Living and dying were simply two points in a circle, intertwined and accepted in this city as part of the great, nebulous, unfathomable whole that said: 'We are one.' *Aham Brahma Asmi.*

Sprinkling ashes into a river

Reportedly, Nehru wanted his ashes sprinkled into the Ganga too. In his last will and testament, he tries to explain why. 'My desire to have a handful of my ashes thrown in the Ganga at Allahabad has no religious significance, so far as I am concerned. I have no religious sentiment in the matter,' said Nehru, according the Press Information Bureau's archive of it on its Government of India website.

Don't mean no disrespect, but that seems pretty disingenuous to me. Is it possible to separate the Ganga from the Hindu religion? If that is so, Nehru could have wished for his ashes to be thrown into any of India's sacred rivers—Yamuna, Narmada, Godavari or Kaveri. But he picked Ganga. Why?

To me, Ganga is all about religion, about Hinduism, about its role in the final rite of passage, about its power to transport, not just from one place to the next, but also from one dimension to the next, about its place as a catalyst of spirituality and expiator of sins. That is what gives this river its potency.

Nehru said that he was 'attached' to the Ganga and Yamuna since childhood and loved its many moods, which is why he wanted his ashes there too. I didn't grow up in North India and have no physical connection to Ganga or jamuna. Ganga, for me, is the stuff of stories, history, tradition and *Amar Chitra Katha* comic books. I am not attached to this river the way I am attached to my hometown, Chennai.

Yet, here I am, standing at the Ganga's edge before sunrise on my second day, trying to will myself to jump in. Part of the reason is the power of hearsay, of myth. I grew up listening about Ganga's greatness. Part of it is the possibilities that the Ganga offers—of expiating sin really. All things being equal, I'd like to improve my odds at accessing heaven by shedding some sin. Jumping into the Ganga, particularly at Kashi, seems to be a good way to do that. Hinduism in that sense is a practical religion. It offers dictums and methods, choices and loopholes by which you can reduce suffering, improve health, wealth and happiness, and have a good death. There are certain locations that offer a kind of bridge between this life and the next. These tirthas or holy places offer a kind of centripetal force: you do good things in these locations and they come back to you tenfold. Prayag, Kashi and Gaya are three such places. They each have specific actions associated with them to help increase good karma. '*Prayaga munde Kashi dhoondhe Gaya pinde*' is the explanation. Prayag: tonsure or shaving of head; Kashi: a search for self; Gaya: offering *pinde* or rice balls specked with sesame seeds to ancestors.

Forbidden love and a river that consumed it

My parents did all three some twenty years ago when I was in the US. They took a train to Prayag or Allahabad, when my father offered *veni-dhaanam*, or a portion of his hair as offering to the river in lieu of completely shaving his head—the prescribed tonsure. They took the boat to the confluence of the three holy rivers: Ganga, Yamuna, and the Saraswati which is supposed to flow unseen by human eyes in the bottom. My father jumped off the boat and immersed himself in the river three times, repeating the mantras after a priest they had hired to propitiate seven generations of dead ancestors on both his maternal and paternal sides. Then, they came to Kashi where they stayed at a small guest house in Hanuman Ghat where Tamilians converge. Each ghat attracts people from a different state. My parents met a Kashi-based Tamil priest called Chellam Iyengar, who took them into the Ganga to do similar rituals. Finally, they went to Gaya to offer pindam or rice balls specked with black sesame seeds as food for their ancestors.

I stand one morning not at Hanuman Ghat but at Panch Ganga Ghat, watching Brahmin priests conduct similar rituals for couples who have come to Kashi. Behind me is the massive Alamgir mosque, built by Aurangzeb after he razed the Vishnu temple, the Bindu Madhva temple, to the ground. It was on the steps of the Panch Ganga Ghat that a poor Muslim weaver named Kabir got his mantra initiation. Apparently Ramananda, Kabir's guru, did not want to take a poor Muslim as his student. Kabir lay down on the steps in the predawn darkness when he knew that his guru would walk down to take a bath in the Ganga. The guru tripped over this particular seeker and uttered the words 'Rama Rama'. This became the mantra that Kabir used for all his songs.

The Panch Ganga Ghat is linked with another sixteenth-century poet named Jagannatha Panditha Rayalu, considered by many to be the last of the great Sanskrit poets. Originally from Andhra Pradesh, Jagannatha moved to Kashi, where he fell in love with a Muslim woman (some say that she was a Mughal princess). When the families refused to accept the lovers, Jagannatha sat on the steps of the ghat and sang a paean called 'Ganga Lahiri': fifty-two verses in praise of the river Ganga. With every verse, the river rose by one step, till it finally reached the step where Jagannatha sat, and enveloped the poet and his Muslim lover into her cool embrace. It is a great story. Perhaps Jagannatha composed the poem during the monsoon season when the river's flood waters would have risen anyhow. No matter. 'Ganga Lahiri' is still sung in Kashi today.

Kashi, Jericho or Byblos

This is my first visit to Kashi even though, like many Indians, it has been part of my vocabulary and psyche since birth. When my grandfather lay dying, one of the things at his bedside was a small copper pot of Ganga water, collected at Kashi and to be poured into his lips when the soul left the body. My mother performed this act, and to this day gains solace from it.

Today, Kashi is like any other dusty town in North India—a hodgepodge of streets, tightly packed buildings, street signs askew, chaotic, honking traffic and the obligatory cow in the middle of the street looking bewildered but determined not to leave its spot.

Gowdulia Circle is the main meeting point when talking to guides. Four roads lead away from it: one towards the Kashi Vishwanatha temple, one towards Dasha Ashwamedha Ghat, and two others towards bazaars and shops. Rickshaw-wallahs sitting on three-wheeled cycles, like a child's tricycle on steroids and just as gaily painted, call out to tourists. Policemen in khaki ineffectually wave the honking cars and scooters around. It could be any dusty North Indian town, but it isn't.

Kashi claims to be the world's oldest continually inhabited city. Unlikely. That status probably goes to towns in the Levant—Jericho, Aleppo, Faiyum or Byblos—some of which go back to 4500 BC, as compared to Kashi's 1800 BC. A fair claim is that Kashi is the oldest city in India. Duck into one of the small by-lanes that branch off the main roads and it feels like Bethlehem, Jerusalem, Nizwa (Oman), or any other ancient town in Mexico, Egypt, Morocco or Rajasthan. Cobblestone streets, tiny alleys, shop fronts selling silver jewellery, locals in loose, long clothes, perfect for the tropical weather, hurrying on urgent errands, picking their way through cow dung, stagnant water and stray dogs curled up on the street.

The streets are tiny, and wind through a bewildering maze of shops and houses. One entire street sells paneer, one sells kachoris, one sells silver, one sells hand-stuffed beds, and to round it all off, there is hearty lassi and paan. Food—sacred and otherwise—is everywhere in Kashi.

Fried food for breakfast

I am standing at Vishwanath Misthan Bhandar in Visheshwar Ganj. It is 8 a.m. and I have just done yoga and pranayama with a hundred strangers on the banks of the Ganga—led by a female teacher who shouted, scolded and coaxed us into stretches, bends and submission. Just show up at Assi Ghat at 6 a.m. if you would like to partake. Suitably lubricated, my body is ready for its next round of lubrication.

At Vishwanath Misthan Bhandar, four men sit outside, frying stuff. Have you heard the sizzle of a jalebi early in the morning? It is the most beautiful sound in the world. Chopin's 'Nocturnes' have nothing on the twin sounds of a jalebi and a kachori sizzling in oil right next to each other. I stand with the milling crowd outside, waiting and licking my salivating mouth. It is my turn. I hold out ₹10 and get two leaf bowls. An impassive man ladles aloo sabzi into one leaf bowl, and the kachori in another. Now comes the dilemma. How to stand, balance these two bowls in one hand and eat with the other? The others around me are doing just fine having years of practice. If I could be born again, I would come back as a *Kashi-vasi* (Kashi resident), not necessarily for the good karma but for the terrific kachoris. I have had kachoris in Jaipur,

Haridwar, Delhi and Bengaluru. So far, the ones in Kashi are the best. They are fluffy, not brittle. They hold their round shape and have a respectable amount of dal. They collapse like a bubble when you tear them open. The best part is the aloo sabzi: a trite tangy, just enough spicy, and piping hot.

Behind me, milkmen on mopeds are readying for the day, with milk cans topped with kusha grass (Desmostachya bipinnata), also called darbha, to keep the milk ritually pure. A man is inspecting the milk in one to see if it has been watered down. He dips the green grass into the milk to check if it drips with good consistency. Once the inspection is done, the milkmen drive away to sell the milk to homes or the government booth.

The only way to make a kachori better is to mix it with jalebi. Best of all however is to eat kachori—jalebi for breakfast, if possible, every day.

Cannabis, cookies and ghee

Once breakfast is done, I go temple-hopping. At the Sankat Mochan Hanuman temple, hot *laal pedas* or red pedas are brought out. Devotees buy boxes of them to take to Lord Hanuman and then distribute to those gathered. I stand in line, awaiting my share. A lady in a purple sari hands me one, then seeing my face, she gives me another with a smile. 'Jai Hanuman,' I say and pop one into my mouth. She looks pleased.

'My daughter conceived after eating ten of these pedas,' she says. 'They are a fertility tonic.'

I stop half-bite. Is this why India is overpopulated? Too late. The peda is delicious. The trick to a good peda, and I speak as someone who has never made a peda in her life, is the consistency. It has to melt in the mouth, but you should be able to chew the last bits, like a cookie. You should make those popping sounds that babies make when they relish food. In Tamil we call this *naaka chappi kotti*, which is like saying 'making clicking and clapping sounds with your tongue'. A good peda should make your tongue clap.

At the Annapurna temple across town, someone is serving sesame rice, perhaps because it is Saturday. Karnataka, where I live, is home to several 'rice varieties', or 'chitra-anna' as we call it: coconut rice, lemon rice, tamarind rice, curd rice and, best of all, *bise bele bhaath*, which literally means a hot lentil–rice mixture. Sesame rice is not often made or served. It is a delicacy and an acquired taste. I acquired it in Kashi. The recipe is simple: roasted and ground black sesame seeds, red chillies, curry leaves, some urad dal and a good helping of asafoetida. Grind it all up and mix with hot rice. Here too, the leaf bowls make their appearance. If you like the thick viscosity of good sesame oil, you will love sesame rice. It is great for vegans because it contains a ton of calcium.

At the Kashi Vishalakshi temple, this wide-eyed goddess is served some ghee-dripping *besan ka sheera* as prasadam. The sponsor of this prasadam ladles out a spoon to a line of devotees, including myself. My mother is a devout Devi worshipper. She has often said that the goddess has a tender neck, almost translucent in its delicacy. Any food given to her ought to go down her throat without any obstruction that would cause her delicate neck to turn red. It is a great image that gives permission to including an eye-popping amount of ghee into temple food.

All this eating has made me thirsty. The great thing is that you can get thandai with bhang in Banaras on an average day. You don't have to wait for Holi to indulge. Shiva, the ascetic, loved his bhang, made from the leaves of the cannabis plant. At a government bhang shop, I nervously watch the vendor pour a respectable amount of this green concoction into the glass before adding chilled milk laced with crushed nuts, sugar and saffron. The resulting drink tastes like milk, but with a slightly bitter aftertaste. It is supposed to be hallucinatory. I end up giggling a lot, and wake up the next day with what feels like a hangover.

The other dish that is a signature of the city is not as potent. Banarasi paan is a digestive. I grow betel leaves in my garden. *How different can this be?* I think, as I stand in front of a tiny shop and ask for a paan.

'With zarda or without?' asks the vendor.

Zarda comes from tobacco. It is addictive—gives a high. How bad can it be? With lightning fingers, the vendor smooths open a bright green betel leaf. He throws in several items: betelnuts, lime paste, fennel seeds, a pinch of zarda, rose petal jam or *gulkandh*, and fruit currants. He folds it into a triangle, sticks in a clove to hold it together, and hands it over to me. I have eaten paan before, but this one has oomph. As I chew, I can feel myself getting lightheaded. The juices flow down my throat, inducing a pleasant sensation of relaxation. I smile beatifically and thank the vendor.

'Careful,' he says as I stumble out. '*Sambhaalke.*'

I wave my hand and keep walking. It's a beautiful day.

I don't remember very much of what happened after that, except that I, much like a Hindi film heroine, woke up in bed.

The forest of bliss

Kashi in the predawn darkness is magical. From the boat, the outlines of the two banks of the Ganga are visible, but not much beyond that. Birds chirp, a temple bell clangs, the oars slap softly into the water. On the shore, the dim outlines of the buildings can be easily be mistaken for outlines of trees. It looks like Ananda Vana or the Forest of Bliss, its most ancient name—one that was given by Shiva himself, according to the *Kashi Rahasya* (Kashi's Secret) a sixteenth-century text. The text says that in Kashi, Shiva lingas are everywhere, self-creating and self-perpetuating.

This is true. Wherever you look in Kashi, it seems there is a linga. There are tiny street-side temples, 33,000 of them by one count, each of which holds a linga. Our guide stops at a shop selling cigarettes, chips, paan and other miscellany. We peer behind the bottles to find a small stone linga sitting next to the shopkeeper. Homes contain lingas, as do street corners. Black lingas are painted on walls, ceilings, buses, autorickshaws and tricycles that carry pilgrims from temple to temple. More than anything else, Kashi is Shiva's city, his chosen place, one that he vowed never to forsake.

Much of the mythology about the city comes from the *Kashi Khanda*, a thirteenth-century book of 11,000 verses in praise of Kashi—itself part of the massive Skanda Purana, which talks about Kartikeya, the son of Shiva and Parvati, but also describes the various pilgrimage sites of India.

Like much of this type of literature, the stories come in the form of a conversation between a husband and a wife—in this case, a short sage named Agastya, and his wife, Lopamudra. The sage lists all the Hindu sacred sites that are capable of giving the four *purushartha*s, or the four objectives/goals of human life. They are *dharma* or righteous duty, *artha* or wealth and prosperity, *kama* or love, and *moksha* or liberation. He proceeds to list out the names of these places. They are Prayag, Naimisharanya, Kurukshetra, Gangadwar, Avanti, Ayodhya, Mathura, Dwaraka, Badrikashram and Purushottam Kshetra. But nothing beats Kashi, he says.

The other story involves the sage and his wife meeting Skanda or Lord Kartikeya. When they sing his praises, Kartikeya replies, 'I can go to any part of the world that I wish, but here I am, doing austere penances so that I can reach Kashi. I haven't yet been successful. If anyone thinks that he can attain Kashi just by performing austerities, he is wrong. Kashi cannot be attained until one has the blessing of Shiva, Lord Mahadeva. And if you are fortunate enough to reach Kashi, you would be foolish to leave.

'O Agastya and Lopamudra, you both are fortunate to have lived in Kashi. Please let me touch your body, which has acquired immeasurable holiness due to its proximity to this holiest of cities.'

Having said this, Skanda reverently touched Agastya's legs as if he were touching the sacred soil of Kashi.

One more reason why Kashi is so important in the pantheon of Hindu holy places.

The primeval shaft of light

It was in Kashi that the first jyotirlingam or Shiva's shaft of light appeared for the first time, something that I read about in Diana Eck's comprehensive book *Banaras: City of Light* (published by Alfred A. Knoff in 1982). The twelve jyotirlingams comprise one of many Hindu pilgrim circuits, along with visiting all the Krishna temples and the four *dham*s (the top pilgrimage destinations) in the north, south, east and west. My mother wants to visit all twelve jyotirlingams before she dies, and every now and then, we plot her itinerary together—to Ujjain, Aurangabad, Dwaraka and other locations where Shiva's shaft of light made its appearance. Kashi, and I didn't know this, is the original one.

It happened at the beginning of the Kali Yuga, which is the age we are living in now. Hinduism's view of time is expansive and would make productivity mavens who want to account for every minute of the day freak out. We have *kalpa*s, *manvantara*s and *yuga*s. The shortest is the yuga, which is like 4,32,000 years or some similar ridiculously high number. At the end of each age, there is massive destruction, dissolution, then equilibrium, after which the process of creation begins again.

For our purposes, we can say that it happened in the beginning of time, which was the end of the previous age. There was nothingness. Shiva resided alone. He longed for company. So he created Narayana or Vishnu, who slept in Yoga Nidra (yogic sleep) on the milky ocean on a bed made of the coils of a giant serpent. From Narayana's navel sprouted a lotus on which sat Brahma. In the vast expanse before time and creation, Brahma thought he was all-powerful—the original human. He grew proud.

Vishnu said, 'Hey, you are not the all-powerful. Shiva is.'

They fought for many eons—a 'clash of the titans', 'battle of egos'—type quarrel.

Suddenly, amidst these two warriors appeared a great big shaft of light that pierced the heavens and then beyond and stretched downward till infinity. Vishnu and Brahma stood stupefied and humbled at this shaft of light.

'Who are you?' they asked. 'And why have you chosen this place to appear?'

'I am Vishweshwara, and this place is Kashi where I will live for this age and the next,' said the glowing shaft of light. 'People who come and visit me in this sacred city will be absolved of their sins and attain liberation from human bondage.'

There was more. 'When the next *pralayam* (apocalypse) happens, when the earth gets swallowed up by torrential floods and never-ending flames, Kashi alone will be held aloft on the tines of my trident. I will never forsake this city, and for this reason, it is called Avimukta (Never Forsaken).'

No wonder the people of Kashi have a certain je ne sais quoi about them. If I lived in Shiva's chosen city, the place that he has pledged to save and cherish no matter what, I'd feel pretty complacent too, as I eat my piping hot kachori breakfast. '*Kashi ke kankad Shiva Shankar hain*,' they say. In every stone in Kashi lies Shiva.

Merely living in Kashi assures protection, and on top of that, you have 33,000 temples to pass by and pray to, plus the 100 billion Shiva lingas that are supposed to be in Kashi. Heaven is guaranteed. The people of Kashi are aware of this. As we walk up and down the gentle slopes of Kashi, our guide smugly says that we are walking on the three forks of Shiva's trident, the one that will hold Kashi up above the swirling flood waters at the end of time. He glances at me as if to say, 'Top that.'

The city which Gods didn't want to leave

In another version of this story, Brahma and Vishnu decide to find out the top and bottom of Shiva's shaft of light. Brahma turns into a bird, flies upwards and Vishnu takes the form of a boar and starts digging deep downwards. To no avail. Neither is able to reach the top or bottom. On the way to the top, Brahma sees a *ketki* flower falling down. He persuades the flower to lie on his behalf. When the two contestants meet back at the centre, Vishnu admits that he has not be able to touch Shiva's feet. Brahma lies and says that he has seen the top of Shiva head. In anger, Shiva chops off Brahma's fifth head with his finger nail. But to Shiva's horror, Brahma's skull is now stuck to his hand. Reason: Brahma is a Brahmin, and Shiva has committed the great sin of chopping off a Brahmin's head. *Brahma hathya*, they called it.

In Hinduism, there are five great sins—the *pancha mahapaapa*. They are stealing, drinking alcoholic beverages, killing a Brahmin, lusting after your guru's wife and associating with people who engage in these activities. This was probably written for young men who lived in gurukuls. The only woman they probably saw was their teacher's wife. In today's world, it could probably be rewritten as getting drunk, killing people, stealing, having extramarital affairs and keeping bad company.

Shiva, the ascetic, killed a Brahmin—Brahma. As penance for this sin, Shiva wandered the earth for twelve years, using Brahma's skull as a begging bowl. In the end, he entered Kashi and the skull fell off. Shiva danced in delight. He was freed of this great sin—as is anyone who enters Kashi. For this reason, it is called *kapaala mochana*—shedding of the skull. The logic is that if Kashi could help Shiva shed his sin, it can help anyone reduce their karmic load.

It wasn't just Shiva who was attracted to Kashi. Every god is believed to reside here. To understand this, we have to go back in time to a virtuous king named Divodasa, who ruled Kashi. 'Every kingdom needs only one ruler,' he said. 'So if you want me to rule, Shiva must leave Kashi.' So the gods persuaded Shiva to leave Kashi. Which was fine, for a while. Then Shiva started longing for Kashi. He sent his *gana*s or minions to Kashi to persuade Divodasa to let him return. Divodasa refused. But the ganas were so taken up by Kashi that they stayed back instead of returning to Shiva. Same was with the yoginis or female goddesses that Shiva sent, with the devas, the sun, the moon, the air and water gods. Pretty much all who came to Kashi didn't want to leave. Brahma then came and asked Divodasa to do ten *ashwamedha yagna*s or horse sacrifices at the ghat that still bears that name. The hope was that failing in such an arduous task would shame King Divodasa into leaving Kashi. But King Divodasa was successful even in that. Finally, Vishnu came in the guise of a saint and sowed the seeds of depression and dissatisfaction into this virtuous king. 'Ask Shiva to come back to Kashi,' said this saint/astrologer/Buddhist monk (it varies in the tellings). 'Only then will you be happy.' The king invited Shiva back to Kashi. A delighted Shiva returned to his city and has never left since.

The Muslim invasions

Kashi's 'misfortunes', as Diana Eck says in her book, began in 1194. Muslim invaders, led by Qutbuddin Aibak, looted the city. By some accounts, 1,400 camel-loads of cash, gold, silver and jewellery were carried away as loot from the city. This trend continued. The Hindus kept rebuilding the temples; the invaders kept attacking. Mughal Emperor Akbar provided some respite, but this changed with Aurangzeb's ascension to the throne. Eck claims in her book that he destroyed some of the most important temples, including the Vishweshwara and the Bindu Madhava temples.

Today, the tiny lanes around the mosque and temple are tightly patrolled. I stand in a long line without mobile phone or camera, waiting to gain entry into Vishwanatha temple. Inside, the Shivalinga is small, relative to the monumental myth that surrounds it. I carry some milk and a *bilva* leaf, known to be Shiva's favourite. I pour the milk on the lingam and am quickly hurried out by the police and priests guarding the entrance and exit.

It is in the Kashi Vishwanatha temple that the *sapta rishi* (seven sages) aarti occurs at around 7 p.m. every evening. Shiva taught these seven sages or seven preceptors the secrets of yoga and then asked them to spread it in the seven corners of the world. The sages were sad to be leaving Shiva. So Shiva taught them the sapta rishi aarti. Doing this, he said, would bring them close to him, and allow them to feel his presence. The sapta rishi aarti is still done every day for this reason. Hindu rituals, in that sense, are like software coding: you do this and you get that. If this, then that (IFTTT). Several spiritual teachers have talked about how rituals build up spiritual energy, which is their purpose after all. Watching the sapta rishi aarti at the Kashi Vishwanatha temple is a surreal spiritual experience. The priests chant words that originated in the Sama Veda and are set in the Hindustani Raga Shree. Seven of them sit in a circle around the small lingam. They hold stacks of flickering oil lamps that they move in a synchronized way. Temple bells clang. All of it builds up a certain vibration that even the most sceptical non-believer can feel. 'What they build up in this temple in this one hour is phenomenal because they have a method— that is what a ritual is,' says Sadhguru Jaggi Vasudev in his book *Shiva—Ultimate Outlaw*. 'Whoever conducts it, if it is done right, it will work, because it is a technology. These priests maintained the process. They kept what is of some sanctity to them, and it still works fantastically.'

Creating stacks of energy through light and ritual

Yogis can create good energy through years of self-cultivation. Rituals are a mass-market approach. They have been codified. Priests follow the code. Their actions create a certain impact on the devotees who stand witness. Godliness being transferred to the masses who don't have the wherewithal to engage in austerities or yoga. Ritual as a software code.

The practice of observing god in this pleasing, flickering light induces *shanta-rasa* or peacefulness when done in solitude. The weird thing is that temples with their noise and chaos also create a certain peace for believers. The logic is to see inner light in this outer light, to submerge the ego into nothingness like how camphor burns, leaving nothing behind (somewhat akin to what contemporary artist Alwar Balasubramaniam talks about in his untraceable sculptures that evaporate into nothingness).

The sapta rishi aarti at Kashi Vishwanatha temple induces, if not ego-sublimation, at least an element of contemplation. Perhaps it is the way the priests chant the words; perhaps it is the power of those flickering flames.

The sapta rishis are seven sages, but they are also preceptors who appear at the beginning of every Hindu age and give rise to all humans. Each age has a different set of seven preceptors. It bugs me that there are no women linked to these sages because how can you create the human race by yourself? These sages weren't celibate by the way, even though pictures of them show old men with beards, monk-like in appearance. The seven original Vedic age rishis were Vasishta, Vishwamitra, Agastya, Gautama, Bharadwaja, Jamadagni and Atri. The age that we are living in now is called Vaivaswata Manvantara (or the age of Vaivaswata Manu) that is enfolded into a longer time span called Sweta Varaha Kalpa. The Hindu age of Kali that we are living in now, or Kali Yuga as it is called, lasts 4,32,000 years.

The Hindu unit of time is mind-bogglingly micro and macro at the same time. Yugas multiply into kalpas, which in turn make up manvantaras, which all end up as a day in Brahma's life.

In our time, the seven sages, who are worshipped with the aarti in the Kashi Vishwanatha temple are Vasishta, Vishwamitra, Gautama, Bharadwaja, Jamadagni, Atri and Kashyapa (who has taken Agastya's place).

The eighty-four places along the river

Walking along the ghats is the best way to experience Kashi. There
are eighty-four ghats on the Ganga, an auspicious number chosen
presumably by multiplying the twelve zodiac signs or *rashi*s into the
seven sheaths that a human body is supposed to have. Today, only
about thirty ghats remain. Of these, five are especially important:
Assi, Dasha Ashwamedha, Manikarnika, Panch Ganga and
Adi Keshava.

The ghats are a hive of activity in the morning. I follow a couple
as they walk down the steps into the Ganga. Both stand in waist-
high water, take a handful of the Ganga water, hold it cupped in their
hands, stare at the rising sun, mutter some prayers and gracefully
offer it back to the river. I force myself to follow suit. I have come
dressed for a dip in the Ganga—in light, easy-drying clothes. I stand
at the water's edge.

A few minutes later, I turn back resolutely and walk up the
steps. I cannot do it. I cannot bring myself to jump into her brown
depths. Mind has won over myth, at least for now. At the top of
the ghat, under a banyan tree, sits a snake charmer. I sit before him
and watch him play his flute to make two snakes curve and dance
sinuously. It is a quintessentially Indian scene: a snake charmer
wearing a turban, behind him a vermilion-streaked banyan tree,
and behind it the Ganga.

Taking a holy dip

Kashi is the only place where the Ganga changes course. From her
origin in Gaumukh in the Himalayas, the 2,510 km long river flows
southward, except in Kashi where she makes a sweeping U-turn and
flows northward as if back to her source or as if—as the people of
Kashi say—she cannot bear to leave the city.

On my last day in Kashi, I stand on the banks of the river Ganga before dawn, trying to figure out how I feel about the place. It occurs to me that I love this river. I love the impetuous imagery of young Ganga descending from the heavens; I love the fact that she purifies, not just the body, but also mind, heart and soul. Just seeing the Ganga makes me happy in a way that makes no sense. The Danube is much more picturesque; the Seine just as poetic; the Potomac certainly far cleaner. Then why am I drawn to the Ganga? I go back to Nehru's beautiful words in his last will and testament. 'The Ganga especially is the river of India, beloved of her people, round which are intertwined her racial memories, her hopes and fears, her songs of triumph, her victories and her defeats. She has been a symbol of India's age-long culture and civilization, ever-changing, ever-flowing, and yet ever the same Ganga.'

As the sun rises, I start walking into the river. The Ganga is icy cold. The orange orb that is rising on the horizon beckons me forward. Keep going, I tell myself as I feel the spongy earth underneath me. Remember the saints and scholars who have walked in this path. The Buddha probably bathed in this river, exactly at this very spot. As did Shankara, Ramanuja, Madhva and every Hindu philosopher worth his salt. They took a dip in this holy river and achieved enlightenment. Poets and prime ministers paid homage to the Ganga. In Kashi. Don't be afraid. Think of your insignificance in the grand mythology that surrounds this holiest of Hindu cities. Who am I, a mere mortal, in front of this river of eternity? The waters rise up to my waist, then to my chest. I stop thinking and keep walking.

'F**k faecal coliform count. F**k bacterial overload. *Jai Gange,*' I mutter.

And then I hold my nose, close my eyes, purse my lips tightly and plunge into the river.

How was it? Well, I am here, aren't I? Writing all this stuff.

Takeaway

Kashi is the Holy Grail for Hindus. Spend a few days in Kashi, and if it resonates with your heart as it did with mine, you don't leave it behind. Kashi stays with you. And although I didn't realize it then, it was the beginning of my journey into the realm of faith.

There is a phrase that is now commonplace. You hear it in meditation apps and yoga studios. The phrase is 'open your heart', and it always caused me to roll my eyes because it was usually said in a foreign accent on some mindfulness app, usually accompanied by words such as 'chakra healing' or 'yoga pose' or 'Om'.

Just because it is a cliché doesn't mean it isn't true. There are people with open hearts. Some part comes from *sadhana* or effortful practice, be it mantra-chanting or daily yoga. My mother has an open heart because she wants it and wills it. This doesn't mean that she is perfect or saintly—far from it. It is just that she has allowed her intuition to flower because she listens to the unconscious mind. She allows thoughts and feelings to bubble up, and pays attention. Most of this happens after her daily puja. And that ultimately is the gift of any mystical or faith-based practice.

What faith does is nudge you from the rational mind into the realm of feeling and emotion, into what Carl Jung called the unconscious mind. What Kashi did for me was speed this along a bit. The people I met, the way they lived, the sights I saw, and, above all, the pervasive presence of the Ganga, enveloped me with their hoary history and ancient mysticism.

You begin a garland with a single flower. You begin a pilgrimage with a single step. Kashi was my first step into the realm of the heart and emotion. And just like you don't exactly know when a lotus flower begins blossoming, I didn't realize the significance of Kashi in my journey till months later.

Kashi was a gift. She was the first letter of the alphabet in my journey, the mother who held my hand and sent me off. For that, I will be eternally grateful to this luminescent city.

Moksha Prakashi Kashi.

3

Ajmer: The Islamic Saint Who Welcomes Hindus

I AM STANDING OUTSIDE the main shrine of the Ajmer Dargah (a Sufi shrine), listening to a spirited group of qawwali singers perform. Their voices are entreating, their eyes sincere, rising up to search for the divine. They sit cross-legged and pray, using their hands to express the strength of their feeling. They aspire towards rapture, to forget the self. They seek oneness with God, a quest worth undertaking—the only quest worth undertaking for some people. Non-believers, though, have to begin with the sombre, and what some might call silly, question: What is God?

When you think about it, God is such an abstract concept, which is probably why humans gave labels and names to Him/

Her/It: Mohammed, Jesus, Mary, Kali, Hanuman, Durga, Buddha, Zarathustra … the list goes on.

Religion, rather all religions, were an effort by early humans to wrap their head around this nebulous idea of the cosmic controller. When early humans confronted events that shocked, awed and confused them, they had to explain it somehow. A child gets hit in a road accident and dies. Why? Who can explain the timing of it? Why now? Why this particular child? Religion, I am guessing, was the answer that early humans came up with when they got hit by the proverbial truck or the Paleolithic version thereof. Why did the lion kill my son—of all people? Why now, when he was making off with that eligible Homo sapiens beauty in the neighbouring hunter–gatherer group? Questions that have no answer. Ergo, religion. Religion was—is—the human search for answers, a way of justifying the inexplicable happenings of the world, much like scientists do today—except now science is looking for alien life and cloning genomes, while religion has climbed down from its pioneering expedition into the soul and, to quote Karl Marx, become an 'opium for the people'.

A syncretic shrine for Muslims and Hindus

Ajmer is the home of Sufism, a spiritual order that originated in the Middle East. The Ajmer dargah, popularly known as Ajmer Sharif, is arguably one of India's most popular shrines, attracting some 1,50,000 pilgrims daily—from all over India and the Middle East. Hindus visit this shrine in large numbers, believing that it can grant wishes and solve problems.

Ajmer used to be called Ajay Meru or Ajay's Hill. Named after Ajayraj Chauhan, who built a fort here in the twelfth century, this was an important kingdom for the Chauhan clan. In contrast, Dilli to the north was a small town at that time. Ajay Meru occupied a strategic gap in the Aravalli hills of the area—with the trade route to the west and the Ganga river basin to the east. It was from here that successive generations of Chauhans fought Muslim invaders.

Today, Ajmer is known for its Sufi connection, and the Mayo College, built to model Eton in England in terms of educating Rajput princes.

Jalāl ad-Dīn Muhammad Rūmī is perhaps Sufism's most famous poet, thanks to numerous translations, and Turkish writer Elif Safak's novel *The Forty Rules of Love*. The novel tells the story of how Rumi became the student of Shams Tabrizi, a Persian Sufi dervish. When Rumi died, his son, Sultan Walad, founded the splendid Mevlevi order, also called the 'whirling dervishes', who perform this type of spinning in the name of remembering Allah or what they call *zikr* (or *dhikr*). They have been channelling the divine through dance ever since. Scholars say that one of the purposes of the whirling is to induce altered states of consciousness, which, you could argue, is the purpose of all religion.

Dance, when you're broken open.
Dance, if you've torn the bandage off.
Dance in the middle of the fighting.
Dance in your blood.
Dance when you're perfectly free.

—Rumi

Like Hinduism's bhakti cult, the philosophy behind Sufism is the idea of *tawhid*, a complex Persian word that symbolizes the primal root, the foundation from which we all spring. Sufism believes that we have become cut off from this primal connection to God.

All human action—the whirling, the singing, the poetry—is an expression of the devotee's longing to return to this root, to restore the connection. This is why the annual *urs*, officially the death anniversary of a Sufi saint, is celebrated as joyfully as a wedding because Sufis believe that death reconnects the soul with its primal root, with God.

The word *urs* comes from the Arabic word *uroos* and means 'wedding'. When a saint dies, as Khwaja Moinuddin Chishti did in Ajmer, he achieves *wisaal* or the ultimate union with the beloved. Realize that they don't say 'union with God'. Instead, they view God as their beloved. This intimate, all-encompassing lover-like connection is what differentiates Sufism from its parent religion, Islam. William Chittick, a leading translator of Islamic texts who studied at the University of Tehran, has described Sufism as the 'interiorization and intensification of Islamic faith and practice' in his book, *Sufism: A Beginner's Guide* published by Oneworld Publications.

Ganga Jamuna Sanskriti

For a Hindu, it is easy to understand and access Sufism through its music and its tolerant, enveloping tenets. Indeed, millions of Hindus visit the Ajmer Dargah every year, clad in colourful saris and sporting bright red bindis. 'It is a Ganga Jamuna *sanskriti* (culture) here,' said a Hindu devotee to me.

This then is the distinctive beauty of this dargah. It is not just open to people of all faiths, it welcomes them. If you have a wish or *mannat* that you want fulfilled, a prayer that must reach God, an offering of thanks that you want to give, you are welcome here. And people come from the four corners of the world, carrying baskets heavy with flowers—a ring of roses interspersed with marigolds, an aesthetic that is distinct to Indian places of worship. The heavy scent of *desi gulab* or indigenous red roses (Rosa damascena) fills the air.

Devotees bring nuts and fruits. They carry blankets and shawls to place on top of the tombstone. They tie strings with objects on a stick that extends across the empty cauldrons where food is cooked. The hanging objects offer clues to human frailties and wishes. There is a metal house, a cradle, a hand, a comb, each symbolizing a desire for a job, marriage, children or wealth. People throw in money and rice grains into the empty cauldron. At the side of the cauldrons are metal containers filled with sacred food that has been cooked early in the morning. The *kesaria bhaat*, as it is called, is orange, and consists of broken wheat, sugar, ghee and dried fruit, all stirred together for hours before being distributed to the faithful. It is vegetarian, although legend has it that Emperor Shah Jahan mixed with the vegetarian food the meat of a Nilgai or Blue Bull that he would shoot while hunting.

Dargah and the Mughals

The dargah's link with the Mughal emperors is close, and spans generations. It was Emperor Akbar who ordered the first giant cauldron to be built. It is called Badi Degh (or big cauldron) and can cook a whopping amount of food. Akbar pledged to come to Ajmer on foot if he won the battle of Chittorgarh. When he won, he kept his promise and walked to Ajmer, where he distributed food from the big cauldron. Some say that the Badi Degh cooks 125 *maunds* (a unit of mass in Arabia and Persia) of rice, a quantity that can vary from 11 kg to 80 kg and more depending on location. Let's just say that food from Badi Degh can feed about 15,000 people.

Not to be outdone, Akbar's son, Jahangir, ordered the construction of the smaller cauldron, called *Choti Degh* (small cauldron). He ordered that this food be distributed to 5,000 people, taking the first offering himself, after which his queen, Noor Jahan, and the other women of his harem, followed suit. This kind of largesse was typical of the empire-building Mughals. Today, moguls of a different sort, from hedge fund managers to business magnates, pay the dargah to have food cooked and distributed. Typically, this happens during the urs every year, or to mark a special occasion.

From Iran to Ajmer

Khwaja Moinuddin Chishti, the saint who is enshrined in this dargah, was born in the Sistan region of Iran. His life followed the fairly standard trajectory of most great spiritual leaders. Pious family? Check. Interested in spirituality from a young age? Check. As a boy, he prayed and meditated instead of picking fruit from the famous Iranian orchards.

Moinuddin's next experience is something I would have liked to have. While working in his orchard, which itself is an experience not to be sniffed at, given the legendary quality of the melons of Iran, Moinuddin had a visitor. Being a well-brought-up child, he greeted the spiritual man properly by kissing his hands, and gave him fruit. The mystic, whose name was Sheikh Ibrahim Qandozi, was impressed by the pious nature of the boy. He took out some *khul* from his pocket. This is described as the dregs of sesame seeds after the oil is extracted. Some historians say that this was bread. Anyway, the mystic man put this piece into his mouth, chewed it a bit and then put it in Moinuddin's mouth. The boy lost all connection with the current world and went into a mystical trance. This event caused the scales to fall from Moinuddin's eyes. He went into the divine realm and realized the true nature of things.

After this experience, there was no turning back. Moinuddin left for Bukhara, back then a great centre of learning, where he finished his education. After that, it was onward to Samarkand to study philosophy, theology and grammar. In Baghdad, he met a great Sufi mystic who became his guide and teacher for twenty years. It was here that Khwaja Moinuddin Chishti received the instruction to go to Hindustan or India.

Ajmer at the time was a great amalgam of many faiths. It was the pleasure resort of emperor Shah Jahan, a far cry from the dusty and grey town that it has become today. Khwaja Moinuddin Chishti set up his spiritual order using Ajmer as the base. He became known as Garib Nawaz for the compassion with which he treated poor people. He spread Sufism throughout north India, gained many disciples and, most importantly, established the Chishti order that continues to this day. His real achievement was to make his faith accessible to all.

Both inclusive and exclusive

Religions evolve through a somewhat contradictory impulse: by defining and differentiating themselves. It is one of the things that bothers me about faith. You'd think that prayer or connection to the divine would make you see the world as one—all people as your own. Most religions advocate this notion of treating everyone as your brother or sister. Except that the deeper people go into religion, the more they seem to define themselves through ever-narrowing parameters, be it Sri Vaishnavism or Seventh Day Adventist. Religion doesn't expand the self even though every great text advocates it. It causes a narrowing of boundaries in a sense so that you begin affiliating yourself with a Pentecostal order or a specific guru. You call yourself Sufi or Mahayana or Orthodox or a Sai devotee. You view other orders, even if they belong to the same religion, with some amount of suspicion. 'All religions are the same,' you say piously, while hobnobbing with other acolytes of the same order.

The relationship between what some call 'mainstream Islam' and Sufism reflects this trend and is fraught in this way. Sufi practitioners emphasize that Sufism originated in Islam, that early Sufi thought was directly drawn from the Koran, except that it was internalized.

Dance as a route to God

Internalization is a word that comes up often in Sufism to explain its tolerance to all faiths and the use of song and dance in worship. The twelfth-century Muslim theologian Al Ghazali has a wonderful passage in his treatise, *The Alchemy of Happiness*, in a chapter titled 'The Use of Dance and Music as Aids to Religious Life'. The fact that he has to defend music and dance speaks of his desire to make Islam and Sufism compatible with one another, which leads to the conclusion that they were diverging, even as early as the twelfth century.

In the chapter, Al Ghazali says, 'The effect of music and dancing … fan into a flame whatever love is already dormant in the heart, whether it be earthly and sensual, or divine and spiritual.' Makes me want to go out and dance.

There is more that Al Ghazali defends. 'As regards the erotic poetry which is recited in Sufi gatherings, and to which people sometimes make objection, we must remember that—in such poetry mention is made of separation from or union with the beloved, the Sufi, who is an adept in the love of God, applies such expressions to separation from or union with Him.'

When and why did religions become so prudish? A few centuries ago, erotic sculpture and poetry was acceptable on the path towards God. What happened? When did we decide that God required seriousness? What happened to joy?

There is a lot of joy in the singing at the dargah. People sway in ecstasy, some with tears rolling down their cheeks. The whole atmosphere combines sensual bliss with spiritual elevation. It is as faith I believe should be, mixing the everyday with the elevated, the mundane with the divine, the senses and the soul.

I didn't taste the kesaria bhaat though. It was Ramzan when I went. Nobody was eating anything during the day. It seemed inappropriate for me to do so, even though there were several enticing containers full of them.

I was disappointed to have not tasted the food. It was a sign, I told myself. The women in my family use this word when they contemplate visits to temples. The god or goddess has to summon you, they will say. Or summon me back, in this case, I think, to taste the food during urs.

Twist in the tale

A surprising twist emerged as I exited the dargah. My guide was waiting outside. He wanted to know if he could hitch a ride to Jaipur with me. His reason epitomized the Indian web of relationships. 'My daughter-in-law's brother's wedding happened a few days ago and my *samdhi* (the in-laws) have invited me for food after a puja. You like *dal baati churma*, don't you?' he offered as explanation.

Two hours later, we drove up to a small apartment on the outskirts of Jaipur. Inside were about twenty people, all colourfully dressed. Plates were brought. We were the last to eat. They gave us a stainless-steel plate filled with spiced dal, a round ball of cooked wheat dough, which was the *baati*, and a sweet mixture, the *churma*. There was a piquant pickle and some water. We ate quietly. Men came up with additional food to serve. This is what I have noticed in traditional Indian homes. People accord food the seriousness that it is due. In my ancestral village in Palghat, you'd sit on the floor and eat from banana leaves, pretty much in silence. The focus was on the food, and on the eating. The servers would watch and add dishes quietly. This was how we ate the dish in Jaipur. It was delicious, although my driver told me later that he had eaten better versions of the dish. 'You need to cook it on a slow fire, using firewood and cow-dung patties,' he said. 'The smoke gets infused in the dish. That is when the flavours bloom and take on a smoky hue.'

I concentrated on the food. It was delicious.

Was this the Sufi saint's blessing? I may not have been able to eat the kesaria bhaat at the dargah, but here was sacred food after an auspicious ritual being served to me.

I will just have to return here: for the kesaria bhaat of the dargah, and for good, old-fashioned dal-baati-churma made in the village.

Takeaway

After returning from Ajmer, the two memories that stayed with me more distinctly than others were the wonderful smell of the desi gulab (native roses) and and the sight of the whirling dervishes, the precursors of the Sufi mystics and qawwali singers.

Try something at home. See if you can whirl like the dervishes. If you are a kathak dancer, this will be easy for you. But what I am asking and what I attempted was a bit more than a practice or performance. To whirl like a dervish involves a suspension of the ego and a desire to connect to the divine. The Mevlevi Order, founded by Rumi in the Turkish city of Konya, has whirling dervishes who view this as a form of prayer. When I watched them in Konya decades ago, I didn't understand why they placed their hands in a certain way—one hand open to the skies to receive and the other hand pointing to the earth to give and ground. It was only after visiting Ajmer and learning about the Sufi mystic, Shams Tabrizi, that I understood the meaning of this mystical order.

Dance is something fundamental to humans. In today's world, we connect dance with discotheques and parties. Early humans danced in ecstasy though, not to perform or show off, but to express their faith.

It is hard to sing and dance without feeling that you are performing, even if you do it while alone within your home. Try it sometime. Dance like nobody is watching. Go further. Dance in order to connect to the divine. Dance to dissolve the ego. Dance to receive blessings from the sky. Dance to catalyse these blessings into the earth.

Sufism is a beautiful path because it incorporates the senses and beauty. Its wonderful poetry, music and dance touch the soul in ways that are hard to explain—they can only be experienced.

All you need to do is feel. To sing and dance. To open the heart (there it is again). If you are lucky, Ajmer's dargah will propel you on this path. But as a start, you can start spinning round and round in your home.

4

Palani: The Oldest Jam in
the World

CARNEGIE HALL HAS NOTHING on Hindu temples. I think of
this as I stand inside the sanctum sanctorum of Palani Temple,
waiting for the doors to open. I have visited countless temples in my
life, and everywhere the routine is the same: long queues of people,
call them fans or devotees, waiting for hours to get a glimpse of the
object of their adoration, be it an actor, musician or, in this case,
their god. Different queues based on how much each ticket costs,
and the wait for 'show time' when the curtain opens.

The curtain in this case has covered the idol of the impetuous,
youthful god, Muruga, who stands atop Palani Hill, 150 m above
sea level. To reach him, you have to climb 693 stone steps or take

the winding 'yaanai paathai' or elephant footpath through sacred groves. I try climbing up the steps first, but switch to the winding 'elephant path' to save my knees.

As temples go, Palani is accessible. It is not crowded when I visit in July. The barricades that snake around the temple complex for use during Thai Poosam and Panguni Uthiram, the temple's largest festivals, when 2–3 lakh pilgrims congregate in Palani, are largely superfluous now.

It is 6 p.m. on a cool July evening. The heat of the plains far below has dissipated. A crowd waits in the sanctum sanctorum, patiently, agreeably, not just resigned to their lot, but also welcoming it as part of the religious experience. It is part of the hardship or *prayatanam* that devotees endure in order to reach the divine—the religious version of 'eat your broccoli if you want the ice cream'.

Behind the curtain, a silhouette of the god is faintly visible. The priests are doing the *raja alankaram*—dressing him up as a king. An elderly man, called an *oodhuvaar*, is singing free-form verse in praise of the lord. It is remarkable how similar gospel music sounds across religions. The elderly male voice praises and entreats the god to shower his blessings.

Explaining faith through song

Oodhuvaar is a Tamil word, which doesn't just represent singing. It has more weight than that. An oodhuvaar is someone who explains, who transports an important truth through song, who convinces, who makes people understand. The songs that this oodhuvaar is singing are in Tamil: my mother tongue. It gives me joy to listen to the words and understand their meaning. Finally, I can relate to what my husband says when he goes into raptures over Urdu poetry. When I ask for a translation of the Urdu verses, he tries, but says that English simply doesn't capture the nuances of Urdu. Well, the same could be said of ancient Tamil poetry—and here, for once, unlike with north Indian languages like Hindi and Urdu, I understand everything.

When I land in Coimbatore, the place of my birth, and listen to the musical cadences of its Tamil, I feel a confidence and comfort that I never do in North India. Two hours later, I am in Palani Hill. Here too Tamil is spoken with the finesse and intrinsic politeness of the Gounder community that populates this region, their speech as elegant and refined as Urdu. I grew up with these people, and easily fall into the respectful way of speaking, so different from the fast pace of Chennai's Tamil.

Nobody is speaking inside the sanctum sanctorum. They sit or stand quietly, listening to the oodhuvaar. After about half an hour, people twitch and shift, as herds of deer do when they sense an impending event. A corpulent man appears and loosens the rope of the large temple bell. The musicians, a drummer and a *nadhaswaram* player (like a South Indian oboe), start tuning their instruments. The crowd stirs, recognizing that the supplementary actors have taken their positions. Suddenly, without warning, the curtain is swiftly drawn open. The crowd doesn't go crazy exactly. It is more like a collective chant of 'Muruga Muruga....'

People fold their hands into a namaste and raise it above their heads, as if to attract his eyes. They hold their palms out in supplication and to receive his grace. All eyes are on the idol, dressed as a king in purple-and-yellow silk clothes, a bejewelled crown on its head. There are garlands of jasmine, marigold, tuberose and roses. There is the flickering light from countless oil lamps that encircle his image. The temple bell clangs as the priests do the aarti. Drums beat, bells clang, and the singer's voice attempts a crescendo above it all. Unless you are used to it, the sensuality of the experience is overwhelming. The priest takes a multilevel oil lamp with flickering lights and circles it in front of the deity. All of us pray: for success, prosperity, peace of mind and salvation. Everyone's eyes are glued on the Lord standing inside. We are, at this moment, taking *darshan* of the deity.

The central act of Hindu worship

In her book, *Darshan: Seeing the Divine Image in India*, Diana Eck, the religious studies scholar at Harvard who has authored many books on Hinduism, says that this moment, when pilgrims stand before the Lord, is 'the central act of Hindu worship'. It is the moment when you see and, equally important, are seen by the deity. 'Since, in the Hindu understanding, the deity is present in the image, the visual apprehension of the image is charged with religious meaning. Beholding the image is an act of worship, and through the eyes one gains the blessing of the divine,' says Eck.

Taking darshan is like gaining audience with royalty. It happens during a fleeting moment that is charged with significance. So devotees do what they can to gain the attention of the Lord. A friend told me to lift and touch my palms above my head so that the Lord could see me. Although the voice in my head says, *If the Lord is omnipotent, won't he see me without my having to do a thing?* I obediently do what my friend told me to do. The aarti ends. The priest comes out to distribute *vibhuti* or sacred ash to the devotees. The security personnel begin their litany: 'Move on, sir. Move on, lady.' The darshan ends. The moment of communing with God is gone. The line moves on; rather, we are hustled out.

A group of devotees, clad in rich silks, are quietly led from the side to the inner room, right in front of the idol. It is clear that they have paid for this privilege. The priests are deferential. I used to get annoyed that you could pay to gain closer access to God. It irked me on many levels. Wasn't God above all such mundane transactions and bribery? Wasn't devotion enough to get close to Him? Shouldn't He punish those who wielded their wealth as a way of queue-jumping? Weren't the priests supposed to be pure and holy instead of selling access to God to the highest bidder? Instead of trying to wrap my head around such complicated concepts, I should simply view temples as theatre, which they are, and which they do magnificently. The front row is reserved for the VIPs; then come the moneyed class that can score good seats to witness the divine; and then there is the general public. Unlike theatre halls though, the general public doesn't pay for entrance into Hindu temples. They just wait in queues for hours. I have tried long and hard to make my peace with the hierarchical structure of Hinduism, and indeed, all religions. Perhaps I should just bring them down from the pedestal, bring them down from the realm of the divine to the realm of the commercial, view them as a spectacle.

A holy spectacle

All religions do spectacles in a way that could shame Broadway. Perhaps they were the original theatrical form. When people got bored in ancient times, they went to the mosque, church or temple not just to commune with each other and the divine, but also to get their daily dose of excitement: to witness something beautiful in a dramatic setting. The experience is multilayered and multipronged. There is music, dance, elephants, chanting, a colourful cast of characters, and a flow of events that leads up to a highly charged moment with the opening of a curtain.

This format isn't unique to Hinduism though. I recall visiting the shrine of Hazratbal in Srinagar during the Meraj-ul-alam Festival. Thousands of devotees waited in the lawns facing the mosque, unmoving, unwavering in their faith, held in thrall by just the waiting. At the appointed hour, an imam came out on the balcony holding aloft a lock of Prophet Mohammed's hair. Called *moi-e-muqaddas*, this holy relic is displayed only ten times a year. The waiting congregation chanted verses from the Koran, tears spilling down their cheeks. No Broadway play could have achieved that effect, and all for a few minutes of display. Before a casual observer could register the import of what just happened, the imam walked back inside. The waiting crowd sagged as if a rug was pulled out from under their feet. Then they folded up the rugs on which they had been sitting. Everyone quietly dispersed from the lawns of the mosque carrying with them a glimpse of the divine, which after all, is the purpose and signature of a religious experience.

The many changes of costume

At the Palani temple, this special glimpse of the divine happens throughout the day, but most particularly during the six pujas or worships. They start at dawn and end late at night. Before each puja, the curtain is closed and the Lord is dressed and decorated. At 6 a.m., he is in his simplest form: the famed *aandi-vesham*, where he is clad in a simple loincloth as a monk-beggar-mendicant (the word *aandi* connotes all three). In this avatar, Muruga's big ears are visible. Devotees believe that this god with his wide-open ears will heed their prayers. Why else is he depicted that way? The Lord as a keen listener of their woes.

At 8 a.m., Muruga become the *vedan* or hunter, who claimed the lives of fierce demons, but also the heart of the gypsy girl Valli. And so it goes through the day, till 8.30 p.m. when he is divested of the flowers and ornaments of the day for the *palli-paatu* or the lullaby. The worship ends when the idol is moved to a nearby room and put to bed.

Inside the sanctum sanctorum, the worship ebbs and flows. After a while, I go out to the spacious corridors of the many *praharas* or mandalas that encircle the temple. Outside, I find a slim man sitting by himself. We get talking. He name is Senthil, and he is a *miraz pandaram*, he says, and has served at the temple for generations. Palani temple has thirty-two priests and sixty-four miraz pandarams. They work long hours and serve their god and the general public.

In Palani, there is a quaint custom associated with putting the Lord to bed.

'At the end of the day, the accounts are read to the Lord,' says Senthil.

'What does this mean?' I ask him.

'Oh, we tell him things like, "Today, we got 50,000 rupees from the sale of the 100-rupees tickets, and 3 lakh from the sale of *panchamritham*." After all, this is His temple, and he needs to know the day's takings.'

Wouldn't he know it already? I want to ask. *A god can see, through his divine eye, the day's accounts without having them read out to him, right?*

This, then, is the difference between a true believer and someone like me for whom faith is still a question mark. I know believers who look at clouds and see goddesses. I look at clouds and see potential rain. I get WhatsApp and Facebook messages where a circle is drawn around a particular cloud with the note: 'Look at the image of Ganesha in the sky.' I merely think that it is a pie in the sky.

Worship as imagination and playacting

My mom is one such believer, and I often have arguments with her about why it is necessary to do this elaborate set of rituals that Hindus do. Hindu pujas involve *abhishekam* or ritual-bathing, *alankaram* or decorating with flowers and jewels, and *aradhanai* or praying to an idol.

'Why make all this fuss when a simple act of meditation will do?' I ask my mother.

My mother calls prayer *bhavanai*, or imagining. In her view, this playacting—decorating the idol, putting it to bed, reading the accounts to an all-knowing God—nudges the devotee closer to an understanding of divinity.

'Do you think you are like the Buddha?' she asked me one day. 'Do you think you are so evolved that you can simply sit down and realize God? The average devotee needs lots of props.'

The theatre reference again, I thought. The idol and all the actions and objects that surround it—the flowers, the decoration, the rituals, the imagining—are props that help pilgrims on their path to the higher plane.

The props used in Palani are pots made of terracotta or metal, decorated with flowers and coloured thread, and containing a variety of offerings—milk, honey, roses and other flowers—for Muruga. They have specific words: *paal-kudam is a pot with milk inside; then-kudam has honey.*

The warrior and his six houses

I grew up in Chennai, then called Madras, at a time when Hindi was banned. The government in the late 1970s wanted all state-school students to learn Tamil. Within a year, in middle school, I went from learning Hindi as a second language to learning Tamil, a historical fact that I resent, and which impacts me to this day, particularly when I travel to North India and am shamed by my stuttering Hindi.

There has been one unexpected benefit though. Studying Tamil literature has exposed me to the glories of Sangam Tamil verse that seduces the reader through its combination of mysticism, philosophy, eroticism, descriptions of nature and sheer poetic beauty in a way that is hard to convey to the average Urdu speaker—and if I were texting, I would put a smiley face at this point.

A lot of Tamil literature begins with *Thiru*, which is an honorific, like 'Mister' or 'Shri'.

Thirumurugatrupadai, for example, is about Muruga and his six battlegrounds, which are the six sacred hills for Muruga. It dates back to the second century and references Muruga as the killer of many demons. More than anything, Muruga is a fierce warrior who was born to kill as it were. There are references about Muruga in the *Tolkaapiyam*, which is viewed to be the oldest work of Tamil literature.

The most famous Tamil verses on Muruga come from the *Thirupugazh*, literally meaning 'praise of the Lord'. My aunts in Chennai still go to Thirupugazh classes and memorize its words and music. Written by Arunagirinathar, who, like Saint Augustine of Hippo, led a hedonistic life before converting to spirituality, Thirupugazh flows through in an easy Tamil metre with rhythmic musical words. Every Hindu god and goddess has verses of praise. Apparently, there were 16,000 such verses, of which only 1,365 have been discovered.

Muruga is, perhaps more than other gods, linked to Tamil Nadu. He used to be popular in North India as Karthikeya, but the Middle Ages saw a gradual decline in his worship. Today, pilgrims from as far as Mauritius, Canada, Singapore, Malaysia, Indonesia and Sri Lanka—wherever there is a large Tamil-speaking diaspora—come to visit his *aaru padai veedu* or 'six army houses', depicting Muruga as a warrior god. Palani is one of these six hill temples dedicated to Muruga.

He who wields weapons

The Palani hills are an offshoot of the Western Ghats and form the backdrop to the Arulmigu Dhandayuthapani (he who wields the *danda* and other weapons) Temple, as this temple is called. The temple stands atop a hill called Sivagiri, which means Shiva's hill. The one beside it is called, perhaps appropriately, Shaktigiri, or Shakti's hill.

Legend has it that the short Sage Agastya, who is seen in sculptures as far away as Java in Indonesia, commanded his disciple, Idumban, to take two hills from the Himalayas down south. Idumban balanced the two hills on either end of a stick—which ended up being the template of the *kaavadi* that devotees carry for Muruga. When he came to Palani, Idumban decided to rest his feet a bit and set down the two hills. At that time, Subramanya, as Muruga is sometimes called, appeared in front of Idumban and told him that he had claimed those hills. Idumban refused to yeild. A battle ensued. Muruga killed Idumban, whose dying wish was that anyone who carried a kaavadi and walked up to Palani should be granted whatever they wished for. Ergo, the kaavadi that thousands of pilgrims carry to this day.

At the bottom of the hill is the Shanmugha river, now overrun with water hyacinths and weeds. As I walk by, an old woman accosts me. Her name is Muniamma, and she is trying to recruit me to be a movie extra. Muniamma is about eighty, with weathered skin the colour of a coffee bean. She is clad in a soft white cotton sari sans blouse in the fashion of village women in Tamil Nadu. She approaches me as I stand outside the tonsure shed, contemplating whether I should shave my head: an action that I have often considered.

The reason for tonsuring or shaving off one's hair entirely is described in the Skanda Purana, as a dialogue between Shiva and his wife. Shiva says that a man should get his head tonsured whenever he gets an opportunity to visit a holy place because the hair contains all the sins that he has committed. The Chinese on the other hand believe that healthy hair growth shows that he has good kidneys or a good constitution. Shaving off one's hair and offering it to God is common in India, particularly amongst the poor, for whom it is the simplest and arguably most intimate offering to God. It reduces ego, makes you less vain and, in a strange way, defines your features. Muniamma, for instance, is completely bald. She has rubbed turmeric on her head, which means that she has tonsured her hair in the last couple of days. Turmeric is an antiseptic in case the barber's blade nicks your head.

Muniamma and the movie extra

Even though I am wearing a sari, Muniamma has me pegged as a 'jeans-pant Madam', a type apparently in short supply in the area. Her grandson wants to make a rap video to protest the dumping of garbage in the Shanmukha Lake. He needs extras to dance behind him and fill up the screen. Muniamma thinks I am a fair prospect, as long as I change out of my sari into tight leggings.

'Don't worry, nobody will see you,' says the young man reassuringly, if somewhat quixotically. *What is the point of dancing in a video if nobody will see me?*

The grandson's name is Pandu. He hovers behind Muniamma, his eyes glancing around furtively. He is resplendent in a red shirt with gold buttons that stretches across his slight paunch. He wears jeans and a matching red pair of sneakers. On his forehead is a bright red dot, and he is wearing a checked red turban on his head.

After filming, the grandson plans to post the video on YouTube, where he hopes it will go viral like 'Gangnam Style'. He has recruited his grandmother to recruit extras.

Muniamma's recruitment strategy is foolproof. She will make me homemade *kuthirai vaali kanji* for lunch if I dance in the video. So hungry am I to taste authentic village millets that I say yes without asking any more questions.

Kuthirai vaali belongs to the Echinochloa family and is known as barnyard millet. With diabetes numbers rising, millets are all the rage in South India. My cousin drinks them as porridge for breakfast, my mother mixes them in her dosa batter, and my neighbour is trying to fashion millet muffins.

Kuthirai vaal means 'a horse's tail' in Tamil, and for a moment I idly wonder if Muniamma's kanji or porridge will give me the strength of a horse—somewhat like the herb Ashwagandha does according to Ayurveda. Muniamma smirks and says that the effects of barnyard millet have to do with 'night strength'. The effects are more like Moringa, widely touted as an aphrodisiac in Tamil Nadu. 'Your husband will be very happy tonight,' she says with a knowing, if sexist, smirk.

As it turns out, I didn't star in the video. By the time I returned from lunch at Muniamma's house—an excellent kanji that lulled me into a deep siesta rather than give me 'night strength' for an absent husband, Pandu had been called away on urgent business at the mechanic shop he runs with his buddies. One of the motorbikes that had come in for repair 'exploded', he explained on the phone before hanging up hurriedly.

He wants to shoot the video tomorrow, by which time I will be far away from Palani.

I tell Pandu that he needs to find another extra and go back to the hotel for respite from the searing sun.

This incident reminds me of something that most pilgrims forget. For the locals of Palani, life isn't only about god and godliness, although many make a living from Him or Her and the temples that they inhabit. But their life is also about motorbikes or motors that break down, breakout Youtube videos that they want to shoot and women they want to woo. They live, love, work, make movies, run businesses and dupe people. Life, in all its myriad hues, goes on—in parallel with the gods—in these temple towns.

Walking up from the river to the hill

In its heyday, the Shanmugha river was the starting point for the trek up Palani hill. The idea was that pilgrims would bathe in this river before climbing up the hill. I do the same later in the evening. After a refreshing shower, I decide to walk up again. With its green hills and valleys, the area must have been picturesque before the seven million pilgrims who visit Palani annually laid siege to this small town, with over a lakh of them showing up on festivals like Thai Poosam.

In Singapore, where I lived for two years, Thai Poosam was the most popular festival amongst the Singaporean Tamils. The name of the festival comes from the date on which it occurs: during the

Tamil month called Thai, and when the lunar star called Poosam is ascendant in the sky. Thai Poosam is the day of grace and light when divine energies are abundantly present on Earth and are willing to render support if you are determined to end pressing problems of your life. A full moon that brings enlightenment will be in the Poosam or Pushya star that is considered auspicious for spiritual development. The presiding deity of Pushya is Jupiter, who is the guru or teacher and the most benevolent of all planets. Hence, those who ardently seek grace of such planetary alignments will not return empty-handed.

Serangoon Road, the Indian area of Singapore, would be packed with devotees, dressed in yellow clothes and engaging in severe austerities such as nose, tongue and cheek piercings. They would walk over hot coals as a way of appeasing Muruga. It was difficult to watch on TV, let alone do it.

Faith and austerity are closely linked. Monotheistic religions like Christianity, Islam, Judaism involve fasting during certain religious periods. Pilgrimages are part of the religious display where devotees take arduous voyages in order to feel close to God. Hinduism encourages multiple ways of physical hardship and austerity for the sake of religion. You can fast for a day or a month; you can walk up the hill or mountain to meet God; you can stop speaking in order to centre your mind and heart; you can circle the temple for a prescribed number of times; or you can actually weigh yourself against fruits, vegetables, silver, or gold and offer it to God.

Rolling around the temple

In Palani, I witness an even more dramatic act, an intense display of faith: a woman rolls around the temple doing the *anga pradakshanam* or full-body circumnavigation of the temple. An older woman, presumably her mother, walks behind her. Halfway through her circumnavigation, the woman starts laughing, somewhat madly I think. She chants Muruga's name. *'Kandanukku Haro Hara! Muruganukku Haro Hara!'* Temples allow for these kinds of trance-like behaviours. What would seem weird outside seems perfectly normal in a sacred space, and particularly so for this ancient god who was worshiped by tribals centuries ago.

In a fascinating paper, epigraphist Iravatham Mahadevan, who deciphered the Brahmi script and was an expert on epigraphy of the Indus Valley civilization, linked Muruga with Harappan deities. In the paper, Dr Mahadevan said that a Harappan pictorial ideogram or inscription of two intertwined bangles was called *muruku*. It referred to a primitive tribal god conceived as a 'demon' that possessed people and was a 'wrathful killer or hunter'. The interesting thing is that the Harappan people had a 'skeletal deity' with similar traits revealed through 'pictorial depictions, early myths and Dravidian linguistic data'.

By linking Muruku or Murukan with the Harappans, the paper shows that Dravidian Tamils worshipped this god in the earliest mists of time. The Sanskritization of South India converted the demon Murukan into Lord Murugan, and made him a compassionate, handsome god rather than a wrathful, demon-like hunter.

He has a number of names in South India, particularly Tamil Nadu:

- Senthil: The red-faced one
- Kanda: A Tamil variation of the Sanskrit Skanda
- Kumara: Son, in this case, of Shiva and Parvati. Also means prince. Hero of the poet Kalidasa's epic titled *Kumara Sambhavam* or 'The Birth of Kumara'.

- Karthikeya: Son of the Krithika sisters who raised him. After their marriage, Shiva and Parvati engage in a long period of lovemaking. Shiva's seed is too potent for Parvati to carry, so Agni, the god of fire, takes it and dumps it in the River Ganga who then carries the seed to the Saravana Lake. There, a six-faced baby is born and is cared for by the Krithika sisters. The son of the Krithika sisters is called Karthikeya.

- Valli Manaala: The one who is married to Valli, the young gypsy girl who is one of the two wives of Muruga.

- Vela: He who holds a spear or *vel*, using which he killed the demon Soorapadman. The story goes that the demon took the form of a mango tree when he saw that his defeat was imminent. Muruga speared the tree into half. One half became a peacock, which is his vehicle or *vahanam*, and the other half became a rooster, which adorns his victory flag.

- Vadi vela: The one who holds the spear like a stick. Palani town is full of shops with names such as Vel Medicals, Vel Batteries, Vel Condiments and my personal favourite Vel Wines.

- Subramanya: Lord of the serpents

- Shanmukha: Literally means 'six faces'

- Saravana: The one who was born from the Saravana Lake

- Guha: The one who resides in the cave of the heart

The oldest sibling rivalry in the world?

In Palani, Muruga is called by the rather longish name Dhantayudhapani—the one who holds the *dhandam* or staff as his *ayutham* or weapon. This staff or dhandam was used by the rishis (saints) of yore to help with their meditation—as anyone who ever read *Amar Chitra Katha* comic books as a child will recognize. The dhandam is infused with many layers of meanings. Depending on usage, it could mean punishment, a mendicant's stick, a controlled life, or the curse of a saint. The dhandam and the *kamandalam*, a copper pot for carrying water, were the two essential accoutrements of Indian ascetics. By imitating the guise of one with his aandi vesham or beggar-like appearance, Muruga was actually making a point to his parents.

The story goes back to the Puranas and could well be the oldest example of sibling rivalry. It began with a fruit, a *gnana pazham* or the fruit of knowledge. Sage Narada, the troublemaker, came to Lord Shiva carrying this wonderful fruit that would give him the benefits of all knowledge. Shiva, being the loving father, wanted to divide it in half and give each half to his two sons: Ganesha and Muruga. Narada immediately said that cutting the fruit would reduce its impact. He also gave them an idea—of a competition. The two children would circumnavigate the world. Whoever returned first would get the fruit. Immediately, Muruga climbed on his trusty steed, the peacock, and flew off. Ganesha merely walked around his parents, Shiva and Parvati, saying that to him they represented the world. Carried away by this wisdom-laced flattery, Shiva immediately handed the fruit to Ganesha. When Muruga appeared a few minutes later, red-faced from the exertion of circumnavigating the world, he discovered that the fruit had been given to his quietly gleeful brother. So Muruga did the ancient equivalent of 'It's not fair!' Being a god, his version was more than just a childish tantrum. He climbed up a hill and refused to come down.

It took an aged woman-saint named Avvaiyaar to pacify Muruga. She walked up the hill singing, '*Pazham nee appa gnana pazham nee appa.*' 'You are the fruit. You are the fruit of knowledge of wisdom.'

As compliments go, calling someone the fruit of knowledge is pretty up there. Muruga calmed down, but stayed up on the hill. In fact, this warrior lord who has killed several asuras or demons has claimed not just one hill but six as homes for his army. Ergo the phrase *aaru padai veedu* or 'six army homes'.

Five ingredients to make ambrosia

Palani's sacred food is the Panchamritham (or five nectars). The minute I told people that I was going to Palani, the orders came fast and furious. My mother wanted half a kilo of Panchamritham, the temple's famed prasadam. Distant aunts and uncles whom I hadn't spoken to for months suddenly called under the pretext of inquiring about my health. In between, they let it slip that they had heard I was planning a temple trip and that they would love some prasadam. They were so transparent in their 'ask' that I wondered why they had even bothered to call. My mom should have simply said that I should bring back half a dozen bottles to distribute to friends and family.

The logic of why certain temples serve certain prasadams makes for a fascinating exercise in reimagining history. Palani is a hill temple. All the ingredients in Panchamritham are found locally, says Santhana Lakshmi, a schoolteacher and local historian. The five ingredients of the Panchamritham have 'body-heating' qualities as per Indian healing systems such as Ayurveda. The Lord chose them because hill districts are cool and misty, and his devotees would need such nutritious and heating foods in order to climb up the slopes to see him. The other logic is of course the widespread availability of the ingredients in the local area. Just as people climbed Everest because it was there, people made Panchamritham with certain ingredients because they were there.

Santhana Lakshmi is an amazing Tamil speaker. For six minutes she speaks confidently, without stuttering pauses, about the history and culture of the temple. Later, she reveals that public speaking is her true calling. Tamil Nadu has a rich culture of public debate, with men and women participating in equal measure. My schoolmate, Bharati Bhaskar, is a celebrity because of her public speaking and debating skills, all in chaste Tamil. Santhana Lakshmi idolizes her and wants to go on the same route.

Marrying industry with tradition

The Palani temple's Panchamritham-making facility looks like a factory. It is a large building with clean corridors and industrial-size mixers. The raw materials—sacks of country sugar, and containers of honey and ghee—are all stacked separately in different rooms. The largest room holds the stainless-steel mixers. When I walk in, two men are standing aloft an electric lift and pouring the bananas into the mixer. Then comes the brown sugar, which is measured out in large stainless-steel boxes. After some vigorous mixing in multiple large stainless-steel containers, a brown, thoroughly mixed, jam-like substance is poured from a pipe into bottles. The whole thing is automated.

Indians are in two minds about brown-coloured sweets. We don't take to them unequivocally, like Western people take to dark brown chocolate. The Panchamritham's brown colour reminds me of the Deepavali *marundhu* or Deepavali medicine that my grandmother used to make for Hinduism's largest festival, Deepavali. Before eating the abundance of sweet and savoury treats that were prepared and procured for the festival, my grandmother would force us to eat a 'digestive' to prepare the stomach for all the richness it was about to endure. An aperitif if you will.

To a young child, this mixture of jaggery, dried ginger, coriander seeds and other mysterious ingredients tasted pretty rotten. The Panchamritham, thankfully, hides its healing qualities well.

At the other end of the metal pipe sit a bunch of women who collect the bottles of Panchamritham and screw caps on them.

'There is no human touch in the whole process,' says the supervisor proudly. 'The whole thing is mechanized, sanitized and completely safe.'

I'm not sure that this is a good thing, but I cannot put my finger on the reason why. Sacred food as sanitized product is difficult to wrap my head around.

A truck pulls into the large shed nearby. Three men stand on top, unloading unripe green bananas that will ripen gradually in shades of green and yellow. Six women sit on stools on the other side peeling ripe bananas.

'Notice that they don't touch the bananas,' says the supervisor. 'They peel and pop the banana into the container, which goes straight into the mixture.'

The role of the human hand—or leg

Traditional preparation wasn't this way. Fifty years ago, Panchamritham was made by stamping all the ingredients together, like the barefoot grape-stomping that happens in Bordeaux and Burgundy. People used to make pledges to Lord Muruga, stating that they would prepare Panchamritham if he alleviated or solved a problem. They would fast for days and purify themselves. After showering and cleaning their feet thoroughly, they would put all the ingredients into a giant cauldron and proceed to mix it by mashing it with their feet.

'We used to be scared to taste Panchamritham in the old days,' said an aunt of mine in Madurai. 'We didn't want to eat something that other people had stomped on.'

Perhaps this is the reason the supervisor is emphasizing the factory-made Panchamritham of the current day.

The reason that this food gets magical curative properties is not simply the mix of its ingredients. It has to do with the ancient *siddha* saint called Bhogar. Ancient India had three streams of indigenous medicine: Ayurveda, Siddha and Unani. Of the three, Ayurveda is the most popular. Siddha medicine originated with saints called siddhas, and there were eighteen of them. Patanjali, who wrote the yoga sutras, was one. These saints gained tremendous powers through penance and self-control, and these *siddhi*s or gifts are still talked about by Indians today. There are eight such siddhis, known by musical names as *anima-siddhi* (shrink yourself), *garima-siddhi* (make yourself heavy), *mahima-siddhi* (grow large in size); *laghima-siddhi* (become weightless), *prapti-siddhi* (create anything or be anywhere), *prakamya-siddhi* (achieve whatever you desire), *ishitva-siddhi* (control nature), *vashitva-siddhi* (control laws of nature, life and death).

What is the Muruga connection, you ask? Well, Muruga, through his father Shiva, was the guru of the siddhas. He taught them all these miracles. Bhogar was one of the siddhas, and he lived in Palani. In fact, he created the idol of Muruga that is worshipped today.

Legend has it that Bhogar used 4,448 local herbs found in Palani hill to create 'nine poisons' that would elevate the body to a higher plane. Not satisfied with this, he mixed the nine poisons (called *nava bhashaanam* in Palani) to create the one master medicine

that would cure all illnesses. When these nine poisons condensed,
Bhogar shaped them into an idol of Muruga and established it in the
Palani temple. The idea was that the milk, honey, Panchamritham
and other ingredients that were used to bathe this idol would absorb
a little of this master medicine which, when consumed by humans,
would give health and healing. Devotees firmly believe in this
legend. Many will only consume the Panchamritham that has been
used for *abhisheka* (ritual bathing) of the Lord. I, too, dutifully buy
the *abhisheka panchamritham*.

I return to Bengaluru and find myself suddenly popular with
all my elder aunts and uncles. They visit me to have a taste of the
Panchamritham and ask if I have extra bottles to supply to them.
If you haven't tasted Panchamritham, you ought to try it. As my
mother says, 'It tastes like heaven, but is actually a healing potion.
Where else will you get this combination?'

Takeaway

Muruga introduced me to ancient Dravidian gods and goddesses
who haven't been, shall we say, sanitized by Hinduism. Every
state has these quirky ancient gods and yoginis. Tamil Nadu
is full of them. They have names such as Mariamma, Angala
Parameshwari, Muniyandi, Muneeswaran. These are gods
who encourage animal sacrifice. Devotees walk on fire, pierce
themselves and undergo austerities in order to enjoy the boons
that these gods offer. After visiting Palani, I started reading about
these gods. And I began longing for the state of trance that these
gods induce in the faithful.

Have you ever walked on fire? I haven't. But I have participated
in fire-walking rituals after returning from Palani. It involves a
suspension of belief. Athletes do this before a big match. The

Muruga devotees at the fire-walking ceremony would shake and swirl as if they were possessed. Could I achieve this trance state, I wondered? Without drugs?

I did the next best thing. I did the *anga pradakshanam* or full-body-rolling that I observed in the Palani temple. When my daughter was sick, I promised that I would go to a local Muruga temple and roll around the *prahara* or outer sanctum. It ain't easy, but it is doable. It involves a mind-bend. Then again, all religion is a mind-bend, isn't it?

5

Mumbai: Rosh Hashanah with the Bene Israelis

I AM IN MUMBAI to celebrate Rosh Hashanah, the Jewish New Year, at the home of Yael and Ralphy Jhirad. They are friends of a friend and have kindly invited me—a stranger—to dinner at their home. En route, I stop at an aunt's house in Chembur, about half an hour from the Jhirad home in Napean Sea Road, yet a world away in terms of mindset.

When I say that I am dining with Jewish people, my aunt, Viji, blinks and nods in the fashion of people who are faking knowledge—who act as if they know what you're talking about when they really don't.

'Jewish people? Umm ... hmmm, umm ... hmmm,' she says.

So I come right out and ask her if she knows what Judaism is.
Does she know any Jewish people?

'Aren't they like Jains?' she asks hopefully.

'No,' I reply. Hasn't she heard of Jews in Kerala where she grew
up? Cochin had a large population at one time in Jewtown.

'Yes, Jewtown. Where good cardamom was available.' She nods.

I launch into a long speech about how Jews searched far and
wide for a homeland. My aunt tut-tuts in sympathy before bursting
into a cackle. 'And to think that they ended up in India. From the
frying pan into the fire.'

India isn't their homeland; Israel is, I say.

My aunt has lost interest. She is listening raptly to Carnatic
music on the radio.

'Leela Samson is a Jew,' I say quietly.

That makes her sit up. My aunt is an old-school Bharatanatyam
dancer who trained in Kalakshetra, the institution that Samson
headed before being ousted. She admires Leela Samson.

'But Leela looks like a Hindu,' she says.

'She is a Yehudi,' says my uncle who has just walked in. He is
using the local name for Jews.

'Yes, a Yehudi,' I say to my aunt.

This time, my aunt nods more convincingly. She may not know
Judaism, but she knows Bharatanatyam. And Leela Samson is a
great dancer, even though she may be Yehudi.

Do you know a Jew in India?

Many Indians haven't heard of Jews or Judaism, not even Indians
who live in Mumbai, where some 4,000 Bene Israeli Jews live. The
quiet anonymity of Jews in India is in stark contrast to, say, America,
where Jews are a visible, prominent and influential minority.

In Long Island, where my cousins grew up, the top public schools that attracted Jewish families moving to the suburbs in the early part of the century also attracted Indian immigrants a few generations later. The two communities got along. They shared values: a commitment to education, the ability to delay gratification, hard work, a certain pessimism (or fatalism) that comes from being old cultures, and a love of specific types of food—gefilte fish and unleavened bread for the Jews, buttermilk-based *kadhi* and spicy curries for the Indians.

When we lived in the US, some of our closest friends were Jews. We seemed to have a natural connection with them. Here is the thing: all the Jews I know live in the States. I didn't know a single Jew while growing up in Chennai.

Celebrating Rosh Hashanah with the Jhirad family is a tentative first step towards bridging this gap. The Jewish diaspora celebrates it over two days so that it overlaps with the single day that it is celebrated in Israel.

I fly to Mumbai for the two days of Rosh Hashanah. Through introductions from friends, I connect with several Jewish families in Mumbai who give me tips about which synagogues to visit and at what time. Ralphy and Yael Jhirad are prominent members of the Bene Israel community. They conduct Jewish tours, and document Jewish life in India. By living in India as Jews, they experience the intersection of two of the world's most ancient faiths.

How to survive in exile?

The Jewish link to India is both ancient and modern. Its modern avatar began in the late 1980s, when prosperous American Jews became fascinated with Eastern spirituality, much like the Beatles.

In October 1990, eight Jewish leaders came to India to visit the Dalai Lama in exile in Dharamshala. As described in the influential book *The Jew in the Lotus* by Rodger Kamenetz, the delegation expected to listen and learn from His Holiness. Instead, the Dalai Lama flipped things around by asking a question relevant to his people. 'Tell me the Jewish secret to spiritual survival in exile,' he asked. Tibetan Buddhists, said His Holiness, could learn something from the Jews, who had preserved their religion and identity in exile for over 2,000 years.

I am not a scholar, but my understanding of the precursors to Jewish exile goes like this. The siege of Jerusalem in AD 70 had all the elements of war, colonization and subsequent destruction, played out in many cultures time and time again (you'd think the world would have learned by now): high taxes in ancient Rome leading to discord amongst its citizens; growing religious divisions between the Jews and the Pagans, one sect mocking the other; Judas of Galilee forming an extremist political sect called the Zealots— named so because they would be zealous in their faith; infighting amongst the Zealots (somewhat like the infighting between the Indian maharajahs when the British showed up in India), leading to the breaching of Jerusalem; the Roman general, and would-be emperor, Titus, storming the walls and entering the city; the razing of Jerusalem to the ground with the Jews going into exile.

They have wandered the earth for 2,000 years, searching for a homeland, till the formation of the state of Israel in 1948.

What is a faith's core value?

All religions have certain core values—inchoate, not necessarily reflected in ritual practice. Hinduism is known for its tolerance, its acceptance of the many faiths that sought its shores without feeling threatened; Buddhism for its Zen-like equanimity; Judaism is about survival and preservation in spite of obstacles, in exile, and through suffering. The Jews, as the Dalai Lama said, could teach us a thing or two about religious identity and preservation: both in exile and in a secular democratic world where religion seems to have lost its place. As the rabbis told the Dalai Lama, religions today need to make their peace with an increasingly uncaring flock, to stay relevant in a world that is embroiled in religious discord and seemingly has no use for religious discourse.

Inside Outside

The spiritual leaders in Kamenetz's book call these practices—rituals, pilgrimages, chanting—the exoteric aspects of religion. Underneath the exoteric are the esoteric practices, 'the deep attunement, the deep way', known only to a small band of practitioners. Hinduism has tantra; Judaism has the Kabbalah; Buddhism has the *vajrayana* or tantric Buddhism. These esoteric practices include literature, and incorporate lifestyle, chanting, specific breathing and meditation techniques. Sadly, only the sexual element of these esoteric practices has been highlighted and made the object of scorn or vulgarity.

How to combine the exoteric with the esoteric is a problem that most world religions face. Kamenetz's book is an attempt to answer this question through conversations with Jewish Buddhists or JU-BUs (poet Allen Ginsberg is one); and Hinjews, who were attracted to Hinduism. New-age teacher Ram Dass, a.k.a. Richard Alpert, of Harvard University, could be considered a Hinjew. He wrote the book *Be Here Now*—about his association with Neem Karoli Baba and meditation.

What flavour is your halva?

Consider halva: a favourite food in both religions, served during Rosh Hashanah by the Bene Israeli Jews, and during most Hindu festivals by the Hindus. Halva is soft, gooey, rich and full of heart. It could be a person's first food and his last. Indeed, I think babies would eat better if they got halva as their first food instead of that Gerber goo. The recipe itself is fairly simple, but painstaking. The Jewish version involves grating coconuts—a six-hour-long and labour-intensive process. The grated coconut is then juiced and squeezed to get the 'first coconut milk' that sweetens the halva.

Traditional Jewish halva is made with rice flour, all-purpose flour (*maida*), sugar and coconut milk in the ratio of 1:1:2:5. To this, add a pinch of salt. All the ingredients are mixed with a little water. The entire quantity is poured into a large pan and heated over a *sigri* or coal fire. After that, the art is in the stirring. Most Bene Israeli families hire a man a few days before Rosh Hashanah just to sit and stir a cauldron full of halva for hours at a stretch.

Once the halva reaches the desired consistency—hard to describe unless in person—the halva is poured into a large plate. Dry fruits and nuts are sprinkled over so that they stick: skinned sliced almonds, skinned sliced pistachios, pine nuts, sliced hazelnuts and others. The whole mixture is allowed to cool for twenty-four hours.

I have eaten many halvas in my life, but none as good as the one I ate for Rosh Hashanah at the Jhirad home. The coconut milk gave it depth and density without increasing the sweetness.

Casting away your sins into running water

Yael Jhirad is soft of voice and considerate of disposition. When I land in Mumbai, she suggests I go to the Gateway of India at 5 p.m.

to witness Jewish people gather at the seashore for a ceremony called *tashlich*—casting away your sins into running water before starting the New Year afresh. Men symbolically empty their pockets: write out sins, mistakes and misdemeanours on small pieces of paper before throwing them into the waters of the Arabian Sea. In some parts of India, Jewish boys fly kites as a way of starting the New Year from new heights—quite literally. Such gatherings also serve a softer purpose: matchmaking. They allow parents to show off their sons and daughters, resplendent in New Year finery.

New Year in most ancient societies was timed to the harvest. It was a bountiful period, a time to look forward, tempered with some long-term perspective. In Bengaluru, where I now live, families eat bitter neem leaves along with jaggery for Sankranti, the New Year. It's like saying, 'Hey, the New Year is here and it's gonna be good. Hard knocks are part of life and just so you internalize it, we are going to make you eat some neem—the bitterest leaf on earth. Swallow that. With equanimity.'

The Jewish New Year is forward-looking too. The tashlich is a way of remembering the past, shaking off the cobwebs, discarding accumulated sins and mistakes, gaining perspective. This then is what living through a few millennia does to a people: it prevents them from enjoying the moment with the unadulterated glee of an innocent child. It makes them aware that tragedy is around the corner. Ups and downs. It is all just a matter of time. Most Hindus and, I am guessing, Jews, are acutely aware of this. They touch wood while giving a compliment, cross their fingers when someone notices their spate of good luck, and would never answer the question, 'How are you?' with a, 'Fabulous, just fabulous.' As seen in the hilarious film *My Big Fat Greek Wedding* the Greeks spit on a child's head if somebody gives the child a compliment. The best you can get from anyone who belongs to an ancient civilization, whether they are Chinese, Indian or Jewish, is, 'Okay—could be better.' After all, why invite the envious eye?

After the tashlich, the whole congregation goes back to prepare for *seder* or dinner.

Keeping Kosher as sacred food

'The Jewish equivalent of sacred food is keeping kosher, adhering to certain dietary laws in the context of tradition,' says Nathan Katz, distinguished professor emeritus at Florida International University and editor of the *Journal of Indo-Judaic Studies*. 'It is a way of turning ordinary food into sacred food through ritual transformation, which is essentially what happens in Hindu prasadam also.'

I speak to Katz by phone. He and his wife are visiting India 'for love', he says. 'Not for conferences, or research, or with any purpose—but just because we love it here.' Over a few months, they will be travelling along the Himalayas—from Uttarakhand to Himachal Pradesh to Darjeeling to Sikkim and Meghalaya— pretty much all the places I have not visited, despite having grown up in India.

Katz knows the Jhirads 'of course', he says, as do most Jews who traipse through Mumbai.

The Jhirad home is in an inconspicuous apartment complex, no different from the thousands dotting the city. When I walk in for seder at around 8 p.m., there are several people gathered around a table that is brimming with food. Sitting beside me is Michael Oskin from Connecticut. Across the table is Ayelet McDonald, a native Israeli science teacher on a two-year contract with a school in Mumbai. Beside her is Matt Daniels, a thirty-something graphic designer and teacher who grew up in Detroit but has lived in India for over ten years. He and his girlfriend, Meghana Srivastava, run a restaurant, The Verandah, in Goa. Yael's brother, Aaron, is on my other side at one head of the table. Yael and her son, Avniel, sit beside Ralphy at the other end. A few minutes later, Yulia Egorova, a professor at Durham University in England, walks in. Egorova has authored a number of books on Indian Jews, two of them with Tudor Parfitt, whose celebrated study on the DNA of the Lemba in Africa and the Bene Israelis in India made front pages worldwide.

After some small talk, Ralphy, a tall, genial man with an easy smile and a warm manner, begins the proceedings. He is nursing a bad cold, but that doesn't stop him from walking around the table, filling our wine glasses and making sure everyone has enough to eat. Avniel reads the blessings from the holy book.

Family participation—does it happen?

What makes some children participate in religious activities, while others don't? Is it the simplicity of the religion, the fact that it has a single holy book? Or is it the fact that religious rites are conducted in a language that children understand?

Hinduism is at a disadvantage on both these counts. Many of the religious rituals, be it Ganesh puja or Durga puja, involve prayers in Sanskrit. Nobody except the priests is really sure about what to do. When you perform these pujas or prayer rituals at home, even the parents/adults aren't sure about what to do. How do you get the children involved? Each state celebrates different festivals in a distinct fashion, so if you live in a cosmopolitan city like Bengaluru, with neighbours who are from different states, there is no unifying date, purpose or ritual that you can follow. Even Deepavali, Hinduism's biggest holiday, was celebrated in a fractured way in the apartment complex that I live in. The North Indians celebrated it on 11 November, Tamilians celebrated it on 10 November, the government declared a holiday on 12 November. We weren't even sure which day to call to wish our neighbours!

Historians believe that the reason why Hindus don't have a strong religious identity—if you exclude the Hindutva movement—is because they didn't call themselves Hindus until the nineteenth century, or at least until the Muslim invasions of the twelfth century. I think of all this as I watch Ralphy and his son conduct the prayers and read out the blessings in a confident manner. Avniel is so confident in his recitation of Hebrew, I think. Maybe I should teach my kids Sanskrit. But first, I need to learn the language myself.

The meaning of holy fruit

Food is passed around. Each dish has a meaning: A bowl of ruby-red pomegranate seeds for bounty, apples dipped in honey for sweetness, dates which are food from the tree, bananas which are food from the earth, string beans or *rov* in Hebrew, which means to multiply, young garlic with stalks, leafy vegetables, called *karsi* in Hebrew, which sounds like the word *karet*, which means to cut off or destroy. Similarly, the beets are called *silka* in Hebrew, which sounds like *siluk*, meaning removal.

'A lot of the dishes are chosen because of their symbolic meaning,' says Ayelet. 'Because of how they sound.'

'The festival is all about leadership, about being the head,' says Yael. 'So we choose the head of the goat, the head of the fish.'

Preparations for Rosh Hashanah begin weeks ahead of time in the Jhirad household. The Jhirads keep track of when Mumbai's Jewish community does the kosher slaughtering of the meat. Ralphy travels two hours one-way to buy meat from a kosher butcher a day before Rosh Hashanah. Yael scouts the market for greens with

stalks; young garlic stalks are not always available, she says. She
starts stocking nuts, which are expensive in India, for the halva,
makes sure that kosher wine is available—brought from Israel by
obliging friends and family—and invites Jewish visitors who are
passing through Mumbai for dinner at her house. 'I have helped my
mother and grandmother with Rosh Hashanah since I was a child,
so I am pretty organized,' Yael says with a smile.

More food is brought out in large platters: lamb meat, a goat's
head, goat's brain, kidneys, rice pulao, potato chops, chicken curry,
fish head (generally pomfret) grilled with minimum spices. Being
vegetarian, I stick to the rice and eat gargantuan quantities of the
halva.

Everyone murmurs about similarities and differences. Matt
Daniels, for example, is an Ashkenazi Jew, with ancestors from
Poland, Belarus, Ukraine and Russia. The Jews of Mumbai are
Sephardic. 'At home in Detroit, the Rosh Hashanah food is very
Eastern European—very Russian and Slavic,' he says. 'Beef brisket,
chicken soup ... which is called Jewish penicillin.' Their family
makes 'that bizarre Jewish delicacy called gefilte fish during other
holidays, not Rosh Hashanah,' he says.

A lot of Jewish holidays revolve around the triumph of the Jewish
people against their enemies, a reaffirmation of the belief that God
is on their side. Hanukkah celebrates their triumph over the Greeks;
Passover, the Pharoah; Purim, the Persians.

'Every time someone tries to kill us, we eat,' my Israeli friend,
Shai, used to joke. 'They tried to kill us: we won; now, let's eat.'

Faith and Achievement

What makes a religion feel beleaguered and how does it change people
who belong to that faith? Could the Jewish drive for achievement be

linked to the fact that they've always had to prove themselves—to the insecurity that comes from not having a homeland? And could India's placidity and acceptance be linked to the fact that the Hindu majority never felt beleaguered, even though they had reason to—being ruled by foreign masters after the twelfth century?

If you remove Hindu fundamentalists from the equation, the Hindus are not bitter or even fussed about the past. They move on. The ruthless desire for revenge, for redemption, doesn't seem to be part of the Hindu psyche. Is this because Hinduism developed organically in India, and until very recently, orthodox Hindus didn't cross the oceans? When you live in the comfort and embrace of your native land, you become complacent, you develop an inner strength and security (which is part of the reason why Indians who live in foreign lands return to India—to give this comfort to their children).

The only time I felt like I had to prove myself was when I became an immigrant and carried the burden of 'being Indian' on my shoulders. Hindus didn't have to go out and proselytize like the Christians, as if to prove our worth to our faith. Hinduism doesn't demand that its faithful go to war for it. We were not thrown out of a country because of religion, like the Jews were, time and time again. Is this what makes the Hindu tolerant? Is this what gives him or her this unshakeable sense of security?

'Ancient religions like Hinduism and Judaism don't have the inherent internationalism and missionary zeal like the younger religions do,' says Katz, who also happens to be a Jainism scholar.

The Jews may have had to prove themselves, but like Hindus, they don't proselytize. They don't convert people like Christian missionaries did.

I guess that when a religion lasts a few millennia, the faithful realize that converting a few hundred people, or even a few thousand, is a drop in the ocean. Is this why the Bene Israelis didn't convert others to their faith, or get converted, during their 2,300-year sojourn in India? Or did they? Convert, I mean. The question isn't innocuous. Indeed, it is the source of much angst and controversy for the Bene Israelis, not the least because rabbis in Israel demanded proof of identity when Indian Jews immigrated there.

It is close to midnight when we finish. Ayelet, Yulia and I get in an Uber cab together. Chattering like parakeets, we whiz through the quiet, dark streets of Mumbai.

I fall asleep as soon as my head hits the pillow. I have a long day tomorrow that begins at the Keneseth Eliyahoo synagogue.

A quorum to start the service

The next morning, at 10 a.m., I make my way to the Keneseth Eliyahoo synagogue in south Mumbai. Mumbai has about ten synagogues, serving a population of about 4,000 Jews. The Gate of Mercy synagogue, built in 1796, is the oldest. The Keneseth Eliyahoo was built in 1884.

This powder-blue synagogue has two floors, carved wooden doors, stained-glass windows and houses a community centre. Ehud Olmert and Madonna have been visitors. But I, apparently, cannot enter. A guard named Samson stands guard at the entrance and says that prayers have commenced. He is polite but firm. Unless I am a known member of the community, or a friend, they cannot let me in.

On 26 November 2008, a series of terrorist attacks shook Mumbai. Amongst those killed were a Jewish rabbi and his wife, at Chabad House in Nariman Point. Ever since then, security has been tightened at Mumbai's synagogues, particularly during Jewish holidays.

I sit on the plastic chair outside the door, trying to indicate that I am not going anywhere. One of the security guards seems sympathetic to my request. His name is Ruben and he calls his friends at Mumbai's other synagogues, trying to see if he can get me into another service.

'We have lived in India for 2,000 years and not one of our synagogues has been the target of any attack or vandalism even,' he says in between calls. 'This Chabad House comes to India and *boom!* they get attacked. That is the difference between Indian Jews and outsiders.'

I nod and try to reach Yael for help. Her line is busy. I call one of my other Jewish contacts who asks for the name of the guard.

'Samson,' I reply.

'They are all called Samson. Which Samson?'

Thankfully, Yael calls back at that moment. She tells me to sit tight. Her brother, Aaron, is inside the synagogue.

Aaron comes out. With him as escort, I go up the stairs into the prayer room.

'We need at least ten men to start the service, so sometimes, we have to wait for a quorum,' says Aaron.

There are about twelve men on one side, and two women on the other. The men are wearing what seems like a shawl across their shoulders and chanting in a singsong fashion.

I had never paid attention to religious clothes, but watching the Jewish men in what seems like shepherd's clothing makes me think about how Hindu and Christian priests are dressed. It is as if their clothes, which probably made sense when these religions were invented, have been frozen in time. No change since the early years of their evolution. The Jewish shawl over the shoulders reminds me of cold nights under the stars. The inside of Keneseth Eliyahoo is extremely warm. Sweating, bearded men nod their heads to the singsong chant. Still, the synagogue has that preternatural peace that somehow descends on all places of worship: as if thousands of souls who have crossed its threshold have been chanted into submission.

Earlier, says Yael, the three groups of Indian Jews—the Cochinis, the Bene Israelis and the Baghdadi—all had their own synagogues, each with slight differences. But now, the Jewish community in India is so small that they all worship together.

The Cochini Jews were based in Fort Cochin and there are hardly any left now. The Baghdadis spoke Arabic and came from Yemen. They too are a minority compared to the approximately 4,000 Bene Israelis who live in India, mostly in Mumbai.

A shipwrecked people find a new home

The Bene Israeli arrival to India reads like a Hollywood or Bollywood thriller. It began with a shipwreck 2,300 years ago, but like all tales, the seed for this one was laid centuries before that.

The year was 175 BC. In the hotbed that was the Hellenistic empire—Egypt, Rome, Greece and Jerusalem—a mad king named Antiochus Epiphanes wanted to stamp his will on the Jewish people. He outlawed the Torah, the Jewish religious book, declared that they could not circumcise their boy children, and forbade them from keeping *kashrut*, the Jewish dietary laws that are eerily similar to what my orthodox Tamilian grandmothers practised at home.

To escape this persecution, a group of Jews jumped into ships and fled from the Sea of Galilee. They headed East to Cheul, a biblical trading port, to forge a new life. En route, their ship encountered horrific monsoon winds and crashed on to the dangerous 'twin rocks' off the Konkan coast of India. Everyone on board perished, except seven men and, conveniently, seven women. The seven couples were washed ashore to a village called Nagaon near Alibaug. They called themselves Bene Israel or Children of Israel. All Bene Israeli Jews are descendants of these seven couples.

This is where the tale gets murky if Bene Israeli historian, Nissim Moses, is to be believed. Nissim Moses is the author of *Bene Israel of India: Heritage and Customs*. He has emigrated to Tel Aviv from Mumbai, 'not because of Zionism,' he says, but to contribute knowledge about the Bene Israeli Jews to the Israeli homeland.

Moses links the Bene Israeli shipwreck to the Chitpavan Brahmins who live in the same Konkan region. The Chitpavan Brahmins, interestingly enough, believe that they are descendants of people thrown ashore dead—also in the Konkan coast—as a result of a storm. Local inhabitants collected their dead bodies for cremation on a common funeral pyre. Just as the fire was being lit, a Hindu sage named Parasurama happened to pass by. He was on a campaign to destroy the Kshatriyas: the warrior caste of the Hindus. Seeing so many 'fair-skinned healthy corpses', as Moses says, the sage saw an opportunity to strengthen the number of Brahmins in the world. He sprinkled some water on the corpses, chanted some mantras and brought them back to life. The people anointed and resurrected by Parasurama called themselves Chitpavan Brahmins. As a community, they consider themselves superior to the other Brahmins. They have lighter skin, and generally discourage marriage with other castes. Their names are quite similar to Bene Israeli names, something that Moses points out in his book. Aptekar is a Bene Israeli name; Apte is a Chitpavan Brahmin name. 'For all we know, the Chitpavan Brahmins and the Jews came from the same stock of people who were thrown ashore in that shipwreck,' says Moses.

I mention Moses's theory to a friend in Bengaluru who happens to be a Chitpavan Brahmin. You may have Jewish genes, I tell her, expanding on the story.

'You can tell your Jewish friend to go take a hike,' she replies. 'We Chitpavan Brahmins believe that we descended straight from the gods.'

Faith as fountainhead

Moses is unfazed by her reply. His grand theory is that Hindus and Jews come from a common land and common ancestors. He lists forty-three reasons in his book to prove this. Both the Jewish and the Hindu calendars are lunar. Yom Kippur in the Jewish calendar coincides with Durga puja in the Hindu calendar. Purim and Holi occur on the same day. Both the Jews and the Hindus perform marriage rites under a canopy. They remove their sandals while entering a temple or synagogue. They have ritual baths before special occasions. Both religions require the isolation of women during the days of the menstrual period and after childbirth. Their death rites are similar. The Jewish first commandment says, 'I am the Lord.' One of the basic tenets of Hinduism is Aham Brahma Asmi or 'I am the Creator.' Hindu and Jewish ritual objects are very similar. The six-pointed star, Magen David, is also a sacred Hindu symbol. The original name of Abraham was Av Ram (father of Ram, in Hebrew). The *pancha diya*s or five lamps used in Hinduism are similar to the menorah lit during Hanukkah. The design of the Second Temple and the Tanjore Temple of South India are very similar. 'I could go on,' says Moses. 'In the Bible, it says that the Garden of Eden lay in a valley of four rivers. Where do you have four rivers in one valley? In Kashmir. If you look at the descriptions of what Moses saw when he saw the land of Israel, all the descriptions match that of Kashmir.'

Kashmir, in other words, could be the Promised Land—claimed by Hindus, Muslims and now the Bene Israeli Jews, or at least one of their historians.

Moses acknowledges that his theory is far-fetched, that he has trouble selling his ideas to his fellow Jews, both in India and in Israel. An obvious criticism of his grand unification theory is that Hinduism is a polytheistic religion while Judaism is a monotheistic religion, although, as Moses argues, Hinduism's most esoteric philosophy, Advaita, propounds monotheism.

Most scholars refute this theory. 'The similarities between Judaism and Hinduism are purely coincidental,' says Katz. 'If you divide the world into Abrahamic and Dharmic religions, Judaism and Hinduism would be the two great world religions that are older than most. Naturally, there would be some similarities.'

'I don't think that there is a link,' says Ayelet McDonald, my dinner companion. 'A link indicates a common ancestry of some sort. Judaism has developed independent of Hinduism. Both religions are ancient. They share commonalities. If you want to create a calendar in the ancient times, the things you observe are day and night, and waxing and waning of the moon. Naturally you would create a lunar calendar.'

Moses will have none of it. After the destruction of the Second Temple, he says, Judaism went from being a sacrificial religion to one that involved prayer and meditation. 'I have lived First Temple Judaism, which is the form that was followed by my Bene Israeli ancestors,' he says. 'And I have lived Second Temple Judaism in Tel Aviv. I know where the crossover points are. The problem is that you have a number of half-baked Western social anthropologists who come to India to prove their constricted, restricted viewpoints, which are primarily from Second Temple Judaism. They don't want to admit that Hinduism was the primordial religion which other religions borrowed from.'

The origin story: The primordial faith

I am not sure how I feel about the conviction with which Moses speaks. I suppose I should be happy that he considers my religion, Hinduism, the primordial religion, the original faith from which all others spring. But what interests me is his motivation. He has lived in Tel Aviv for decades, his children were born there. He tells me that his daughter had to audition four times to get into ballet school when no other student had to. Clearly, he feels that the Bene Israelis have faced discrimination in the Holy Land. Yet, he has not left. What keeps him in Israel now that his son and daughter have settled in the US? He says that the rabbis are like the 'Jewish Taliban', and that 'Jews, sorry to say, are a very intolerant people.' Then why doesn't he return to Mumbai? Why does the Bene Israeli narrative consume him? Part of it is setting the record 'straight' from a Bene Israeli point of view. That, I get. He wants the Bene Israelis to be the authors of their past and future instead of having it written for them. Bene Israelis, and indeed, Indian Jews, occupy that liminal space where they belong to two cultures or neither, depending on time and circumstance. To be exiled from two cultures is, to say the least, difficult.

Exile, says Palestinian professor Edward Said, is the unhealable rift forced between a human being and his native place, between the self and its true home. It's an essential sadness can never be surmounted.

Where do you come from as a person, as a people? Does this question matter to you? I imagine that any transplanted or transmuted group would have more than a passing interest in this question, for example, Goan or Syrian Christians who track down their Hindu pasts, or Indian Jews who trace back their origins. What made them leave their native land? How did they choose their new home? Was it a chance shipwreck or an intent to sail east? What were their lives like in their new home? These questions seem to have consumed the Bene Israelis, at least since the nineteenth century when Haim Samuel Kehimkar wrote *The History of the Bene Israel of India*. In the book, Kehimkar (who happens to be Moses's great grandfather) meticulously documented the customs and practices of his community, including the arrival of a mysterious stranger who taught them who they really were.

Oil-pressers who take Saturday off

The seven couples that were washed ashore on the Konkan coast began setting up roots. They were stranded in a new land, but slowly began making friends with the locals. Over successive generations, they and their descendants spread across 142 villages. They had lost all their prayer books and scrolls in the shipwreck. They had no synagogues. They did not celebrate Hanukkah, leading many to speculate that their arrival in India 'actually pre-dated the destruction of the Second Temple', according to a piece by Rabbi Jonathan Bernis in *The Jewish Voice*. Then again, as Katz says, Hanukkah is a relatively minor holiday, made famous only because it coincides with Christmas. 'If you are going to forget a Jewish observance, Hanukkah would be it. It is a twentieth-century holiday.' A 'Hallmark' holiday made famous by the greeting card company.

For 1,500 years, the Bene Israelis lived in the bejewelled, beautiful Konkan coast, amidst lush paddy fields, coconut and betelnut palms, and banana groves dripping with dew. Over the course of several centuries, they forgot Hebrew and learned Marathi, the local language. They wore saris, ate Indian food and adopted the customs of their neighbours. During weddings, they drew mehndi or henna designs on their hands. When a woman was pregnant, they fed her laddus to improve the chances of her delivering a son—a Hindu superstition. Brides wore saris and a floral headdress or *sehra*, like the locals.

A favourite wedding dish was the *modak*: sweetened, steamed dumplings, which are part of a game that literally translates to 'steaming of the hands'. A large plate of steaming hot modaks is placed in the centre, with the bride and groom on either side. Whoever can pick up more modaks and move them from the centre plate to their own plate is the winner. The women, with more experience in handling hot food, typically pick up many more of these modaks. Sometimes the bridegrooms want to prove that they are no slouches. With great *josh* or enthusiasm, they would pick up the scalding sweet dumplings and end up needing bandages for their fingers. The next part of the game is feeding each other. The interesting thing is that I did versions of these games for my wedding.

The Bene Israelis liberally adopted local Maharashtrian customs and traditions as they settled into their new homeland. They worked as skilled carpenters, merchants and, most importantly, oil pressers. Yet they clung on to certain religious practices, passed down orally through successive generations. Male children were circumcised eight days after birth; they recited a single Hebrew prayer, the Shema Yisrael: 'Hear O Israel. The Lord our God. The Lord is One'; maintained certain dietary restrictions; and observed the Sabbath, leading them to be called the *Shanivaari Teli*, or 'oil pressers who take Saturday off'. Hindu oil pressers, in contrast, took Monday off, leading them to be called *Somavaari Teli*.

The clues and the conclusion

Centuries passed in this fashion. 'But like a Bollywood blockbuster in which two halves of a locket come together in an emotionally charged climax, the lost children of Israel were eventually discovered,' writes Shabnam Minwalla in the book *Bombay Meri Jaan: Musings on Mumbai*.

Enter a mysterious stranger named David Rahabi, around 900 CE. He watched the oil pressers who took Saturday off and had an inkling that they were linked to Judaism in some way. So he gave the women a test. He spread two types of fish in front of them and asked them which ones they cooked. The women pointed to fish with fins and scales—exactly like the Jews that Rahabi had left behind.

That was the moment Rahabi decided that these oil pressers who looked no different from their neighbours were Jews. He taught them Hebrew and other rabbinical customs. He initiated three men or *kazis* into Jewish prayer rituals and finally gave them a religious identity that linked them to a land that they had fled two millennia ago.

'Unlike every other Jewish community, the Bene Israelis never experienced anti-Semitism for 2,000 years in India,' says Shalva Weil, a Jewish scholar and researcher at the Hebrew University of Jerusalem. 'As a result, they are not as defensive as other Jews. They were quite naturally incorporated into the caste system of India. They were not restricted to a particular profession like in Iran where they were forced to be silversmiths or goldsmiths. The pluralism of India nurtured them.'

'The character of Indian culture—its relative placidity, its acceptance of diversity, and its inherent communalism—have given the Jews a sanctuary the likes of which has never been known in any of the countries of the western world,' says a paper by Daniel J. Elazar, titled 'The Jewish Community of India', on the website of the Jerusalem Center for Public Affairs.

The Bene Israelis versus the Baghdadi

After dinner, I asked Yael why she had never considered immigrating to Israel like many Indian Jews. 'We never felt the need to,' she replied. 'My parents are here. Ralphy's parents are here. They are both well-established families. We are settled here.'

The Bene Israelis, while exiled from their native land, made their peace with the tropical lushness of their landing place and the exuberance of the community that adopted them. Indeed, some of them said that they felt the state of exile when they moved to Israel from India. In India, they were Marathi-speaking sari-wearing Bollywood-loving cricket-crazy folks who looked no different from their neighbours. This state of affairs continued for close to 1,500 years.

In the late eighteenth century, Jewish merchants from Iraq, Syria and other Middle Eastern countries arrived in what was then British Bombay, and quickly established themselves as leading businessmen, opening textile mills and international trading companies. Only about 200 of these so-called Baghdadi Jews remain in Mumbai, with the rest having immigrated to Israel, Britain and the United States. But their legacy endures: synagogues, libraries and schools, many of which serve Jews as well as non-Jews. They also financed the construction of several city landmarks, including the Flora Fountain and the Sassoon docks. 'The arrival of the Baghdadi Jews gave Bene Israelis a sense of community, but also a sense of inferiority,' says Minwalla.

The fact that the British colonial masters classified Baghdadi Jews as 'Europeans' and the Bene Israelis as 'natives' didn't help matters much. This didn't change even after Bene Israeli Jews migrated to Israel after the State was established in 1948. They faced extensive questions—about their parents, ancestors and family tree. They had to furnish documents, even photographs of the family graves. The Israeli authorities would then cross-check everything with their connections back in Mumbai. Minwalla interviewed a number of Bene Israeli families that made this decision to emigrate. 'They felt bad about it. They worried about military service, and the fact that they were not fully accepted as Jews in Israel,' she said. 'But the promise of better pay and income was alluring.'

Are you really a Jew?

In 1964, the chief rabbi of Jerusalem, Yitzhak Nissim, who happened to be a Baghdadi Jew, refused to allow the Bene Israelis to marry other Jews until they provided proof of Jewishness and the fact that they had not been tainted over several generations. 'This was very insulting to them,' says my dining companion, social anthropologist Yulia Egorova. 'After all, one of the reasons they moved was to be part of a Jewish society. As late as 2005, some individual rabbis would prevent them from marrying other Jewish people.'

Hundreds of Bene Israelis conducted a protest in the middle of Jerusalem, because the Israelis were saying that Indian Jews were tainting their blood. Perhaps because of this, the Bene Israelis consider themselves Indians first and Jews second. A few years ago,

I attended a book reading in Mumbai in which author Robin David said that he felt more at home in Mumbai than in Israel. 'I migrated to Israel five times,' said David. 'I always came back.'

Religious identity is complicated. Even Sigmund Freud, the king of complicated, said poignantly, 'In some place in my soul, in a very hidden corner, I am a fanatical Jew. I am very astonished to discover myself as such in spite of my efforts to be unprejudiced and impartial. What can I do against it at my age?'

It must be tough to belong to a minority religion that you feel you need to uphold no matter what. It must be tough to be torn between two cultures, as immigrants constantly are.

'Israel is in our heart. India is in our blood. Every Indian Jew will say that,' says Moses.

From heaven to earth and back—two times

One custom that is celebrated exclusively by the Bene Israelis is called Malida, which is essentially a ritual for giving thanks or to petition. The community performs this before an engagement or wedding, after the birth of a child, for a circumcision, or to request a new job or promotion. Most families do this at home.

The ceremony is in honour of the biblical prophet Elijah, who is viewed as a precursor to the Messiah. Elijah, according to Bene Israeli legend, came down to earth and went back to heaven—two times. The first time was when he revived the seven couples who swam from the sea to the beach. The second time was later when he went up to heaven in a chariot of fire from Khandala, a small town near Alibaug, which has since become a pilgrimage site for the Bene Israelis. During the Malida, offerings of fruit, flowers and specific dishes are placed on the table, after which there is a specific prayer ritual.

The most important offering is made with pounded rice or poha. The pounded rice is soaked in water twice. The water is drained. The softened poha is mixed with powdered sugar and a variety of nuts. Rose petals of different colours are sprinkled on top. A bowl of liver and gizzards is also placed as part of the offering.

Nissim Moses connects it to the tribe of Levi, who received liver and gizzards as part of their priestly offerings.

The Poha dish is somewhat similar to what Hindus make. Then again, who is to say which religion adopted what dish from whom in the long arm of history?

Non-Indian Jews don't subscribe to the Malida ceremony, and, indeed, find it quaint. 'They (the Bene Israelis) would take me to this place on the coast and actually show me the chariot marks from where Elijah flew to the sky,' says Weil. 'It was very cute.'

Lots of scholars, including Shalva Weil, Shirley Isenberg, Nathan Katz and Haim Samuel Kehimkar, have documented the history and customs of the Bene Israelis. One provocative question is their early local name: Shanivaari teli—oil pressers who took Saturday off. Why did they choose oil-pressing as their profession?

Marathi Jews and Moses

In his book *The History of the Bene Israel if India*, Kehimkar theorizes that the Bene Israelis probably descended from the tribe of Levi, since oil-pressing in the biblical time was reserved for the priestly class who served the temple.

Triumphantly for him and other Bene Israelis, genetic evidence seems to support this theory. In 2002, British historian Professor Tudor Parfitt administered DNA tests on the Bene Israel community. His results made front-page news.

'Marathi Jews Are Moses' Kin, Says Study', said a 2002 headline in the Sunday *Times of India*.

From Reuters: 'Extensive DNA testing has found the Bene Israels, clustered in and around the western city of Mumbai, are direct descendants of a hereditary Israelite priesthood that can be traced back 3,000 years to Moses' brother, Aaron.'

'Of the Indian datasets, only the Bene Israel carry the Cohen Modal Haplotype …' said Tudor Parfitt in a 2003 paper titled 'Place, Priestly Status and Purity: The Impact of Genetic Research on an Indian Jewish Community'.

'The CMH is common in kohanim, supporting the legend of the Bene Israel that their founding fathers were seven shipwrecked kohanim,' said Chana Ratner in an article in YuTorah Online, titled 'DNA Evidence for the Bene Israel in India'.

This acknowledgement that they were not just Jews but those belonging to the priestly class was huge for the Bene Israelis, particularly since their history, identity and Jewish 'purity' had been constantly questioned—which itself is something that I don't understand. I can understand your wanting your child to marry someone belonging to your faith, but why go to the level of DNA analysis?

Egorova believes that the Bene Israelis were probably oil pressers by accident, rather than due to the presence of a particular genetic marker. 'There is no such thing as a Jewish gene,' she says. 'All geneticists can say is that the ancestors of the Bene Israelis came from the Middle East, from the Levant.' But having this bonafide certification, as she says, made the Bene Israelis happy.

The black-and-white issue

This didn't mean that all was hunky dory amongst the Bene Israelis themselves, at least in the early part of this century. As Shirley Isenberg suggests in her book *India's Bene Israel: A Comprehensive Inquiry and Sourcebook*, the Bene Israels had their own hierarchy. They divided themselves into two groups: 'gora' and 'kala'. Gora (meaning white) are majority in the community and both parents are of Jewish religion. Kala (meaning black) is the smaller group, where the father is of Israeli origin but mother is non-Jewish. These two groups used to pray together but the Goras didn't accept the Kalas as complete Jews and didn't mingle with them, nor did they marry with them. The Goras also didn't allow the Kalas to hold the 'Sefer' (religious book) or to blow the 'Shofar' (horn).

I heard the Shofar being blown at the Tifereth synagogue, although I could not tell if the young man blowing it was a Kala or a Gora.

The Tifereth Israel synagogue is near Jacob's Circle. The cab pulls up at the address given by Google Maps. I search for what seems like a synagogue but only see what looks like a movie theatre. I get off and walk around, asking shopkeepers for the Tifereth. Nobody has heard of it. I try using the local name: *Yehudi ka Mandir* (the temple of the Yehudis). Still no reaction. The tea-sellers are busy filling glass tumblers with masala and ginger chai. I walk up and down the street and discover that what I thought was the movie theatre is in fact the synagogue.

This time I have wizened up. I don't want to be stopped by any Samson. I wrap my dupatta around my head and boldly walk in. People glance at me but don't stop me from entering. Women, dressed in saris, sit on one side, and the men, dressed in white, on the other side. A young man blows the shofar. It reminds me of the conch that is blown in Hindu temples. In the Exodus, it is written that the blast of the shofar emanating from the thick clouds of Mount Sinai made the Israelites tremble in awe.

Perhaps it is the blast of this shofar, but it makes me wonder: Could there be a connection between Judaism and Hinduism? Is Moses (the historian I interview, not the leader of the Jews) right? These two religions share too many things in common. Did they come from the same source? Where do they go from here?

Takeaway

What I learned from Jewish observances had little to do with religion and more to do with language. I think Hinduism needs to figure out a way to get children involved in doing the pujas. Sanskrit is daunting because most of us don't understand it. As a result, Hindu kids tend to be bored, passive observers of Hindu rituals, both, at home and in the temple. *Could this be changed?* I thought, after watching how the entire table became involved in the Passover ritual at the Jhirad home.

I also began mulling over the exoteric and esoteric aspects of religion. The mixture of beauty, art, sensual and spiritual in the surface-level exoteric practices of all faiths acted like the hook. Or so it seemed to me. Embracing deeper, secretive practices however, was more holistic—rather than dividing faith into the sacred and the profane.

Judaism and Hinduism, ancient religions both, are well equipped to bring mysticism, meditation, music and, yes, sacred food into spirituality—fusing the exoteric with the esoteric.

6

Madurai: Witness to the Apocalypse

IT IS SUNSET WHEN I walk into the Azhagar Kovil, 20 km outside Madurai. Azhagar Kovil means 'Handsome Lord's Temple' in Tamil: a tad immodest, I think, even for Vishnu, the flamboyant Hindu god who is known to enjoy the good life. As it turns out, I may be wrong about the provenance of the name. The hill that cradles this third-century temple is called *Azhagar Malai* or Handsome Lord's Hill. Is the temple named after the hill or vice versa? Likely the latter, for this is a temple of ancient provenance, older than the seventh-century Madurai Meenakshi temple down the road.

A classical Carnatic music song sung by Oscar-nominated musician Bombay Jayashri goes, *'Azhaga ... Azhaga ... Azhaga enru ...'*, which is like calling someone, 'Hey, handsome,' except that this particular endearment is for God and happens to be the ringtone of the temple priest that I am trying to connect with.

Devotional ringtones are a unique feature of India. They are a calling card that occasionally flummox the caller. The man who irons my clothes is an example. Every time he burns a hole through my husband's shirts, I call him, frothing with fury, only to hear his soothing ringtone chant that goes *'Om Namah Shivaya ...'*. My anger dies down. I feel guilty for planning to yell at the man who has such a divine ringtone, which perhaps is the point of his choice, and a smart strategy at that.

The priest whom I am trying to reach has chosen the Tamil song 'Azhaga ... Azhaga' about the god in this temple—composed by a contemporary female composer, Ambujam Krishna, as his ringtone. It is like choosing a Coke jingle as your ringtone if you happen to be an employee at the company: corporate loyalty displayed through choice of ringtone.

The siblings who rule Madurai

Azhagar, also called Sundara Rajan (meaning Handsome King, thus reinforcing the theme in case you didn't get it the first time), isn't as famous as his sister, Madurai Meenakshi, whose grand seventh-century temple down the road attracts about 20,000 devotees every day—a fact that I relish both as a woman and as a sibling. Devotees wait in long queues to get a glimpse of the green-hued goddess. In contrast, Azhagar's sprawling temple with its carved stone pillars, dance halls and spacious sanctum sanctorum is relatively vacant. There are probably 2,000 devotees in total on the day I visit. It doesn't make sense. If the point of a pilgrimage is to commune with the divine, why not choose a less crowded and equally, if not more, ancient temple?

Some of it has to do with resonance. Different gods resonate with different people, and Hinduism with its vast pantheon of gods allows for picking and choosing. Children naturally gravitate towards Hanuman for his strength, and Krishna for his playfulness. Feminists may like the Shakti cult, which focuses on goddess worship; hence the choice to visit Meenakshi, the goddess, instead of Azhagar, the god. And so what if they are siblings? My mother is a Devi worshipper not because she is a feminist but because she likes the maternal, nurturing, forgiving nature of female goddesses. Some gods are chosen for you based on caste and culture. I was born into a Shaivite family that worships Shiva even though I am drawn to the aesthetics and ornamentation of Vaishavites who worship Vishnu. If Shiva is the yogi—the saying goes—Vishnu is the *bhogi* or the lover of good things. The ascetic Shiva likes abhishekam or ritual baths done with water and milk. Vishnu, on the other hand, only likes to be bathed in fragrant sandalwood paste and other expensive unguents; he also likes alamkaram or ornamentation, with sumptuous silks, diamond crowns, gem-studded necklaces, flowers, incense, the works. He would have fit right in with today's metrosexuals with their love for well-cut bespoke Savile Row suits, Tom Ford perfumes and Cleverly shoes.

The politician and the ascetic

The good life analogy applies to the prasadam or sacred food as well. If you like to eat, you might as well make your way to a Vishnu temple. Shiva is often portrayed as an angry god, dancing the *Rudra Tandavam* or the Dance of Fury, holding the dead body of his wife,

Sati, in his arms. Vishnu, on the other hand, is the consummate
performer, taking many avatars to suit the time and place. Shiva can
afford to be ascetic, angry and dismissive, given that he is responsible
for the tail end of the creation cycle. Vishnu, on the other hand,
maintains the order of the universe. He is like a politician and CEO,
weighing the wants of multiple stakeholders, pushing and pulling
the sails so that the boat tilts back and forth but never loses balance,
giving his people the feeling that they are in control, yet handling the
reins adroitly so that both saints and sinners get what they deserve.
Vishnu engages in diplomatic negotiation with gods and demons,
and yet has no compunction about ruthlessly cutting off people's
head with his discus, the *Sudarshana chakra*, when he needs to.

There are temples dedicated to a few of the ten avatars of
Vishnu—with Rama and Krishna being the most famous. There
are also temples for the various forms of Vishnu where he takes on
certain qualities based on myths and stories. One of India's richest
temple, Thiruvananthapuram's Anantha Padmanabha Swamy
temple, has Vishnu resting in *anantha sayanam* or blissful sleep.
Kerala's famous Guruvayoor temple is based on a story where the
planet Guru, or Jupiter, and Vayu, the Wind God, carried this idol
of Vishnu to its location. Another among India's richest temples,
Tirumala Tirupati has Vishnu as Balaji or Venkateshwara.

The last avatar of Vishnu?

Azhagar is not an avatar of Vishnu, although one priest at the temple
tells me that since the god is seen here on a horse, he represents the
last of Vishnu's avatars, known as Kalki. Legend has it that Kalki will
ride in on a white horse, not as a knight in shining armour but as a
witness to the *pralayam* or apocalypse.

My image of pralayam, gleaned, no doubt, from paintings and movies that I watched as a child, shows the earth being submerged by tsunami-like waves and scorched by forest fires—an image not that different from the bleak portrait painted by modern environmentalists who speak of glaciers in Tibet melting and submerging entire plains and valleys.

Indian mythology points at earth as a giant rolling ball sinking into the ocean till it renews itself for the next yuga or time cycle. Thankfully, there are several hundred centuries before this apocalypse, caused either by climate change or the Kalki avatar, kicks in. If this temple houses Vishnu in the Kalki avatar, devotees ought to be thronging this place to pray for redemption and safety when the earth goes to hell. If apocalypse will strike during this earth cycle, called Kali yuga, wouldn't you want to hedge your bets by praying to Vishnu as Kalki? I think about this as I walk around the empty corridors within the temple. Where are the pilgrims and why aren't they here? Why are some temples rock stars—like Tirupati, and even the Madurai Meenakshi temple down the road?

Location, location, location

Some temples do better than others because of their access, location and brand value, while some temples are the benefactors of their own success, leading to a virtuous up-cycle and more devotees. Tirupati temple, dedicated to the same god, Vishnu, is fifty times more famous than the Azhagar temple, even though it is hard to make a case for why you should visit Vishnu in Tirupati when you can just as easily visit him in Azhagar Hill.

A pilgrimage is called *tirtha yatra* in India. The word *tirtha* connotes a sacred place, sacred water mostly—crossing a river and moving to a higher spiritual plane. Tirthas are places where you cross over to the other side physically and spiritually. The word tirtha probably made sense because most ancient temples were located besides water bodies: lakes, rivers or the sea. The point of a pilgrimage was to show God that you had taken pains to visit Him, to think about Him. In that sense, pilgrimages, much like ritual fasting, prayers or sacrifices, are a process of softening the mind to access your faith.

The cynic in me says that they are a transaction with God. It is like saying, 'I worked so hard to come all this way to see You, so you might as well do something for me like getting me that promotion I've been working towards, or finding a suitable bride for my son.'

All of which leads to the big question that really has no answer: why go on a pilgrimage at all if God is supposed to be everywhere?

God's blessing makes food sacred

At the Azhagar temple, the lamp has been lit for the evening's offerings. It is 6.30 p.m., but being July, it is still bright. The *neivedhyam* or offering of food has just been placed in front of the small, golden statue of the god. The fare looks mouth-watering. The handful of us milling around can hardly wait to get a taste of this prasadam after it is ritually offered to him. Is it bad to think of your stomach in the presence of God? How will I ever reach a higher plane if I question everything and think of food all the time?

Food becomes sacred food after it is ritually offered to God with much pomp and ceremony: ringing of bells and Sanskrit chanting. Neivedhyam becomes prasadam after it is blessed by God. The word prasadam literally means mercy or blessing. Azhagar temple prasadam includes piquant lemon rice, bright yellow in colour and specked with black mustard seeds; tangy tamarind rice; sweet pongal flavoured with jaggery, cashew nuts, cardamom and tons of ghee. But the pride of place goes to the Azhagar Kovil dosai, famed in the area for its taste. The word dosai is the correct, South Indian way to pronounce what North Indians mistakenly call the 'dosa'. I will use both terms in this section, depending on context.

The recipe is simple and boils down to one foolproof cooking technique: the dosai is deep-fried in ghee, giving it a richness and depth of flavour that no amount of healthy, low-cal cooking can replicate.

Pounded white rice is ground with whole black *urad* dal along with curry leaves, asafoetida, black pepper and salt. The resulting mixture is deep-fried in deep containers. As is common in temple cuisine, all the ingredients are native to India. Whole black urad dal (Vigna mungo) is an ancient bean, highly prized in India and Pakistan for its bland, nutritive properties. The two most popular breakfast dishes in South India are the idli and the dosa, a fermented combination of polished urad dal and rice. The dosa at the temple doesn't tamper with this black bean.

I ask the priest, Ambi Bhattar, why this particular temple has chosen a savoury dosai as their offering.

'It is a larger version of the *thirumaal vadai*,' he says, that is served at the famous Balaji temple in Tirupati.

'This temple probably wanted to do a larger and grander version, and so they came up with the dosai—at least that is what I infer,' he replied.

The anklets from which Ganga springs

I visit the temple kitchen. Two women sit on the floor rolling a mound of yellow mixture, which contains the infallible combination of flour, sugar and ghee, into balls to make laddus. Two men are deep-frying dosas that will later be sold to devotees for ₹40 a pop.

'Every temple has its special dish,' says Chellappa, one of the cooks. 'Tirupati has its laddu. Palani has its Panchamritham. Azhagar Temple has its dosai. The taste comes from the water that we use. There is a spring called Noopura Gangai, which supplies all the water for this temple. It is what gives our prasadam the distinctive taste.'

The natural spring that gives this sacred food its distinctive taste is at the top of the hill, reached via a steep, wooded path. The way up is gorgeous and quiet, with ancient, arched trees, lots of birds, rustling wind and falling leaves. Close to the top, however, it gets crowded. Whoever says that Indians are unfit and unhealthy ought to visit its temples. People—old and young—bound up the hill, laughing and chatting with each other. The pull of God is greater than the pain in their joints.

At the top is a temple for Rakhayee, a tribal goddess. This spring originates from under the goddess's sanctum sanctorum and is therefore invisible. It flows out through a hole and down the steps of this temple. Hands reach out to scoop up the water. People drink it, then sprinkle it on themselves and over their loved ones. There is a shallow tank that collects the water. One family dunks their naked baby into this tank, amidst all the hands. Nobody bats an eyelid. This is holy water after all. It will purify everything. The baby won't fall sick; he will only get healthier. People dunk empty Coke bottles and fill them with the holy water to take back home. The filth all around is at odds with the supposed purity of the water.

Three women walk by in a jingle of anklets. Seems appropriate in this place. The word *noopura* means anklets. It is a quintessentially Indian ornament. Necklaces belong to every culture, ranging from the ancient Greeks to Zhou Chinese. Earrings, bracelets and hair ornaments too are found in many cultures. Two ornaments however seem to belong to India: one is the *maang tikka*, worn in the parting of the hair in the middle of the forehead; the second is jingling anklets. Of the two, the anklets are still popular in India, worn by women still. The other ornament that is worn on the forehead has been relegated to brides these days.

The anklets that gave the Noopura Gangai its name belong to Lord Vishnu. The story behind this natural spring shows the scale and colour of the ancient Hindu imagination. The story begins with a demon named Mahabali who wanted to conquer the three worlds. So he conducted a grand fire sacrifice or yagna, at the end of which he decided to give alms to a long line of Brahmins. Vishnu took on the form of a small boy. When his turn came, the demon king grandly asked, 'What do you wish for? I will give you anything you desire.'

The young Brahmin boy asked for three steps of land.

The demon king laughed scornfully and said, 'That's it? That's all you want? Why don't you ask for more? I am the master of this universe after all.'

The young boy insisted that all he wanted was three steps of land. (You know what's coming, right?)

The king agreed. 'Go ahead,' he said. 'Take your three steps of land.'

Wrong statement. Before his very eyes, the small boy grew taller and taller, reaching to the heavens, and then some. To infinity, and then beyond. His one foot covered the entire earth. He lifted his other foot upwards so that it covered the entire galaxy.

The king slowly realized that this was no small boy asking for a mere portion of land. This was the Lord himself. Standing in this fashion with one foot on the ground and the other foot on the sky, Vishnu asked Mahabali, 'Where shall I put my third step to fulfil the promise you made me?'

A suitably chastised king knelt on the ground. 'Put your third foot on my head, O Lord, and push my ego into the underworld,' he said.

He who steps over three worlds

As a child, it was thrilling to hear my grandmother recite this story when the electricity went out and the only light came from the flickering candles all around. My cousins and I would sit around my grandmother, our eyes round and wide with wonder, and imagine Vishnu with one leg turned upwards to the skies like a yogi. The moral of the story, my grandmother would say at the end, is that pride comes before a fall. The arrogant king didn't realize that the small boy would be the cause of his downfall when he grandly offered him three steps of land. Figure out how to subdue the ego and all will be well, my grandmother would say, echoing the theme of many Hindu parables.

Trivikrama is a magnificent name that means the victor of three worlds: the earth, the heavens and the netherworld. It is but one of the thousand names of Vishnu that is uttered in the *Vishnu Sahasranamam,* or the thousand names of Vishnu, a chant that is the background score to many a Tamilian childhood, rendered by the incomparable M.S. Subbulakshmi.

It is this Trivikrama name and attendant 'form' of Vishnu that gave rise to the holy water that lends flavour to the food here.

The twist to the story has to do with Brahma, the creator, who sits in the heavens spinning the wheel of life. When Vishnu's foot reached up through the clouds into *Brahmalok* or Brahma's abode,

Brahma did what any quick-witted, self-respecting god would do at the sight of a potential usurper: he calmed things down. He poured water as abhishekam on Vishnu's foot. This water eventually flowed to earth and became the rivers of Hindustan. (The ancient Hindu imagination didn't extend to Europe and the Americas, and anyway, my ancestors believed that crossing the seas was a sin and discouraged it.) The water that Brahma poured over Vishnu's feet became the holy Indian rivers: Ganga, Yamuna, Saraswati, Godavari, Narmada, Sindhu and Kaveri.

The water that washed over Vishnu's anklets took a different path and perhaps physics will have a reason why the water impeded by heavy anklets would make their way south to Madurai and became the Noopura Gangai. Devotees believe that taking a dip in this Noopura Gangai holy water is akin to bathing in the Ganga, or even better, the Triveni Sangam—the confluence of the holiest of India's rivers—the Ganga, Yamuna and the now-dead ancient river Saraswati. No wonder people were dunking newborn babies into this water.

Although I didn't realize it, Azhagar Hill is the site of not one but three temples: the Vishnu temple; the temple of Rakhayee, the tribal goddess; and a temple of Muruga called Pazhamuthir Cholai, which happens to be one of the 'six battlegrounds' of this warrior god.

Beside a water body and beautiful gardens

The appropriate site for a temple, according to Sanskrit texts that deal with the subject, sounds like a real estate developer's dream. Temple sites were chosen based on a few criteria: they had water bodies—lakes, rivers and the like. If they didn't have flowing water, a temple tank would be built and filled with water. Ideally, temples were built near beautiful gardens with blooming lotuses and other flowers—where animals could frolic without fear of injury, where swans, ducks and other birds would fly freely and make patterns on the water and wind. When the nature-worshipping ancients created human-like gods, they brought their love for nature with them and chose to build temples near the best sites. The good energy and harmonious vibes of these places caused the gods to come out to play, say the texts.

Other Shilpa Shastra texts talk about the magnetic resonance of the places where ancient temples were constructed. Some say that a large square copper plate is placed beneath the *garbagriha* or womb chamber to collect the magnetic energies and disperse them to all the devotees that circle the sanctum sanctorum. Perhaps this is why my mother and aunts circle around temples: to increase their magnetism.

Most holy places in the Hindu pantheon—and there are countless—have an accompanying story, specific to the site called *sthala purana*. These are the ancient equivalent of modern success stories. They give injunctions. If you have a holy dip in this pond or this river, you will attain wealth. If you visit this temple on this day, you will be absolved of all your sins. These stories talk about specific people who visited the said temple and attained health, wealth, the love of a good woman, lots of children and success.

Tale with a familiar trajectory

Even today, a specific ritual known as the Sathyanarayana Puja ends with the telling of stories that take a familiar trajectory: So-and-so brahmin had so many troubles; he performed this puja and everything changed: he got gold coins, his son was cured of illness ...

This is the ancient version of modern-day success stories: A kid named Mark started a company. He had many problems raising capital. He worked day and night, dropped out of college, came up with these unusual deals and went nowhere. Then, he met rainmakers and private equity guys (they were called 'holy men' in Hindu myths). The rainmaker said, 'Lose the word "The" from "The Facebook" and just call it Facebook.' The man complied. He moved his business from the shores of the Charles river to another sacred spot beside the mountains of San Francisco. It was called Silicon Valley. In this new land, the man found friends and colleagues. He performed these rites and rituals and was blessed with shares that are now worth—well, who knows how many billions they will be worth by the time you read this.

A pan shatters ... and a new one is made

By the time I come down the hill, it is evening. A purple shamiana has been set up outside. A small gold idol riding on a silver horse has been placed on a raised platform. Some thirty priests stand in front of this idol, chanting Sanskrit hymns with exacting rhythmic cadences called *chhanda*s (poetic metre). A group of us devotees wait under the awning of the shamiana, listening to them and salivating from the ghee-laden smells that waft towards us.

The dosai that is offered to the Lord is much bigger—about the size of a pizza. It is made in a special pan that lends itself to slow cooking. The pan is made of five metals: bronze, brass, lead, copper, gold and silver. In 2009, a calamity occurred. The ancient pan that the temple had used for centuries broke into pieces. The priests consulted astrologers and soothsayers to try to figure out why God had destroyed the pan that gave him his daily meal. My fanciful mind says, perhaps He wanted to be on a diet; perhaps He wanted a low-fat version of his daily offering. But these are modern considerations, not something that would affect a god who had lived on such scrumptious if calorific foods for eighteen centuries.

Eventually, the temple cast a new pan made with five metals. It cost ₹7,20,000.

I didn't see this special five-metal pan that is deep enough to cook a large, pizza-sized dosai. It is not taken out of the temple kitchen. But I did see five large dosais that held pride of place amidst the food offerings that had been placed before a small golden image of the Lord. This is the *utsava murthy* or the 'festival idol', a miniature version of the main deity, usually made in metal, and used during festival parades. The main Azhagar deity, black in colour, carved out of granite, stands over six feet tall within the sanctum sanctorum. There is no way you can move it during festivals when the god goes on a ride around town. The smaller idol outside is but a few feet tall—made of gold and mounted on a silver horse.

Temples are God

There are many manifestations of God within a Hindu temple: a useful thing for a devotee in a hurry. Hinduism has no problem with straightforward and fairly transactional relationships with gods. Devotees go straight to specific gods that occupy the sub-temples around the main temple, depending on need and circumstance. They may approach Lakshmi, the goddess of wealth, to pray that the bank loan comes through quickly. They may circle the *navagraha* or nine planets upon the advice of an astrologer, particularly if they hear that Saturn is in a bad location in their horoscope and will cause a prolonged period of bad luck when all projects fail. Propitiating the nine planets through flowers, milk, oil lamps and food offerings is a never-ending part of the weekly life of believers. Couples may hang a tiny toy cradle on the peepul tree that houses the *Naga* or snake god, so that he stops eating up the embryos that are supposed to grow in the woman's womb, so that they may conceive a baby. Still others simply duck in and do a *sashtanga namaskaram*—make every part of the body touch the ground—in front of the *kodi maram*: a flagpole clad in brass, silver or gold, that stands at the entrance to the inner sanctums.

Hindu temples not only house God; they *are* God. The figure of God makes up the architecture of the temple. The sanctum sanctorum, also called garbagriha, is the most sacred spot in the temple and denotes the God-head. The next circle is the *natya mandapam* or performance hall, with many pillars that make up the body of the God. The entrance to the temple is the God's feet. Different parts of the temple represent different parts of the god, the most sacred being the garbagriha.

Most accessible is the kodi-maram or the flagpole outside the sanctum sanctorum.

The long process of making a flagpole

This flagpole is made by cutting a tall sacred tree, often teak. The bark must have specific auspicious markings, like the shape of the conch that Vishnu holds, or like the serpent that Shiva wears around his neck. The tree is cut slowly to make sure that it doesn't touch the ground. Then comes a slow process of tempering and softening it by soaking it with oil. Finally, the wooden flagpole is covered with beaten metal, often brass, but also silver or gold if the temple is rich. The idea is that all the gods reside in this pillar, with Indra, the king of the gods, at the top. This is why the kodi maram is sometimes called Indra's flagpole. By prostrating in front of Indra's flagpole, a devotee is essentially prostrating in front of all the gods.

If the temple's flagpole offers one quick option for the devotee in a hurry, the travelling miniature idol allows God to come to your doorstep when He or She goes for a ride around town during festivals. It is this utsava murthy who is receiving the food offerings when I visit Azhagar temple. The Lord is also listening to long Sanskritic words of praise: songs and poetry that pay homage to this god and this temple, considered one of the 108 *divya desham* or Divine Places of Vishnu.

Memorizing long texts

In a 2015 paper published in the journal *Neuro Image*, a team of scientists from the Center for Mind/Brain Sciences at the University of Trento, Italy, studied the brains of 'professional Vedic Sanskrit Pandits' in India who were used to memorizing and reciting 40,000–1,00,000-word oral texts, and discovered 'massive grey matter density and cortical thickness increase' in the brains of the Vedic priests, somewhat similar to what was seen in London taxi drivers, in previous studies. The paper, which is available online, is fascinating, not only because it describes how the Vedic priests' brains changed, but also because it talks about the subjects and their training.

The typical student at a *veda pathshala* or veda school is almost always male, says the paper. They memorize the exact pronunciation and invariant content of the Vedas and Vedangas (subtexts), starting as young as age eight, with twelve being the average age of the initiate. The Vedas, identified in the study as 'late bronze/early iron-age oral texts passed down for over 3,000 years in an unbroken tradition in India', form the core of the knowledge of these young priests. Passages are memorized and practised for eight to ten hours daily for at least the first seven years. During this time, the young Vedic students master a very specific type of recitation, with exact intonation and accompanying hand gestures, totalling about 10,080 hours, over the course of their initial training—certainly over the

10,000 hours that Malcolm Gladwell made famous. These oral texts are long: 40,000–1,00,000 words, relative to the 38,000 words in the Book of Genesis.

The unusual thing about this study is that the young boys who participated in the study did not come from 'traditional family lineages of reciters,' thus proving that their brain's memory component became larger—physically—because of their training.

Unlike China, which chooses its athletes based on body type and propensity, the boys in the study were chosen with no entrance exam, nor any selection criteria that tested good memory. In other words, the training of these Sanskrit scholars is a triumph of nurture over nature. Which means that you and I could potentially do this too—if we wanted to increase the size of our brains, one path would be to memorize long Sanskrit texts.

Monkey-chasing and mass feeding

At the end of the prayer ceremony, containers of sacred food are offered to the Lord with much pomp and circumstance—the ringing of bells, the loud chanting and the chasing away of the monkeys who populate the temple. Finally, the chief priest brings out the blessed food to the waiting populace. First comes the sweet pongal. We swallow it with gusto. It is delicious, but no different from the ones we make at home. Then comes lemon rice: same—very good, but I could just as easily have made it myself. Tamarind rice: better than usual. Then again, this is a Vishnu temple and Vaishnavas are known for their tamarind rice. Then comes the pièce de résistance: the dosai. The priest brings out small pieces of the dosai and distributes it to all of us. I greedily take a bite. It is unlike anything I have ever eaten, with a bite of black pepper, redolent with ghee, hearty with the girth of whole black urad dal and rice, and flavoured with green curry leaves. The cook attributes the taste to the water from the Noopura Gangai, but I cannot taste this distinct water.

Priests and their routines

After the ceremony, I approach the priest whom I've been chasing all day. His name is Madhavan, and he is a very busy man. Madhavan is no different from many of the priests I have encountered at temples. But over the course of the next few hours, as I interact with him, I gain new respect for the priestly class. Sure, they size up devotees based on wealth and stature. Sure, they arrange for special passes or access to the deity in exchange for cash. But in that, they are not different from many 'fixers' in other areas. I hold priests perhaps to an uncommonly high ideal. They work uncommonly long hours, waking up at 3 a.m. to do the pre-dawn puja and ending their day at midnight when they put the god to bed. For this, they get paid very little. No wonder they entreat rich devotees to give them a little something in exchange for special rituals: a commission model approach in a profession that isn't necessarily lucrative. As I think this, I catch myself. Am I getting co-opted into the whole religious worldview? Is this search for sacred food turning me into one of those Indians whose only prism through which to view life is Hinduism and spirituality?

Of medium height, medium build and exuding a pleasant disposition, Madhavan should have been an investment banker. He has the cheerful, smiling countenance of someone who has had long practice in recognizing and massaging opportunities as they come.

When I tell him that I'm a journalist, he says, 'Good. Very good. May God be with you.'

Over the next hour, I find him to be unfailingly courteous. He anticipates people's needs and delivers to their wishes with an artless transparency—in the hope that his delivery of their desires will lead to good things, not just for the organization that he represents— the temple—but also for him, personally.

I tell him that I want a sound bite from him, an interview if possible. He replies that he needs to do the *sandhya vandhanam*: the evening prayer of the thrice-daily practice that devout Brahmins are supposed to do every day. Madhavan tells me that he will return after his ritual and talk to me. He races up the stairs to what I imagine to be the priest's office, which actually is part of the third-century edifice. It is 7.30 p.m.

Half an hour later, an assistant summons me into the room. There are ancient, carved pillars in the room, overlaid with a ceiling fan, tube light, and all the accoutrements of an office.

Madhavan has just had a bath. His long hair is tied with a towel that hangs like a low chignon on the nape of his neck. He is clad in a white dhoti and is dressing up for the evening rituals: applying the sacred chalk (*thiruneeru*) and red kumkum on his head as well as on his arms and chest. It is both decoration and identification.

Madhavan's dressing-up ritual is just as intimate, except that I am a stranger—a woman at that—watching a priest get dressed. It reminds me of my maternal grandfather who adorned his head with the same design.

The Shiva–Vishnu dichotomy

Although I belong to an Iyer family, which worships Shiva, my maternal grandparents belonged to Tirunellayi village (former election commissioner Tirunellayi Narayanaiyer Seshan is my mother's first cousin) where the Brahmins had Vaishnava proclivities. I know this because every time the priest said '*Parameshwara Preethyartham*' during the *homan* (fire rituals), my grandfather would interject. 'Say *Narayana Preethyartham,*' he would correct him.

It wasn't 'As *Parameshwara* or Shiva wishes' in our family; it was 'As Narayana wishes'.

My maternal grandfather's caste marks were a vertical white '*naamam*' shaped like a cup, in the middle of which was a red vertical line. He had a box with all his tools: a thin stick for drawing the marks, a block of what looked like chalk, a red herbal dye for the middle red line and a sponge with which to correct stray lines. Every day, after his bath, my grandfather would sit down in front of the mirror and draw these lines on his forehead with great relish. Every day, during my summer vacation, I would sit beside him and watch.

Madhavan's decoration lines on his forehead are the same as my grandfather's, only more elaborate—somewhat thicker and longer. He also streaks similar lines on his arms and chest. As he dresses up, he talks about the temple: about its provenance, the story behind its appearance and architecture. He tells me about the Kalki avatar of Vishnu, about the special pan which was used to make the Lord's prasadam, and about the blessed water from the Noopura Gangai that gave taste and fragrance to all that it touched.

After the interview, Madhavan insists that I have dinner at the temple.

'But I have only just eaten the prasadam!' I protest.

He will have none of it. 'You have a long way to drive to Madurai,' he says. 'Why don't you have a little bite at the priests' dining hall?'

From dawn to midnight

We walk out of the priest's office. Madhavan is mobbed by multiple parties. One group has come from Mumbai and wants special access into the sanctum sanctorum right away—at 9 p.m. Another group is waiting to collect the sacred food for which they had paid money last year. A third wants to contract with him to do a special puja for their daughter's wedding next month. Madhavan is a whirligig.

He calls out to a junior priest who is walking by. 'Take this group to the sanctum sanctorum right away and make sure that they have a relaxed darshan,' he commands him.

He turns to the group and his tone changes to one of customer-friendly hospitality. 'Please go with my boy over here,' he says. 'You will be taken care of.'

He quickly arranges for the second group to get their prasadam from the temple office, and grabs an official calendar to fix a date for the special puja for the girl's wedding, all the while making sure that I don't slip away so that I can have dinner at the temple.

After the swirl of instructions, he runs towards the building on the other side of the temple. I follow suit.

Inside, in front of a black idol, there is dinner being prepared for the priests. Puris are being rolled out by two men. A woman stands behind a curtain frying papads to serve with the hot *bisi bele bhaath* (the words translate to 'hot lentil rice'); there is potato curry and dal to go with the puris, and curd to finish the meal.

Madhavan fusses around me, making sure that I get a banana leaf on which to eat, and a glass of cold water. He instructs the lady in charge to make sure that I get a good dinner.

'Please eat. I have to go for the Lord's procession,' he says.

He yells for an assistant who comes out riding a motorbike. Madhavan jumps on the pillion seat, waves at me and takes off towards the entrance of the temple where the Lord is being carried out for some fresh air and village sights.

It is 9.30 p.m., and Madhavan's day is nowhere near over. The whole group will come back at around 11 p.m., the priests will have dinner together, then they will go home—only to wake up at 3 a.m. for the next day's prayers. Whatever you may think about their fixing and brokering, the stamina of an average priest is pretty high.

Food for the gods and priests

The food is piping hot and extremely flavourful. These priests eat well. The dal is yellow *moong*, bland, with just ginger and salt for flavour. The potatoes are cooked in the South Indian style—they aren't runny. Best of all is the *bisi bele bhaath* with a dollop of ghee on top. I eat with relish even though I am really full.

As I walk out of the temple after the meal, I see the group in the distance going around the village. The utsava murthy is being taken out on a procession so that the Lord can see his people. There's a group walking in front, singing songs and beating drums. The priests walk on the sides and behind, chanting the Lord's praises, even though it is after 11 p.m. How many times during the day will they keep doing this?

The moon is high in the sky. The air smells of neem flowers and mango leaves. I am sated from the food and the conversation, ready for bed. As I drive out of the temple, I wonder when the Lord is going to call it a night. I have a date to keep the next day: a date with a green-hued goddess who carries a parrot on her finger ....

A few weeks after returning from the Azhagar temple, before lunch one day, I quietly went into the guest bedroom and squatted on the floor. I was alone in the house and I wanted to do the *aachamanam* the way I had seen it done. At the very least, it would be an exercise in squatting.

I placed the silver bowl (called *pancha patram*) in front of me and poured a teaspoon on my cupped palm. I threw my head back—

good for the thyroid, my doctor had said—and poured the water into my open mouth.

'Achyuttaya namah,' I muttered silently and swallowed.

'Anandaaya namah.' Swallow.

'Govindaaya namah.' Swallow.

I wasn't sure what I expected to gain by doing it, but it felt good, even though my knees hurt. After drinking this water purified by the accompaniment of mantras, I stood up.

And then, I walked back to the dining room, sat primly on the table—set for one—forked some salad and popped it into my mouth.

Swallowing water before beginning a meal is a specific Hindu ritual called aachamanam. As a child, I would watch my grandfather do this.

The ritual itself is very specific. You sit on your haunches—which is tough in itself. Then you cup your hand, fold your index finger so that it touches the base of your thumb, and drink water from the part where the hand meets wrist: the *brahma granthi* as it is called. Now that I am studying mudras, this notion of using specific portions of your hand to alleviate specific ailments is interesting to me.

Squatting on the floor on your haunches activates all the acupuncture points in the feet. My cousin, who is a Vedic scholar, says that the reason for this custom is a little more innocuous. People used to do the aachamanam while sitting by a river, he says. They would take hands full of the flowing water and pop it into their mouths. Sitting on your hunches was the best way not to get your clothes wet.

In a typical aachamanam, you pour teaspoons of water on your right palm and drink up while mentally saying the different names of Krishna. Say one name, then throw your head back, swallow water once. The idea is that the water reaches not just your throat chakra, but also your heart chakra.

The devout believe that this combination—saying the name of the Lord, then drinking water with devotion and gratitude—not just purifies the food that you are about to eat, but also cures all mental and physical ailments.

Predictably, women aren't supposed to do this ritual, and predictably, that's what got me interested in doing it in the first place.

Takeaway

How do you drink your water? Traditional Indians drink water without having the container touch their lips. It helps that they drink from stainless steel tumblers with rims so that the liquid pours into the mouth without any spillage. This is how all the elders in my family drink, whether it is hot coffee or cold juice. They throw their head back and pour the liquid in.

Recently, I have started doing this. On my computer desk is a blue glass bottle gifted by my brother. Every now and then, I sip water from it. A few weeks ago, I tipped my head back and poured the water in, like I was taught to do as a child.

Unbidden, the names of the Lord that my grandfather would recite as he did his aachamanam, came to my mind.

'Keshava, Narayana, Madhava, Govinda, Vishnu, Madhusudhana, Trivikrama, Vamana, Sreedhara, Rishikesha, Padmanabha, Damodara ....'

As long as I recited, I kept pouring the water down my throat. These days, we are told to keep track of how much water we drink— 'a minimum of 2 litres per day' is a common dictum. The problem is to force yourself to drink enough water in one go. I found that reciting Sanskrit mantras while drinking water distracted my mind and made me drink more.

This practice has continued. When I feel thirsty these days, I do the pour (or the waterfall), not the sip. If I am alone, I actually squat on the floor, pour water down my throat. Tilting my head back is a change from staring down at my computer.

I hope it will help my chronic hypothyroidism.

7

Jaipur: Singing and Dancing, Hindu-Style

THE YEAR: AD 1669. King Mirza Jai Singh, a courtier in the Mughal court, sends a messenger to the temple priests at Vrindavan with some chilling news. Emperor Aurangzeb has turned his gaze towards Vrindavan. In short order, his army will invade the temple and destroy everything inside, including the precious idols of Krishna.

Flee, says the message from the Rajput king to the temple priest, Shiva Ram Goswami. *Take the idols and flee. Go via adjoining Bharatpur. The hardy Jat king, Surajmal, will give you safe passage. Once you get to Jaipur, the idols will be safe. Aurangzeb's army dare not invade Rajputana.*

The man who is recounting this incident is Thakur . Singh, who has converted his family mansion into Dera Manda a boutique hotel in Jaipur. Like many Rajasthanis, he recounts the past as if it were in the present.

'The sad thing is that Aurangzeb was 82 per cent Hindu,' he says. 'His mother, grandmother and great grandmother were all Hindu princesses. Yet, he treated the Rajput princes with vengeance because they sided with his elder brother, Dara Shikoh, in the succession effort.'

Grab an idol and flee

As Aurangzeb's army prepared to march to Vrindavan, each of the temple priests grabbed an idol of Krishna, wrapped it in diaphanous white cloth, and fled into the mists of the night. After a treacherous journey that lasted months—they travelled on bullock cart and camel in the stealth of the night; hid in caves and valleys—the four idols reached Jaipur, where they make their home and are worshipped under the names of Govind Dev, Radha Gopinath, Radha Damodar and Radha Vinodhi Lal. The fifth idol, Madan Mohan, accompanied a princess of Jaipur who got married and moved to Karoli. She was 'so attached to Madan Mohan Ji that she wanted to take him with her to her in-laws' home, but her father would not allow the idol to be moved,' recalls Durga Singh. The Lord conveniently appeared in her father's dream and instructed him to send the idol along with the girl, and so it came to be that Madan Mohan moved to Karoli.

Radha Damodar was returned to Vrindavan in the eighteenth century, although a mirror image (*pratibhu*) of it remains in Jaipur. Two idols have stayed in Vrindavan: Banke Bihari and Radha Raman.

All of which leads to my first question: who are all these Krishnas and why do they have so many names?

'It is all part of the *Gaudiya Sampradaya* (Gaudiya cult),' Durga Singh explains.

'Like Srinathji?' I ask.

'Srinathji is part of the *Vallabh Sampradaya*,' he replies, foxing me further.

Variety is the spice of life—and faith

The problem with a polytheistic religion like Hinduism is that it is hard to keep track of its regional, if rather glorious, variations. As a South Indian, born into a traditional Shaivite (Shiva-worshipping) family, I grew up with the sayings of Shankaracharya, poetry of Annamacharya, songs of Deekshitar, and the milk-soaked, hand-drawn Kalamkari textiles depicting images from Hindu mythology. Traditional feasting and fasting in South India took the form of the Sathyanarayana Puja and Varalakshmi Vratham. I know little about the Gaudiya or Vallabh cults that flowered in North India.

Many South Indian Hindus, I would wager, remain wholly ignorant of how their faith finds expression in North India. The Radha Krishna cult, for example, which spread like a lotus petal from Mathura, or Vraja/Braja/Brija as it is called, remains a mystery to many folks in Tamil Nadu, caught up as they are in the temples of Tanjore. I had to look up what Vraja meant. It is the area around Mathura where Krishna grew up, where the young prankster lived and loved.

The cult of Radha and Krishna gave birth to some of North Indian Hinduism's most sensual pleasures in the fifteenth and sixteenth centuries. This was when the poet Jayadeva composed the emotionally charged and erotic *Gita Govinda*; also when the songs of Surdas, Ravidas and other poets were sung in front of the Krishna idol of Nathdwara; when miniature paintings portrayed the pranks of Krishna; and the folk dances emulated the *Raas Lila* or Krishna dancing with the gopis or village girls. The temple of Govind Dev is one expression of the Radha Krishna cult.

Gods and kings

Govind Dev Ji Ka Mandir is Jaipur's most famous temple. It isn't nationally known like other Krishna temples, be it at Vrindavan, Dwaraka or even Nathdwara. But ask anyone in Jaipur for its most sacred site and chances are that they will point to this temple.

It lies behind the City Palace, within the old city, near the Hawa Mahal. Perhaps its fame comes from its proximity to royalty. Every royal function, be it a wedding, birth or death, is accompanied by a visit to Govind Dev, who stands with his flute in a temple that still retains the makeshift feel of a Lord who has taken up residence in a new land in a hurry. This temple began as a transplanted abode that turned permanent thanks to local devotion.

All of Jaipur wakes up to worship at Govind Dev Ji's temple, say the locals. On the day I visit, early one morning, none of Jaipur is present. It is 7 a.m. Exactly four people are sitting in front of what seems like a large stage curtain. They sit cross-legged, muttering prayers, humming songs. Sparrows chirp. A sadhu sits on a chair, welcoming the rising sun. The air is cool, the atmosphere quiet—or what passes for quiet in India. Used to the maze of corridors and multiple sanctums of South Indian temples, I assume that I have stumbled into the wrong location.

'Where is Govind Dev Ji's temple?' I ask a seated man.

He stares at me as if I am mad.

'This is Govind Dev Ji's temple,' he says, waving his arm around.

I look but cannot see any idol—only a large curtain like the one spread in front of construction sites to cover up the work in progress.

'Where is He?' I press.

Turns out He is behind the large curtain, which will open at 7.30.

To pass the time, I decide to visit a few nearby temples. Why can't I sit still and meditate like the others? Why must I rush from temple to temple? If it is connection with the divine that I seek, isn't it better found by staying put rather than seeking?

Of butterflies and joy

Happiness is like a butterfly, said one slogan that I heard when I happened to be unhappy. *If you chase after it, it will fly away. Only if you stay still will the butterfly alight on you.* Not true, let me tell you. I've tried staying still and no butterfly ever alights on me.

The question holds weight though. Do you seek the Lord or let Him or Her come to you? Most religions advocate a kind of intense passivism, which seems like an oxymoron, but is not. Saints wander from place to place in a kind of delirium, filled with intense longing for divine grace, seeking some kind of awakening or enlightenment. Quixotically, it is only when they surrender that they get hit by the bolt of religious salvation. By that token, I should be sitting and waiting for the bolt of lightning.

Too late. I am in the Toyota Innova, driving towards the Birla temple, or rather the path beside it where a large orange Ganesh holds court. A sacred ficus tree streaked with vermilion—echoes from past tribal blood sacrifices, according to Hindu scholar, Diana Eck—stands in the centre of what feels like a courtyard. On one side is the Ganesh temple. Beside it are two sweet shops selling laddus of various types: those made with desi ghee are more expensive, as are the creamy ones shaped like modaks, Ganesha's favourite sweet.

What can I offer you?

I haven't figured out my stance with respect to offerings for God. Flowers will get crushed, sweets will aid and abet India's rising numbers of diabetics. And really, does the god partake of all this stuff? The offerings of money, clothes, food or flowers end up in the pockets of the priests or the temple. So why do we persist carrying these objects as an offering to God when He doesn't need a thing and only wants us to be pure of heart?

Rationalizing it this way—*or am I merely being lazy or stingy?*—I walk into the temple empty-handed. I stand before an orange Ganesha, whose broad features make him look like the mouse who is his *vahana* (vehicle), and then walk to the Shiva temple a few yards away.

This Shiva temple is a small neighbourhood shrine, much like the scores of tiny temples dotting India's cityscapes. Devotees walk in carrying water in copper pots and pour it on the Shivalingam that lies a little below the ground. Access to the idol is a great advantage in North India. In South India, the average devotee wouldn't dare touch the Lord's idol. You need an intermediary in the form of a priest to carry your entreaties to the higher plane— somewhat like the mother in a traditional Indian household who mediates between the children and the strict, distant father. In North India, however, direct access is permitted. You can touch the Lord, bathe him with water and shower him with flowers. It is intoxicating, like freely entering a forbidden space, like cavorting in the school principal's office.

I find a copper pot full of water just sitting there and carry it towards the Shivalingam. Two others beside me are doing the abhisheka—pouring water on the Lord's head. Doesn't he ever get a cold, I wonder as I follow suit. Half of me wishes that I hadn't just picked up what was easy and available, but instead, gone the extra step of actually opening the tap outside and filling my own pot. It is called *prayatnam* in Sanskrit; it means effort; and it was a word I heard a lot growing up. Only if you do some prayatnam will you reap the reward, was the saying.

Does my little ritual hold water, figuratively speaking? Does it carry weight with the Lord, or will he consider this a shortcut and deduct marks? Will I get the full benefit of this particular abhishekam? I suppress my angst and concentrate on the pour. I gently aim for Shiva's black granite lingam, then a marble Parvati who sits across him, then Nandi the bull. For good measure, I pour water on the snake's hood over the Shiva lingam, and on Shiva's trident. When I am done, I go outside, fill water from the tap and leave the copper pot where I found it. The circle is completed. Hopefully I will get the benefits.

Singing off-key

As I walk back into Govind Dev Ji's temple, I hear the sound of singing. Fifty devotees are standing in front, waiting for the curtain to open. They are singing a bhajan in a spirited if slightly off-key chorus. I stand with the women on one side. There is no pushing or shoving. All temples should have a wide, broad opening to allow for panoramic viewing by the throng of devotees. The tiny entrance of South Indian temples is poor design. Devotees have no choice but to push through.

The curtain opens swiftly. Everyone raises their arms like in a rock concert. The singing continues. Some of them are swaying, some dancing with their arms in the air. Before Bollywood choreographed how Indians ought to move, before rock bands like Indian Ocean made Indian youth fist-pump and head-bang in a way that was no different from what could be seen at a Western rock concert, this was how Indians made merry, sought joy and engaged with song and dance—at temples, with bhajans.

Ecstasy born of faith

Two months ago, at an ancient Muruga temple in Bengaluru, a similar bhajan happened. My mother invited my daughter and me to go along. A crowd of people sat cross-legged on the ground, singing along with the musicians on stage. Half an hour later, the singer began a popular bhajan on Krishna.

Radhika Manohara Madana Gopala
Shyama Sundara Madana Mohana
Brindavana Chanda Hari…

The singing gained momentum. The drumbeats became faster. A few people in the audience stood up, lifted their hands and began dancing. My mother reached for my daughter's hand.

'Shall we also dance?' she asked.

Embarrassed, my daughter shook her head and pulled back her hand.

My mother's face crumpled.

The bhajan went on.

A week after this, I accompanied a group of teenagers, including my daughter, to a concert by a visiting British rock band called Poets of the Fall. The atmosphere was joyous, even delirious, with some

10,000 kids dancing non-stop for what seemed like four hours to me: the tired chaperone to six giddy teenagers.

These kids had no problem dancing at a rock concert, but could not bring themselves to do it at Hinduism's version of a rock concert, aka, communal, large-scale bhajans where devotees gathered to sing and dance.

My daughter associated religion with enforced seriousness that didn't tolerate her cracking a smile, with boredom that came from standing in long queues at stuffy temples, listening to chants that she didn't understand, with sombre rituals where she was permanently in danger of being wrong: 'Don't put the lamp *there*. Put it *there*. Facing *East*.'

Caught up in mores that make no sense, rules that have no reason and rituals that have no meaning, Hinduism, for many, becomes a bed of nails, bereft of joy, lightness and pleasure. It is that way for my children, and used to be that way for me. Even today, when there is a puja or a *homam/havan* (fire ritual) at home, everyone gets tense before the priest shows up. Do we have all the ingredients? Have we prepared the sacred food in the proper way? Am I wearing my nine-yards sari right or will it slip? Where is the joy in all this? Where is the fun and laughter in religion? If fun is what children are after, could religion be made that way? Could it morph into a mode that allowed for pleasure?

The singing and dancing congregation at Govind Dev Ji temple provided a potential road map. People were grinning, swaying from side to side, smiling, raising their hands, clapping and moving in time to the music. It was the Indian dance idiom, folksy and informal, exuberant yet spiritual, completely different from the sexy twirls and seductive shakes created by Bollywood and imitated by countless diaspora from San Jose to Stockholm. I ought to incorporate more song and dance with prayers at home, I thought.

Third time is a charm

Krishna's marble idol looks modern to my eyes, used as they are to dark, carved, stone images in South Indian temples. But the image is over 5,000 years old if legend is to be believed. The image was carved by Lord Krishna's great grandson, Bajranabh (or Vajranabh), the last king of the Yadu/Yadava dynasty, according to lore.

Bajranabh made an idol, and showed it to his grandmother, who said that the feet looked like Krishna but that was about it. That idol was named Madan Mohan—he who travelled with the princess to Karoli.

Bajranabh tried again. His grandmother, a stickler, said that the chest looked like Krishna. They called it Gopinath of Jaipur.

The third was a perfect match and won the grandmother's approval. It became Govind Dev Ji. The three idols were buried under the sands of time, quite literally, till about 500 years ago when a saint–savant named Chaitanya Mahaprabhu sent two disciples to the area to rediscover Krishna's playground—the places described in the ancient book, the Bhagavatha Purana.

Apparently, one of the disciples, Roop Goswami, found cows shedding their milk on a particular mound. Underneath were the idols that were first established in Vrindavan before making their way to Jaipur.

Glimpses of the divine

Like most temples, there are seven daily openings of the curtain, or *jhanki* (glimpses of the Lord) as they are called here, beginning at dawn and ending late at night. The 7.30 a.m. one is full of office-goers who pray here before heading out to schools and post offices, offices and shops to begin their workday.

The priest begins doing the aarti: waving a lamp with a single wick around the idols. In front is the sacred food offering: piles of sweets—orange, yellow and white—arranged like a pyramid. The pride of place goes to the laddu-prasadam, sold in the premises as the temple's signature offering. After the parikrama or circle around the temple, I go out to the sales counter and buy a couple of laddus for ₹10. They aren't as tasty as Tirupati laddus, but for some reason, I cannot stop eating them as I walk outside. By the time I get into the car, I have polished off both the laddus.

Religion through community is a new thing for me. Prayer, particularly at South Indian temples, is a solemn, solitary act, even though throngs of people surround you. It is between you and your maker. The singing and dancing at the Govind Dev temple are nothing if not communal. Gujarat, of course, takes it to another level with the garba during navarathri: joyous communal dancing on the streets, in building societies, grounds and auditoriums, with step routines rangings from two steps to 1,000 steps and more.

In South India, I didn't have these communal religious celebrations. I wish I did though, because they fuse joy with faith.

Joyous abandon and communal music

As I walk out, I run into Durga Singh's wife, Usha. She agrees to show me the other three temples, which have the idols that made their way from Vrindavan.

After a quick stop at the Radha Damodar temple, we make our way to the Radha Vinodhi Lal temple, up a flight of stairs and hardly visible from the road. We are the only ones there. The priest rouses himself, decorates the idols and invites us for the puja. At the end of the short ritual, he hands us a bowl filled with *rabdi* as prasadam. Usha is delighted. 'This is not just prasad, but *mahaprasad*,' she says. 'This is not made for general consumption, but specifically for the Lord. We are so fortunate to get it today.'

The rabdi is delicious. Made with whole milk that is slowly boiled till it condenses into a thick, sugary liquid, with dollops of cream and nuts, it reminds me of South Indian payasams, but tastes a whole lot better. Or maybe it is just the novelty of it.

Our last stop is the Radha Gopinath temple. Right outside, I find a shop selling my 'desert island' food. There are mounds of savory *bhujia sev*, deep-fried into thin strips of flour, flavoured with mint, green chilli, red chilli and salt. I could eat this every day if I were stranded in a desert island. But religion comes before food, so we hurry into the temple.

The sound of music fills the air. A music troupe, comprising only women, are sitting in front of the idol and singing. There is a drummer, a tambourine player and other accompanists, all clad in colourful saris. They sing with spirit, with joy. In that moment, I'm envious.

Takeaway

I sit down with a group and follow the leader. The songs are easy enough. Bhajans are simple to follow. Indeed, that is their purpose. Unlike these women though, I am unable to lose myself in the Lord's song and dance. I am still held hostage by my rational mind.

'The one thing which we seek with insatiable desire is to forget ourselves, to be surprised out of our propriety, to lose our sempiternal memory and to do something without knowing how or why—in short, to draw a new circle,' said Ralph Waldo Emerson in his essay, 'Circles'. 'The way of life is wonderful. It is by abandonment.'

These singing women give me a glimpse of this abandonment. They sing with their eyes open, yet lost to the world, smiling and making merry. In their minds, they seek refuge in the Lord. They have abandoned their egos and surrendered themselves to his mercy. As a result, they are able to dance like nobody is looking and sing like nobody is listening (which nobody is, by the way, because in bhajans everybody sings together and nobody needs to listen to each other). To achieve this kind of abandonment from the chores of everyday life, without the help of drugs, is to my mind, one of the greatest 'uses' of religion.

My guru in this area is the 15th century Bengali mystic, Chaitanya Mahaprabhu. In photos and paintings, he is singing and dancing, leading devotees, holding two *khartal*s (musical instrument) aloft, his face smiling in bliss. This flow state is achieved through forgetting the self, through connection with the divine. It is achieved via music and dance but also through intense faith.

Faith is a funny thing. It gives you the 'flow' state, but takes things in return. You cannot be rational or sceptical if you want to feel this flow-state faith. You have to surrender: called *sharanaagati* in Sanskrit.

Surrendering to a higher power is a way of life that involves trust and belief. It involves acknowledging that you are not in control. Perhaps you were never in control. Then what? Do you act? How do you act? When do you stop and give up? It turns out that surrendering to God is not as simple as doing nothing. That doing nothing is harder than it looks.

Most people understand surrendering to God after walking through fire, figuratively speaking. When all seems bleak and life seems to be a series of insurmountable obstacles, you figure out that (at some point) you are not in charge. What to do when you have exercised all options? When you cannot 'manage' the situation to your advantage? You have no choice but to surrender to a higher power and pray—try to align yourself towards it. That is the position I am in now.

There is a lovely YouTube video of a hurt condor—a majestic bird with wings like Jatayu. It has been nursed back to health. There it stands at the edge of a cliff, fluttering its once-broken wings. There is a chasm out in front. The inner voice says, 'If I step off, I will fall.' The condor steps off the cliff. And it flies. Is that surrender? I don't know. I haven't stepped off the cliff yet.

8

Goa: Dancing Under the Stars on Christmas

I T IS CHRISTMAS EVE in Goa. I am with Luis Ribeiro en route
to a village dance. Luis is a photographer who covers parties for
the local papers. Tonight he is off duty, but he nevertheless carries
his camera because, he says, you never know when a celebrity will
show up.

Silver Bells, the outdoor dance hall in Sangolda, is prettily lit.
Ribeiro greets friends—a kiss on each cheek for the women, a
handshake or hug for the men, depending on the level of friendship.
He hands me a gin and tonic from the cash bar and goes to mingle.

The hall is full of couples and families. The women are decked
out in long dresses, and the men in either suits or black tie. A band

comes onstage and begins to play—the fox-trot, the rumba, the samba, the swing. To my surprise, the floor fills up with couples, the men as graceful as the women. One twosome cradle a baby as they waltz. Little girls in flouncy dresses and boys in jackets and trousers freestyle in between the adults.

I observe a couple dancing cheek to cheek. They are plump and not particularly attractive but move with impeccable rhythm and grace. After the dance, I follow them out to the bar and compliment them on their dancing.

'Oh, if you went to as many church socials as we did, you'd dance well too,' laughs the woman.

Ribeiro comes back and greets them. No surprise. In Goa, everyone knows everyone else.

'Time to go to church,' he announces.

So we all troop down through the lanes to the church, rising like a spire in the darkness. Inside, there is a pleasant hush. We walk in slowly and take our places in the pews. Some kneel, some sit. The organ starts playing. A familiar song begins.

'Oh come all ye faithful.'

Mangling the Lord's Prayer

I grew up with Christianity. By which I mean, I grew up in Christian schools all my life. The first thing that my father taped was me mangling 'The Lord's Prayer' in my toddler's high-pitched voice. Since then, I have knelt on the floor with nuns at St. Antony's school in Chennai praying for forgiveness and redemption, walked into the chapel at Women's Christian College in Chennai to listen to the choir and spent pretty much every Christmas eve at churches all over the world—from the Vatican to Velankanni (a shrine in interior Tamilnadu), from Barcelona to New York, from Bangalore to

Boston, lighting candles and listening to music. To me, Christianity is linked to music, the magnificent sound of the organ and a sense of peace and orderliness within churches, quite in contrast to temples. This is not to say that the faith is without contradictions.

My first inkling of the contradictions in Christianity came in Memphis, Tennesse, where I was an art student. At a Gay Pride march, one of my friends encountered a Christian woman who asked Lisa whether she wouldn't mind stepping aside to learn about the Bible. Homosexuality was abnormal, said this earnest and attractive young Christian woman, pointing to the holy book. Being gay was against nature and against god's will.

Lisa wasn't fazed. She listened to the Christian's lecture and delivered a line that I will not forget.

'Sure, I will come aside with you. Either you will save me or I will seduce you.'

Where spirits live alongside humans

When I recounted this to Wendell Rodricks at a conference in Mumbai later, he laughed out loud. 'I am so going to use this line,' he said.

Rodricks has since, tragically, passed away. But it was he who opened the fusions and contradictions of Goa for me, beginning with our first meeting ten years ago, when I went to interview him for an article.

He and his partner, Jerome Marrel, were living in a beautifully restored mansion in Colvale. It will now become the Moda Goa museum.

'Goa has a special vibration, a Latin feel,' said Rodricks. 'It sees no problem in mixing religion with fashion, food and faith. It is one of the few states in which Hindus and Christians recognize their common past.'

What do you mean, I asked.

A lot of the Goan aristocratic families honour their Hindu past by contributing to Hindu temples, said Rodricks.

We were sitting outside his bungalow, under a lovely arching banyan tree. It was the eve of a fashion show. Rodricks was sketching and describing the model line up to his manager. A man brought us breakfast: fresh fruit juice, green tea, and oatmeal on a stylish wooden tray. Five dogs lounged around Rodricks's feet, occasionally nuzzling his Prada sandals. Marrel sat on a balcony above us, reading. It was a cozy domestic scene.

Rodricks bloomed as a designer after moving back to Goa, he said. His love for his home state is tangible and visible in his last book, *Poskem*.

He took me around his village, describing his life as 'part lotus-eater, part globe-trotter.'

'In Goa, spirits live alongside humans,' he said. 'Mysticism is a way of life. People aren't constrained by the rigid boundaries of faith.'

This layering of a Hindu past with a Mediterranean soul, of Latin beats with sitar strings, of Indian spices with European stews is part of what makes Goa so irresistible. Goa is what India is and could be if it sheds the 'narrow domestic walls' that Tagore talked about.

The roadside shrine

It is in South Goa that I discover Christ, or rather Mother Mary. Most people prefer North Goa, where the action is. The seashore at Baga, Calangute and Candolim is full of sunbathing bodies, sometimes nude. Masseurs and reflexologists ply the sand. And as the sun sets, nightclubs like Britto's and Tito's pump out music.

Leaving Baga, you encounter rice paddies and palm groves. White egrets take flight from lotus ponds. Crocodiles swim amongst the mangroves. Europeans on scooters speed down the narrow rural roads, dodging chickens, cows, dogs and pigs. I chase them on my rented Vespa, determined to find their secret hideouts. Which is how I end up at the end of a long dirt road at what looks like a roadside shrine inside which a beautiful Mother Mary is ensconced.

There are a line of people waiting to pray to her. I join the line and get chatting with the folks. They are carrying fruit, flowers, candles. But that is not what is unusual. There are women wearing sarees and bindis, there are women in hijabs and there are women in dresses too.

When I ask why they are waiting in line, one of them says, 'This is the most powerful shrine in all of Goa. Offer something to Mother Mary and your wishes will be answered, even if you don't know what those wishes are.'

So I stand in line with the rest of them. The heat is intense. My head is throbbing. And frankly, I don't know why I am waiting in line.

When it comes to be my turn, I kneel and rest my head on the cool marble feet of Mother Mary. Perhaps it is the intensity of the prayers all around me, but I feel touched by grace.

Cut off from shackles of history

'Portugal did Goa a great favour,' architect Gerard da Cunha once told me. 'We were cut off from the shackles of Indian tradition. We were forced to look outside.'

Since there was no blueprint to evolve, Goans created one themselves. They were a trading port for the Greeks, Romans, Arabs and Europeans. This meant that they were forced to interact with the outside world far earlier than the average Indian. Goans are therefore friendly, laidback and not overly fussy about faith or food.

Visit any temple, church or mosque and you will find some sort of hybrid culture. Trance music and tranquil beaches nudge type A personalities into subdued sublimity. The heat and, yes, the hashish encourage a languid pace of life and a state of mind that Goans call sussegado: a life of leisure.

Combined with this love of the good life is a commitment to the past. Many aristocratic Goan families including the late great cartoonist Mario Miranda honour their Hindu roots. When I interviewed him before his death, Miranda told me that his ancestors promised to deliver a sack of rice and a hundred coconuts to the local Durga temple at the start of each harvest. He kept this promise till his death, even though all the family lands had been disposed off, and Portuguese was his mother tongue.

Cleaving away the past is not the Goan way. Instead, Christianity here is tempered by the thick trees, Pagan rituals, harvest festivals, village elders who talk to spirits and rituals borrowed from Catholicism, Hinduism and mysticism.

It could well be a blueprint for all faiths.

9

Thiruvananthapuram: The Elephant God's Fried Dumplings

ONE OF THE FRUSTRATING and perplexing things about religion—all religions—is the petty hypocrisies and double standards that seem to go with the territory. Of course, this is because most of us hold religion and religious types to a higher standard. Because the faithful pray, we expect them to be better than us. Because they have an intimate and direct relationship with God, or so we think, we expect them not to be morally frail and pedantic. When they are, we feel disappointed, and occasionally angry.

While growing up, this was one of my biggest problems with my Hindu faith. My grandmother, for instance, would pray every day, but she would have no problem bargaining with the vegetable vendor to the point where she essentially cheated him out of his livelihood.

Visiting temples brought a whole other set of contradictions and complexities. At the larger temples like Tirupati and Guruvayoor, we essentially had to buy our place in front of God by bribing the priests with silks, nuts, fruits and money. What was the point, I often complained to my mother, of teaching truth and honesty, while engaging in the religious version of match-fixing?

Crossing over to munificence

Hinduism calls pilgrimages *tirtha yatra*. *Tirtha* means 'crossing over', and the idea is that you leave behind the mundane travails of everyday life and move to a higher plane, a sacred space. Many temples have a metal sculpture of a tortoise below the kodi maram or flagpole in the central courtyard. The idea is to emulate a tortoise, which pulls back all its limbs into its shell when touched. Similarly, when entering a sacred space, devotees are encouraged to pull back their senses, control their mind and raise their thoughts to a higher plane.

The problem in India is that most large and ancient temples don't necessarily encourage the peace and tranquillity that comes with such a crossing. Indeed, they are as transaction-oriented as betting on the turf club, or at the Bombay Stock Exchange. There is the shouting, the jostling to catch the eye of the right priest so that you can slip in between the crowds and stand in front of the main deity for at least a minute. There is the fee that you need to pay the priest so that he will treat you well the next time you visit; and there is the ignominy of being crushed amidst hundreds of sweaty bodies who are intent on communing with the divine by elbowing or crushing the feet of the person next to them. There is the hurried communion with the main idol before the priests start rushing you to move, to carry on.

Churches, especially old, ones are quieter and lend themselves to communion with god. Visit St. Paul's Cathedral in London, or the Basilica of Santa Maria Novella in Florence, and you can sit quietly in one of the pews, collecting your thoughts and reflecting on the divine in repose.

Congregations are another matter, however. The politics of any religious cult (and I grew up being exposed to several) are unbelievable. People sniped at each other, sniffed for back channels to get close to the guru, and engaged in a kind of one-upmanship that bordered on the childish ('I chanted more mantras than you'). They demeaned themselves in front of their teacher, their sycophancy so obvious, and so sickening to my youthful eyes.

The politics of religion

Even if you took a guru out of the equation, religion ended up being a highly political exercise. While living in Connecticut, I became part of a group of Indians who wanted to build a temple in Fairfield County. This led to a beehive of problems. The North Indians wanted a marble temple, with a priest from Varanasi, and Radha Krishna idols as the main gods. The South Indians wanted Balaji or some South Indian god, like Muruga. There was bickering, and difference of opinion, on everything from the architectural style to the types of sacred food that could be offered. Eventually, the discussions fell apart and divided the community. The only god that was acceptable for both the South Indians and the North Indians was Ganesha or Ganapathy, as he is traditionally known.

What is it about this god that makes him endearing and worshipped pan India? Is it the elephant head? Is it the rotund stomach that makes us feel at ease and less guilty about not going to the gym? Is it his beatifically broad face and curved trunk? Or is it because he reflects an animal that we have grown up with? I'm not sure. Whatever the reason, the only god who seems to bring Indians—all Indians—together is Ganapathy. Why is that?

It is this question that I am attempting to answer at the Ganapathy temple in Kottarakara, Kerala. An hour from Thiruvananthapuram, Kottarakara Temple is an anomaly. Kerala is known for its Shiva temples, its Krishna temples and for its Devi temples known in the state as Bhagavathy temples. Ganesha temples are rare.

Kottarakara is unique, not only because it is a Ganapathy temple, but also because it houses a Shiva temple. 'The son has become more famous than the father,' says the priest of the temple, a smiling man called Mohan-Thirumeni. Thirumeni is an honorific given to Kerala priests.

Tour guide to a temple

One of the first people I meet is a woman named Ganga. I immediately dismiss her, I'm ashamed to say, as 'one of those temple types'. Her home is opposite the temple and she is clad in a simple sari. She has been deputed by my uncle in Chennai, who specializes in temple visits. This is normal in my family. We have people specializing in jobs that are absolutely essential to our lives but have no economic value altogether. Growing up, everyone in my family flocked to a septuagenarian named Vaithi for anything to do with astrology. Vaithi's skill was not necessarily the accuracy of his predictions but the fact that he was willing to doctor horoscopes to suit the situation.

There was another man who was simply called 'Storeroom Mama'. He appeared like clockwork just before marriages and took charge of the storeroom to make sure that the caterers were not taking off with an extra coconut or mango.

Visiting temples too was a preoccupation in my family. Depending on the location, relatives were called to ease the way. When my in-laws heard that I wanted to visit Kottarakara, they immediately called relatives, who knew not just the temple opening and closing times, but also shortcuts, such as which priest to approach for what favour. It was thus that I met Ganga who knew everyone in the temple.

Moving your eyes to mimic a demon

Ganga and I stand at the entrance of the temple, chatting desultorily. Turns out she is a kathakali dancer. She plays male roles, she says, and usually prefers to play the villain in any dance drama. Her favourite role is that of Ravana, she says. I ask for a demonstration and she obliges me. Before my eyes, I watch her scrunch her eyes and pull down her lips. Her face and upper body gain girth and gravitas as she turns into a demon. She shakes her body, face and head. At the end, it takes her a minute to calm down. I am stunned by her transformation. But, perhaps, I shouldn't be surprised. After all, kathakali was invented in Kottarakara by its ruling prince. Before kathakali was invented, the dance form in vogue was called Krishna Natyam or Krishna's dance, based on the life of Krishna. When the prince of Kottarakara invited a dance troupe to perform in his kingdom, the *zamorin* of Calicut (a term coined, supposedly by Ibn Battuta, for the monarch of Calicut— now called Kozhikode) twirled his moustache and made a snide remark about how the Kottarakara princes couldn't appreciate the sophistication of Krishna Natyam. Now, the normal princely thing to do in such situations is to either wage a war or kidnap the dance troupe in question. But the royalty in Kerala were different. They were aesthetes. The prince of Kottarakara decided to invent a dance form in response to the snide remark from the neighbouring zamorin of Calicut. Rather than use Sanskrit verses for the dance, he used the local Malayalam language, albeit a highly Sanskritized version called Manipravalam—a mixture of Malayalam and Sanskrit. He called this Ramanattam, or Rama's dance, based on life stories of Rama. Years later, a refined form of this dance was presented to the world as kathakali.

Kathakali, I have to say, takes a while to get used to. Every time I went to Kerala for holidays, my uncle in Kottayam used to take a gaggle of us cousins to a kathakali performance as if it was some kind of treat. Before long, every cousin developed a mysterious and unexplainable stomach ache on the evening of the performance and had to bow out, until it was only I—naïve and uncomprehending—who was exposed to this 'profound art form', as my uncle would say.

Kottarakara has a museum of classical arts—a musty building—which contains the nine expressions or the *navarasa*s of kathakali as part of the display. The museum is most definitely not a 'must see'.

Jaggery and rice flour fried in ghee

Kottarakara temple is known for its *unni-appam*, or fried dumplings made with rice flour, coconut, jaggery, ghee, dry ginger, cardamom and squished banana—a local variety known as *palayan thodan*. These are loosely mixed in giant vats and fried in ghee or oil. On a slow day, the temple makes 50,000 such dumplings, a number that can rise to 1,70,000 during festivals, according to Mohan *thirumeni*. Unusual for temples, these unni-appams are cooked in front of the deity, in an alcove, rather than in a separate, sometimes secret, chamber.

How a temple chooses its offering has to do with myth and locally available ingredients. So it is with the Ganapathy temple of Kottarakara. While this particular elephant-headed god is known for his fondness for modaks, here in Kerala, he dines on unni-appams.

It all began when the king did not have a child, was 'issue-less', as the local books say. He prayed to Ganapathy saying that he would offer a garland of these unni-appams if a child were born. God granted his wish, and he garlanded the Ganapathy with unni-appams.

How the Ganapathy came to the temple is an older legend. It involves a carpenter, beloved in this area, known as Perunthachan. While sculpting the bottom of the jackfruit tree, Perunthachan discovered that he had sculpted a Ganapathy—unconsciously and perhaps by accident. He asked the priest of the Shiva temple if he could install the Ganapathy idol there and was refused. So he walked to another local Shiva temple and secured permission from that priest. That temple had not just Shiva, but also Parvati, Shasta or Iyappa, and also Muruga. The carpenter installed the Ganapathy idol in this temple, which is now known as Kottarakara temple.

The priest divined that Ganapathy was hungry and decided to offer the unni-appams not just to Shiva, but also to Ganapathy. And so it came to be that these sweet dumplings are prepared at the temple all through the day.

Some thirty-two men work in shifts to produce the unni-appams. It is tedious, hot work to sit in front of a stove for hours, pouring the liquid, forking out the cooked buns, and sprinkling them with sugar—day after day after day, all in service of the Lord.

As for the unni-appams—have them hot. They are delicious.

Takeaway

There is a term that is used in Hindu philosophy that fascinates me because it links Advaita with psychology. The term is *vasana*, and it refers to desires, impressions and patterns of behaviour that a yogi must discard in order to evolve to a higher spiritual plane.

At Kottarakara, I thought about this term a lot in connection to art and sculpture. The carpenter carved a log and unconsciously made it into the image of Ganesha who was then—after many perambulations—installed in a temple that belonged to the father, Shiva. Call it intuition, call it desire, call it unconscious wishes, or call it vasana—such patterns were becoming commonplace in the shrines I visited. Indeed, temples allowed or encouraged my vasanas to surface.

Consider Ganga, for example. She who danced the male-dominated kathakali and she who played the role of a demon named Ravana. Ganga reminded me that while all religions are patriarchal, there are ways to overcome or at least sidestep these archaic practices. She also brought up an old vasana: why was I so pissed off with patriarchy? Why did these discriminations affect me in a way that didn't affect other women my age? Was it the merit of a women's college education? Or were these old vasanas that were surfacing?

'Why can't women say the *Gayatri Mantra*?' I asked a Hindu priest once.

The priest replied in what I thought was masterful flattery: 'Women are like goddesses themselves. Why would you need to chant mantras? It is as if you are singing an ode to yourself.'

I wasn't convinced. Women aren't allowed to do many things in Hindu rituals. We can't be priests; we can't chant the Rudram and other sacred hymns; we can't do the aachamanam, and we can't perform the havan/homam or fire sacrifice. Some women however just go ahead and do all these things. Ganga was one. My mother was the other. And I could be too.

Don't get mad, get even, says the billboard.

Just do it—even if 'it' is chanting the Rudram.

10

Amritsar: Food, Community and a Holy Book

THE FAMILY STANDING IN the long, snaking queue to enter Harmandir Sahib, or the Golden Temple of Amritsar, is arguing. All around are people prayerfully singing kirtans (devotional songs), but this father and son, united by their pink turbans but divided by their accents, are arguing.

'I am a Sikh in my heart,' says the boy who looks to be about sixteen. 'Why do I need to wear a turban to prove it?'

'Because wearing a turban is one of the five tenets of our faith. You should be proud of it, not ashamed of it,' replies the father.

In Sikhism, five items are considered necessary to be carried or worn by the devout. The five 'Ka' as they are called include the *kada* or metal bangle, *kesh* or unshorn hair, *kangha* or comb, *kachchha* or undergarment and *kirpan* or dagger. Together, they form the identity of a Khalsa follower of the Sikh way. Of the five, the turban holding together the kesh remains the most visible embodiment— and the focus of this family's quarrel.

'Who says anything about being ashamed? I just think that religion should be private, not something to shout from the rooftops,' says the boy.

'Have the kids at school been bullying you again?' asks the father.

'Dad, that was in third grade; I can handle it now.'

'Talk some sense into your son,' says the father to his wife. She stands with the resigned wariness (and weariness) of long-suffering spouses who have seen this argument before. She adjusts her dupatta and continues muttering prayers.

The people in line stare at the father and son unabashedly. Indians, by and large, have no respect for quaint notions such as personal boundaries or private space. We embrace strangers, quarrelling families included. If the watching group could have jumped in and offered advice to the young lad, they would have. His accent is indecipherable to them though, which handicaps the crowd somewhat.

Suddenly, the queue moves forward. I sail forward, enveloped by a crowd of Sikhs. This is my first visit to a gurudwara. I am already favourably inclined to a faith that worships a holy book.

The inside of the gurudwara has that strange combination of hush and buzz that is the hallmark of places of worship. Sikh music is beautiful. I hear it in the background as I move through the sacred spaces of the gurdwara. Roses are scattered around the *Guru Granth Sahib*, the primary and living scripture for the Sikhs. Devotees move around, almost in a haze, praying and submitting themselves to the divine energy inside.

After spending half an hour inside, I walk around the Amrit Sarovar (lake of nectar) that was excavated by Guru Ram Das in the 16ᵗʰ century. This lake, from which Amritsar takes its name, has waters that are considered healing by Sikhs, many of whom come from far away to take a dip in its waters. One of the verses in the Guru Granth Sahib instructs devotees to wake up early, meditate on the godhead and bathe in the waters of the Amrit Sarovar.

The marble walkway around the lake is a hive of activity. In one corner is a group of volunteers handing out glasses of water. In another are pilgrims resting under the eaves. Men and women step inside the tank to purify themselves. And finally, there is the entrance to the feeding area: the *langar*.

A sanctuary through food

The communal kitchen at Harmandir Sahib is large, yes, but curiously and disproportionately small given the number of people it feeds every day. Nearly 50,000 people eat here on an average day. The number rises easily to 1,00,000 on festivals. Given these eye-popping numbers, the kitchens where all the food is prepared are relatively tiny—about the size of a small Mumbai flat, but with none of the accompanying squabbling. In fact, the cooks here are supremely serene.

There are two kitchen areas. One is where the dal is cooked, in vats large enough for three grown men crouching on top of each other to fit inside. The second kitchen is where the roti assembly takes place. It is here that I find my way to—a South Indian of dubious culinary prowess, determined to prove my worth to volunteers who have perhaps been rolling out rotis ever since they could hold a rolling pin.

All religions are linked to certain ideas, which end up becoming stereotypes associated with them. These are core philosophies of the faith that are believed by the faithful. Christianity and Zoroastrianism are linked to service through the establishment of schools, orphanages and hospitals. Buddhism is linked with the idea of Zen, mindfulness and meditation, all of which are the catchwords of current neuroscience. Sikhism is irrevocably linked with community and feeding. No other faith is as generous and welcoming of the hungry as the Sikhs are, even though every faith has feeding the poor as one of its tenets. Indeed, by some accounts, the idea of langar itself was borrowed from the Chishti Sufis who popularized this practice all over India in the twelfth and thirteenth centuries. The Persian word *langar* represents an asylum or sanctuary for the poor and destitute.

Guru Nanak's genius lay in not just adopting the practice of feeding the poor, but also making it egalitarian—controversial, given India's caste proclivities at that time. The idea that people could sit together and have a meal, regardless of caste, creed, gender, class or religion, was revolutionary in sixteenth-century India when Sikhism was born. Today, however, the notion of langar is intertwined with Sikhism. What makes the practice so special is not just the fact that thousands of people sit beside each other and partake of a meal, but also the fact that hundreds of people cook together in a community kitchen. It is this kitchen that is my first, if tentative, stop when I enter Harmandir Sahib.

Chopping vegetables and rolling rotis

The sound of the langar kitchen is the clattering of thousands of plates, cups and other stainless-steel vessels being washed in the dishwashing area. Chants play in the background as volunteers separate plates from bowls and tumblers. I quickly walk to the other parts of the kitchen area. People sit in circles—chopping garlic, slicing onions, peeling carrots and potatoes, pulling off cauliflower florets from its stem, and carrying large bowls of chopped vegetables to the other section where they will be cooked in even larger containers than the dal vats. An entire section is devoted to rotis, and it is here that I eventually settle, attracted by its warmth and comforting fragrance.

There is a clear division of labour. Some people simply roll the dough into small balls, another group presses them into perfectly round flatbreads, and the third group pops them over the flame to create fluffy rotis. I, ambitiously and foolhardily, sit in the rolling section. Almost immediately, a young, turban-clad boy brings me a plate of evenly divided dough. I begin rolling. It starts to look like the map of India.

A kindly woman sitting next to me says, 'I think you need to start again.'

I collapse my roti that looks like the map of India into a round ball of dough and begin again. About ten tries later, my roti too becomes round and even. *I have to come all the way to Amritsar and sit in a community kitchen in order to learn to make a perfectly round roti*, I tell myself ruefully. The approving smiles from the people all around me makes it worth it.

Adjoining the dal and roti kitchens are the washing area and the food-prep section—humming with activity. All together, they are smaller than the dining halls where 5,000 of the faithful sit cross-legged on the floor to eat a simple but tasty meal of dal, roti, sabzi and sweet *kheer*. I join the queue that waits to enter the dining area. We are waved through in batches, and quickly—if undignifiedly—grab our spot on the floor.

An assembly line of volunteers serves food and collects discarded plates with a humility that is a paradoxical hallmark of this warrior faith that emphasizes standing tall in the face of obstacles. *Miri* and *Piri* they are called: twin actions that are represented in the intertwined swords. The word *miri* comes from the Persian word *amir*, and represents royalty, wealth, nobility and kingship. The word *pir* refers to a Sufi holy man. In the Sikh context, it represents the *sant sipahi* or warrior saint: perfectly apt, given the history of how Sikh gurus have had to stand up to Islamic rule and (it must be said) torture.

Two elder Sikhs collect finished plates and toss them like Frisbees into a giant vat. The leftover food is separated and the plates handed over to the washing area.

I too hand over my plate and walk out of the langar area.

Takeaway

How do you determine the strength of belief? Adherence to a religion can be the baseline. Adherence during times of global turmoil, when one faith is under siege, usually from members of a different faith, is tougher. Toughest of all is sticking to your religion during times of great personal crisis.

Back home in Bengaluru, I talk to my Sikh friends about their religion. As with all religions, the strength of personal belief is complicated and varying. Hardship can cause an increase in belief or it can be viewed as a betrayal, causing the devotee to forsake God forever.

One friend tells me about her parents who began their life as devout Sikhs. They lost their only son to a road accident when the boy was but twenty years old.

'Instead of questioning their religion or feeling betrayed by the God that they had worshipped for so long, my parents gained all their strength from Sikhism,' said my friend. 'It was their life raft during the time of extraordinary hardship. Not once did they question their faith. Indeed, it was their religion that saw them through the loss of my brother. It kept them sane. It allowed them to survive, to live.'

Isn't this why the faithful cling to God? Because they cannot make sense of the crises and events that confront them? Because they realize that much of life is beyond their control?

Telling yourself that you are an atheist is simplistic, in my view. To gain succour from an imperfect faith and an elusive God offers the greatest spiritual (and psychological, as per recent studies) reward. Sikhism may be dominated by the idea of a warrior saint, but for the average devout Sikh, it is a peaceful path that keeps them from turning their rage outwards or inwards even when life deals them a devastating hand.

And that ultimately was the lesson I learned from Amritsar.

11

Puri: The Juggernaut That Moves a Chariot

I AM GOING TO Puri to experience *Maha Bhog*—the pinnacle of all prasadams, the Lord's food, which will be served to his devotees with his blessings. It is kind of a futile exercise really, because I will not be allowed into the temple kitchens.

As someone who was kept out of the cricket fields by the neighbourhood boys while growing up, I smart at this discrimination. In Puri though, this isn't about gender. No outsider is allowed inside the temple kitchen except the 1,000 male cooks who make fifty-six different kinds of offerings—called *Chappan Bhog*—to serve to the gods *six* times a day.

The list of dishes isn't just fifty-six; it runs to the hundreds. The Lord, along with his family, likes variety. The sweet dishes alone are of over fifty types, including several types of laddus, *malpua*, kheer and *rasagulla*, making this a diabetic's nightmare. Thankfully, there are also boiled-rice dishes, lentil-based ones, vegetable curries, and their permutations and combinations. Food is central to worship in this temple because, you see, Lord Vishnu dines here.

It is a great exercise in imagination to connect an activity with worship in the four greatest Hindu pilgrim sites, the *Char Dham* as they are called: Rameswaram, Puri, Dwaraka and Badrinath. Four abodes of God. They were created by Adi Shankara, an eighth-century young genius who grew up in Kalady, Kerala. Shankara, the story goes, wanted to become an ascetic. His mother wouldn't allow him. One day, while bathing in the river, a crocodile caught hold of his leg and didn't let go. Shankara told his distressed mother that the crocodile would let go of his leg only if she were to let him go and become a monk. His mother should have questioned the whole story. Why would the crocodile hold her son's leg without simply biting it off or killing the boy? But a mother in distress doesn't think. She said yes. The crocodile opened its jaws. Like Jackie Chan walking away from a bombed car, Shankara walked away from the jaws of death, quite literally.

India in the eighth century was dominated by Buddhism. Shankara travelled the length and breadth of India, trying to rejuvenate and revive Hinduism. He established ashrams and pilgrimage sites all over India: a kind of tourist-cum-religious circuit. Puri was one of them. Lord Vishnu is said to take a bath in the seaside temple of Rameswaram in South India; then He comes up to Puri for a meal; from there He goes onward to Badrinath where he meditates for the welfare of humanity; and finally he retires in Dwaraka. Since he

eats in Puri, this temple serves Maha Bhog or the Lord's food to all
devotees. That is why food is a big deal in this temple. It is the place
where Lord Vishnu dines.

Cooking by mathematics and scale

The kitchens are vast—spread over an acre. If you stand on the
roof of the Puri library across the street from the temple kitchens,
and bend over till you almost fall down, you can see the courtyards
leading into the kitchens using a pair of binoculars. This is where
200 junior cooks, who are not yet allowed to enter the kitchens, do
the prep work. They grate hundreds of coconuts—a tiring, thankless
job, made tolerable by chanting the name of the Lord; they chop
a mountain of vegetables; and wash the earthenware pots that are
used to cook. Inside, it is said, are multiple rooms—some say nine;
others say thirty-two. Here, 500 main cooks or *suara*, as they are
called, do the actual cooking along with 300 assistant cooks. Even
by Indian wedding standards—where thousands of guests are fed
in one go—the production capacity of the Puri temple kitchens is
staggering.

There are 752 *chulha*s or stoves, lit only with charcoal and wood,
as was done in the olden days, imparting a dense, smoky flavour to
the food. These stoves made with mud and brick are hexagonal—and
tantric—in shape. They are quite large—about 4 feet in diameter—
and equally deep. On the floor of the stoves is a nine-chakra yantra
or drawing. Every morning, before the fire is lit, the sun god and the
fire god are invoked through chanting and havans (a ceremony that
is essentially a way to feed the fire god—with a specific mudra or
hand gesture that is used when the samagri or offerings are given to
the fire god. Ghee is poured gently, like feeding a child, in the end
called 'purna-ahuti' that is the culmination of the ritual. The havan

is therefore a key Hindu ritual that is an invocation, an invitation, an offering and—in the Vedic past—a sacrifice.)

All the cooking is done in earthen pots, which are stacked on top of each other in groups of nine, cooking the food in a kind of sequence. Nine is an oft-repeated number in rituals. There are the *navagraha* or nine planets, *navadhaan* or nine grains, *nava durga* or nine Durgas, and so on. Things that take the longest to cook, like rice, are stacked in the bottom pots, while lighter vegetables that cook easily are placed at the top. Only indigenous vegetables and fruits are used, which means that the list of vegetables that cannot be used is long. No potato, tomato, green chilli, cabbage, cauliflower or any other foreign vegetable. Coconut, ghee, rice, dal or lentils, milk and milk products—curd, paneer, and others—are used in abundance. Molasses and date palm are used instead of sugar, black pepper instead of green chillies, rock salt instead of iodized refined salt. Spices such as cardamom, cinnamon, raisins and saffron flavour the sweet dishes, while mustard seeds, fennel seeds, cumin seeds, fenugreek seeds, ginger, asafoetida, turmeric and tamarind are used for the savoury dishes. Oil is used for deep-frying certain dishes, mostly sweets. Much of the food is boiled or steamed in earthenware pots over long periods of time with drip-holes for the excess water. Slow cooking at its best, just as it is done during the *shraadham (or shraadh)*, the annual ceremony to worship ancestors within families.

Why the secrecy?

I am not sure about the point of all the secrecy. Is it because outsiders will make the kitchens ritually impure? It is certainly not to protect the recipes, which are simple and involve a combination of ingredients in well-known proportions and slow-cooking over a wood fire. The dishes are fairly standard: a variety of rice dishes, flavoured with milk, lemon juice, tamarind and curd. There is khichdi, a bland mixture of rice and lentils, vegetable curries, a variety of dals made with different local lentils and flavoured simply with salt, ginger and turmeric. Green bananas or plantains are a particular favourite, as are locally available gourds. *Raita* (a variety of curd) made with radish or winter melon (*lauki*) are served in the summer months. Drinks made with milk, jaggery, dried ginger, buttermilk and fruit juices are part of the offering, as are a whole variety of sweets. There are no complicated techniques—Ferran Adria's kitchen this is not. Any cook in India could make any of these dishes with her eyes blindfolded. Then why the secrecy?

The very fact that I am asking this question shows that I don't get it, according to believers. In a Hindu kitchen, food isn't just about ingredients and techniques—it is about the energy and intent of the cook or cooks.

In Puri, the flavour of the temple food comes from the quality of the local ingredients, the water from 10-feet-deep temple wells called Ganga and Jamuna, the slow cooking and, most important of all, the purity of intention of the cooks. 'Thought stamps,' they call it in Tamil: *Enna pathivugal.* It means that the thoughts of the cook or even a random passerby can stamp themselves on the dish, thus affecting its 'energy'. This idea is beautifully illustrated in the movie, *The Ramen Girl* where the chef's ramen noodles make a sad man laugh because he cooks with that intention.

Indians are obsessed with how a dish is made—not just the ingredients used and the cooking techniques, but also the mood and character of the cook and his environs. If the cook is angry, my grandparents used to say, the diner will get heartburn. If the cook is hungry and salivates at the food that he is preparing, the person who eats will not be able to digest the food properly. A cook is sad—the dish that he prepares will cause tears in the eater. A cook is mad—the eater gets aggressive after the meal. And so it goes. It is not just the cook. The thoughts of anyone who is around the food can get 'stamped' on the food and affect the eater. For this reason, babies are spirited away and fed in private. The logic is that young souls are extremely sensitive to other people's energy. Having someone stare enviously at a baby's delicious food will give the infant stomach ache. My grandparents were extremely careful about where they ate, carrying home-cooked food across long distances rather than risking eating food that was cooked improperly. If you ate at the home of a person who has made his money improperly, through bribes, for instance, then his bad karma would come to you through the salt, they would say. My grandparents, needless to say, would have a huge problem dining at modern restaurants—with yelling cooks, macho energy, flaring egos and flying swear words. In their mind, the temperament of the cook translates directly into the quality of the food that he is serving. A serene disposition is essential for the food to nurture body, mind and soul. This is why temple cooks are told to do two things: enter the kitchen with a full stomach so that they don't salivate at the food that they cook, and chant the name of the Lord while they work so as to induce a peaceful disposition. In Puri, they go further. They believe that Mahalakshmi, the consort of Lord Vishnu, actually cooks the food. They are mere prep and line cooks who do the work. The actual flavour comes from Lakshmi's hands.

'You can hear the jingle of her anklets in the kitchen,' one cook told me.

Offering the food to the deities involves dance and balance. The cooks carry a long bamboo pole on which hang two rope baskets at either end. Once the food is cooked, the cook lassoes the top of the earthenware pot with a wet jute rope, lifts it up in one swift motion and places it inside the rope basket. He places two or three more pots atop it. The same applies for the other rope basket. Once this is done, he places the middle of the bamboo pole on his shoulders and begins a sinewy, even walk—hips shaking from side to side—from kitchen to the sanctum sanctorum so that not a drop of food spills on the ground.

'Even if we think for one second that we had anything to do with the making of the food, our pots will shatter en route to the garbagriha,' said the cook. 'For this reason, we have to tame our egos at all costs. We have to be mere vessels, carrying out the work of the goddess.'

Temperament, not talent

I guess this is why temple cooks are different from the average Morimoto or Daniel Boulud, who love putting their name not just on the dish but on the entire premises. The talent in temple cooking is not just about technique; it is about temperament, about taming your ego. You have to be pure of intent, joyful in nature, chanting the name of the Lord in total supplication.

Legend has it that the food carries no fragrance on the walk from kitchen to garbagriha or womb chamber, a more appropriate name than the usually used sanctum sanctorum. Once it is offered to the gods, it smells divine. In Puri, the food is first offered to Lord Jagannath, then to the goddess, Bimala, his wife, before carrying it out to the devotees.

Each cook and his family get a portion of the prasadam. This is their livelihood. They carry it to the Ananda Bazaar or Pleasure Market and sell it to the approximately 5,000 devotees who visit the temple daily. On festive days, of which there are many, this number swells to about 1,00,000 people. The Jagannath Puri temple is the largest vegetarian, *sattvic* kitchen in the world—one that no outsider has ever entered.

The town that gave English a word

In 1810, Robert Southey, a somewhat effeminate-looking British poet laureate who belonged to the Romantic school, wrote an epic poem called 'Curse of Kehma' with a shorter poem called 'Jaga-Naut'.

> A thousand pilgrims strain
> Arm, shoulder, breast and thigh, with might and main,
> To drag that sacred wain,
> And scarce can draw along the enormous load.
> Prone fall the frantic votaries in its road
> And, calling on the God
> Their self-devoted bodies there they lay
> To pave his chariot-way.
> On Jaga-Naut they call,
> The ponderous Car rolls on, and crushes all.
> Through blood and bones it ploughs its dreadful path.

This poem—even though it is fiction—bothers me on many levels. The term 'wain' refers to the chariot and the poem is about the Rath Yatra, the annual procession when Lord Jagannath's chariot is pulled by devotees. Although crowds still gather for the Rath Yatra, Southey imagines and writes about a time when the chariot rolled over devotees, killing them in a rather brutal fashion.

The poem that makes a judgement without offering context. It highlights an imagined tragedy without making a mention of the religious devotion that anchors the practice. Most of all, it is a third-rate poem that resorts to rhyme to hide the fact that there is no deeper meaning than a description of an event.

Southey's fame has been justly eclipsed by his contemporaries, William Wordsworth and Samuel Coleridge. He, however, gave the world the term juggernaut. The etymology of the word does no justice to the god. Juggernaut refers to an unstoppable, somewhat menacing force that gains momentum and causes death, ostensibly because throngs of devotees are crushed under a chariot's wheel during the annual Rath Yatra, improperly translated as the Car Festival.

First of all, and I didn't know this, it isn't one god but three. Jagannath, the main deity of the temple, is a form of Vishnu. He stands with his brother, Balabhadra, and his sister, Subadhra. A *rath* is a chariot, and *yatra* means a journey. The Rath Yatra is a journey by chariot, not a 'car festival'. It is a trip that the three siblings make to their aunt Gundicha's home for rest and relaxation, for restoration. They have fallen sick and have to be cared for.

Who came up with this idea? Gods are taken in procession through villages in many temples. But the idea that gods fall sick, and have to be cared for by a maternal aunt, are nifty embellishments forming the background of one of India's largest human congregations.

Hundreds of thousands of people stand witness to the Rath Yatra. The road between the Jagannath and the Gundicha temple, therefore, would give any broad French boulevard a run for its money.

Tantric roots of the temple

At 45,000 square feet, the temple complex itself is large—not as large as some of the Big Temple in Tanjore, Tamil Nadu, but of respectable size. The *vimana* or tower is 215 feet high, and in the evening, a type of temple *sevak* (service-giver), called Garuda Sevaka, climbs up to the tower to tie pieces of cloth on the flagpole. People can buy this offering and these men tie their hopes and dreams on top of the temple tower, without so much as a belay, safety rope or harness.

Inside the temple complex, there are numerous shrines for Surya, the sun god; for Lakshmi, for Shiva, and perhaps, most ancient of all, the goddess Bimala or Vimala. Some say that her shrine predates that of Jagannatha, proving that Puri was an important place in the Shakti or goddess cult.

Perhaps because I grew up in Kerala, I am fascinated by the tantric roots of the goddess cult. Kerala and Bengal are two important centres for tantrism. Tantra co-developed in Buddhism and Hinduism in the 1st century C.E or A.D., and incorporates a variety of practices including mudras (hand gestures), mantras (chanting), pujas (rituals) and yantras (diagrams) to pay homage to a variety of gods, goddesses, and yoginis. In Puri, tantra worshippers belonging to the Shakta cult (goddess worshippers) come to pay obeisance to the goddess, Bimala, whom they consider more important and more ancient than Jagannatha.

To get to see the god, Jagannatha, you have to wait in a spacious hall in rows of ten or more people. North Indian temple entrances are broad, particularly in comparison to the tiny openings of ancient South Indian temples. The security men shoo you in and the crowd moves in unison towards the massive deities that stand on a pedestal above eye level. What do they think of this surge of humanity coming towards them, I wonder.

There is the white Balabhadra, the red Subhadra, the black Jagannatha, and slightly behind them, the red Sudarshana, which is

Vishnu's chakra or destructive discus that chops off evil-doers' heads with impunity.

The temple priests urge you to touch your head to the feet of the idol of Jagannatha, and make an offering. The air is cool. Every now and then, a group of temple cooks bring in food for offering and then take it out to sell in the Ananda Bazaar.

I sat one evening under the banyan tree and ate the prasadams that I bought from the priests. There were a variety of rice dishes, brinjal flavoured with coconut shavings, dal and a sweet. I would like to tell you that the food was delicious. It probably was, but it isn't memorable. The sceptic in me believes that the quality of the food is watered down because of the aggressiveness of the priests and their economic needs. But flavour isn't really the point of this food. After all, you can have bad food at a five-star hotel. This is food that has the breath of God; it is a symbol of his mercy and munificence.

The temple kitchen in miniature

You cannot enter the kitchens of the Jagannath Puri temple. But you can see a miniature version of this type of cooking at the Anantha Vasudev temple in Bhubaneshwar. This jewel of a temple sits across a broad, beautiful temple tank. Inside, several small kitchens prepare food for the Lord every day using humble ingredients: local rice, yellow *tuvar* dal, yellow pumpkin, brinjal, yam and other indigenous vegetables—all cooked over wood fire, and served in the eating section adjacent the temple.

At 11 a.m. on a rainy morning, the kitchens were busy. There were no metal pots to clang. Men in checked towels sat behind wood fires, stirring mud pots full of ingredients. A few hours later, the cooks carried earthenware pots of steamed rice, dal and vegetables into the temple. They offered the food to the Lord before selling it to the devotees. Wouldn't the Lord like to eat something different once in a while? I wondered.

How to make ancient rituals modern without losing their essence?

Tradition and seed preservation

It is easy to be flippant or cynical about temple food: the same list of dishes, cooked in the same way over centuries, feeding masses of people via the Lord. What other virtue does it have? An important one has to do with the preservation of indigenous seed varieties. At the Jagannath Temple, for instance, one of the offerings is made with green paddy. For green paddy to be available throughout the year, specific seed varieties that ripen at different times must be grown around the temple. At the very least, this promotes biodiversity. India used to have 1,00,000 varieties of rice. Today, most of us eat Basmati and, in the South, Sona Masoori rice. Temple kitchens specifically choose local and indigenous varieties of rice, such as *matta*, *njavara*, red rice and parboiled.

Today, dining locally and seasonally is the buzzword. Restaurants like Noma in Copenhagen make a virtue of foraging for local herbs and ingredients. Most traditional societies used to do just that. The problem is that much of this traditional food, and I speak mostly for Indian food, is not necessarily tasty. On Amavasya or new moon days, elderly South Indians eat only indigenous vegetables such as plantain or green banana, pumpkin, yam, Indian beans such as *avarekai* and *karamani*, and green leafy vegetables such as moringa and amaranth. Traditional Hindus fast on Ekadashi—the eleventh day of the waxing or waning moon. They break their fast with food that contains no tamarind and bitter greens such as agathi keerai and dried sundakai or Turkey berry. Both are, shall we say, an acquired taste. Mashed potatoes with a dollop of butter is not.

Some festivals are linked to specific fruits or vegetables. Both *undhiyo*, the Gujarati delicacy, and the *kootu* made during the month of December for a south Indian festival called Tiruvadirai used only those vegetables that were available during that month: cluster beans, field beans, yellow pumpkin, yam, green banana and tender lentils still in the pod. These are all vegetables that have natural properties to keep the body warm, which serves to offset the cold of December. Similarly, the amla—Indian gooseberry— renowned for its vitamin C, comes in the month of Karthigai/ Kartika (mid-October–mid-November). It arrives in the markets when the weather turns cold, causing colds and flu. Eating this amla during this month staves off the sniffles. My mother calls this amla *Vidya-arambha Nellikai*, or 'gooseberry to start the learning season'. Or the gooseberry that comes to fruit during a particular day called Vidya-arambham or Vijaya-dashami or the last day of Navaratri.

In Maharashtra, certain wild greens are cooked during Rishi Panchami. Indeed, every part of India has specific dishes, recipes, pickling techniques and ingredients that are linked to festivals. All of these would be forgotten were it not for festivals, temples and tradition. To the questions 'Of what use is tradition?', 'Of what use is temple cuisine?', the answer is: To encourage frugality, local and seasonal living, to intersperse feasting with fasting and, yes, to eat well, not just in the rich, paneer butter masala type of cuisine, but also in the simple, sattvic sense. Food that is light, easy to digest, and spreads like lightning through your cells causing them to dance with delight; food that sparks your neurons and magnifies your mood; food that calms you down and lets you think clearly.

Our ancients believed that food was potent. It was Anna Brahma—food as a creator.

Tribal totem from the mists of time

Who is this god for whom all this food is made? Jagannath is one of the most interesting gods in Hinduism. Everyone claims him: the Vaishnavites or Vishnu worshippers, Shiva and Shakti worshipers, Buddhists, Jains, and tribals. Everyone seems to have a connection to this dark skinned god by the seashore with his round popsicle-red eyes and frozen rictus smile. Wooden arms, stretched in front, to give and receive, prompting generations of saints and sinners to rush into towards this lord, seeking mercy and blessings. Chaitanya Mahaprabhu, the influential teacher who founded several spiritual orders, went into paroxysms of delight upon seeing this god. He ran into the garbagriha and fell senseless with delight. Or a tribal totem. Which is how this particular god originated.

The history of Jagannatha-Purushottama, and yes, I realize that I am throwing in a new name here, is a fascinating blend of religion, statecraft and devotion. In the chessboard that was India in the tenth century, there were kings who wanted legacies, religions that were jostling for supremacy, teachers who wanted to convert kings and their subjects, and devotees who could choose religions like a voter chooses parties. Puri was the stage on which all these dramas were acted out.

Blue beating heart

The origin of the idol is the subject of many tales. My favourite comes from Sarala Dasa, the fifteenth-century Odia poet who wrote his version of the Mahabharata. In it, he imagines Krishna's death. The actual way that Krishna dies is somewhat innocuous. A hunter named Jara sees Krishna's foot sticking out from behind a tree, imagines it to be the ears of a deer, shoots and kills Krishna. A disconsolate Arjuna comes along and tries to cremate his friend. But Krishna's heart doesn't burn. As always, a divine voice echoes from the heavens. It tells Arjuna to tie Krishna's heart to a log and throw it into the ocean. Over eons, this log floats all the way around from the west coast of Dwaraka to the east coast where Puri is located.

Jara, the hunter who had killed Krishna, is reborn as a Shabara tribal man named Biswa Basu. He discovers a congealed blue stone—Krishna's heart—in the forests around Puri, and worships this giant stone as Nila Madhava. A local king called Indradyumna hears about this miraculous blue rock that is being worshiped by tribals. He wants it for himself, as kings are wont to do. So he sends a Brahmin priest, Vidyapati, into the forests to discover this blue idol. The only problem is that the tribal hunter refuses to reveal the location. So the Brahmin stays with the tribal hunter, Biswa Basu. He 'falls in love' with the daughter of the tribal man—either by design or not. As the new son-in-law, he begs his tribal father-in-law to take him to see the blue idol. The tribesman blindfolds the Brahmin and takes him deep into the forest. But the Brahmin is smart. He drops black mustard seeds all along the trail. He waits a few days for the yellow mustard flowers to sprout and retraces his steps back into the forest to where the idol is hidden. Once he discovers the spot, he rushes to King Indradyumna to tell him the location. The king gathers up his forces and goes towards Nilachala or Blue Mountain. He goes to the cave, but the blue stone idol has vanished. A disconsolate king makes a bed of *Kush* grass, lies down on it, and declares that he is going to fast unto death. That night, the blue Lord appears in his sleep. 'Build a large temple for me,' says the Lord. 'Go to the seashore. You will find a large log of wood with markings that include a conch, a chakra, a mace and a lotus (*shankha chakra gada padma*), the four things that are carried by Lord Vishnu. Carve this log into four idols and install them in your temple.'

The king builds a giant temple by the seashore. He tries to have his men lift the log, but even an entire army cannot move the thing. The king decides to kill himself—again. That night, the Lord appears in his dreams—this is getting to be a habit.

'Have my tribal devotees help your soldiers lift the log. Only then will it move,' says the voice.

Many people, one faith

This confluence of efforts—by the tribals, warriors and Brahmins—brings the log into the precincts of the temple. This continues to this day. The servitors of Jagannath temple include tribals (who are the cooks) and Brahmin priests.

Okay, so now the log is in the temple. But there are no images of the gods. The kingdom's finest sculptors come to convert the log into the four idols. Every time they touch the log, their chisels break. Finally, an old stranger walks in. He says that he will carve the log into the four god images so long as nobody disturbs him for twenty-one days. You know where this story is heading, right? The old man takes the giant monolithic log into the temple, shuts the door. Days go by. The door isn't opened. What is the sculptor doing for food? A concerned queen orders that the door be opened after fifteen days. When the door opens, the sculptor has vanished. Of course, he is the Lord himself. The half-finished idols are installed at Puri temple. The black one is Jagannatha, the yellow one is his sister, Subhadra, the white one is his elder brother, Balarama, and the last one is the Sudarshana chakra held by Lord Vishnu. Was this story made up to explain the ancient, tribal, almost totemic images of these idols? Or do the idols look this way because events occurred exactly as the story described?

Jagannatha. The literal translation is Lord of the universe. But you see, and this is where the story gets complicated, that isn't his name. He has many names and incarnations, this God. When I said that everyone claimed him, I wasn't kidding.

Perhaps the most authentic claim comes from the tribals or adivasis, who view the Jagannatha trio as gods who were tribal in origin. Many reasons are offered as proof. Scholars have talked about the 'unfinished, premature, aboriginal, savage, exotic look' of the deities, the use of wooden idols that look like totems in tribal cultures—rather than the more common metal or stone sculptures of gods, the continued practice of including tribal priests in the Jagannath cult and, most important of all, the cooking style of the Jagannath kitchens where food is boiled with very little use of spices, similar to the tribal cooking style. All this does not stop other religions from claiming this god.

Hindu, Buddhist or Jain?

'Jagannatha is primarily a Jaina institution,' said Pandit Dr Nilakantha Das, who has been awarded the Padma Bhushan. The sacred food in Puri is called *Kaivalya*, which is similar to the Jain notion of salvation. Most Jain tirthankaras have names ending with '*natha*', such as Rishabhanatha, Neminatha, Parsvanatha, and Gorakhanatha. Why not Jagannatha? After all, Jainism had spread all over Kalinga—the earlier name for Odisha. There are accounts of one king conquering this land and taking away the *Kalinga Jeena* or Jain idol. So, in fact, the argument goes that Jagannatha is Jeena Natha.

The Buddhists too claim him, stating that the three idols represent not Hindu gods but the 'three jewels' or *triratna* that are the central principles of Buddhism: buddha, dhamma and sangha. The most interesting Buddhist claim has to do with an unknown substance called 'Brahma' that lies inside the navel of the main idol, Jagannatha. Hindus say that it was the original blue stone, but Buddhists say that this Brahma is Buddha's tooth relic that was brought from Kushi Nagar, where he died, to Puri. Buddhists say that the *snana yatra* (bathing ritual) and *ratha yatra* (chariot journey festival) are Buddhist in origin. A Buddhist temple in Nepal is called Jagannath temple. When Buddhism got absorbed into Hinduism, its images, idols and ideas were usurped and subsumed. Buddha was nothing but an avatar of Vishnu, sang the poet Jayadeva, who—no coincidence—was from the area around Puri.

Prior to the eighth century, scholars say, the area around Puri was Buddhist. Along came Shankaracharya, whose goal was to make Hinduism flower in India again. He went to the four corners of the country, established *matha*s, engaged in long debates with Buddhist scholars and won them over to his faith. Simultaneously, he tried to reform Hindus who were caught up in empty rituals and the rapidly congealing caste system. Puri was one of the epicentres of the battle that Shankara waged against the Buddhists. He succeeded. For a while. Wave after wave of religious change washed over India during that period, usually in a reaction to what happened before: Jainism of the third and fourth centuries, followed by Buddhism in the fifth to seventh centuries, then the Advaita philosophy propagated by Shankara in the eighth century, followed by an upsurge in Saivism or Shiva worship in the tenth century, which is where we encounter a charismatic, controversial king who built the current temple of Jagannatha in Puri.

From Shiva to Vishnu

The interplay between statecraft, religious dominance and influential kings plays a role in the hoary history of this temple. Consider the builder of the current temple, as it stands today. This wasn't King Indradyumna, the man in the ancient tale, who sulkily decided to fast every time he encountered a snitch in his devotion. The king who built the current Jagannath temple was a hardy, mixed-blood monarch named Anantha Varman Chodaganga Deva. His mother was a Chola princess, Raja Sundari. His father was a Ganga king called Rajaraja. He ruled in the eleventh century, for seventy-two years, beginning as a minor and then giving up his throne at a ripe age.

In ancient India, kings seem to be involved in three activities: warring against each other, marrying each other and performing giant sacrifices to consolidate their power. So it was with this king, Chodaganga, who had the blood of the virile Gangas and the stalwart Cholas in him. He was fighting off neighbouring kingdoms, trying to expand his kingdom, rein in a diverse citizenry who were all engaged in intense religious activities—as was typical in those days before Facebook or even television. People prayed and procreated. That was about it. Chodaganga, like his Ganga ancestors, was a staunch Shaivite or Shiva worshipper. That changed when he encountered a South Indian Vaishnava saint named Ramanuja, who had come up north to convert more people into Vishnu worshippers. Anyone who says that Hinduism is a passive religion without evangelicals is living in the wrong era. In the eleventh century, there was a king who worshipped Shiva, a saint who wanted him to worship Vishnu, and a fickle public.

Scholars argue over whether Ramanuja succeeded in making the king convert to being a Vishnu worshiper. They point to inscriptions and seals where Chodaganga refers to himself as *Parama Maheshwara* (one who worships Shiva) at first, and then later—after conversion—as *Parama Vaishnava* (one who worships Vishnu). What seems to be true is that Odisha was at the crossroads of multiple faiths in the eleventh century. For me, the most fascinating of these is the God that they called *Purushottama* or noblest man. Not Jagannatha, you ask? Wait, we are getting ahead of the story.

Highest amongst individual souls

'He drew patterns on her pitcher-like breasts with a paste of musk and saffron.' That's what stood out, particularly since the verse was describing a God. The actual verse by the tenth-century dramatist, Murari, is more detailed and of a beautiful rhythm, even for a non-Sanskrit speaker.

Kamala kuca kalasa keli kasturika patran kurasya…

And so it goes in one long breathless sentence.

'Oh, all ye spectators assembled on the occasion of the yatra or voyage of Purushottama, the exalted one who is like a new sprout of the dark green Tamala tree growing in the forest, who resides near the salty ocean, who is like the big blue sapphire which decorates the head of the three worlds and who sports with Kamala, the goddess Lakshmi, by drawing patterns with the paste of musk and saffron on her pitcher-like breasts…'

The god that Murari was talking about is Purushottama or Vishnu. I read this verse in a 1,000-page book called *Cultural Heritage of Odisha*, Volume XII, Puri District, Special Volume, put out by the State Level Vayasakabi Fakir Mohan Smruti Sansad,

Bhubaneswar, and sold for a mere ₹300. It is required reading for anyone interested in the Jagannath cult, Odisha, or Puri. In an essay titled 'Concept of Purushottam in the Agamas', scholar and professor G.C. Tripathi describes how the god that we all now call Jagannatha wasn't really Jagannatha at all. His earlier name was the equally complex Purushottama. Purusha means individual soul. Purushottama means highest amongst individual souls, or divine soul.

Descriptions of Purushottama with his consort, Lakshmi, is what Bertie Wooster would call 'ripe stuff'. In one commentary by Raghava Bhatta in the fifteenth century, Purushottama holds Lakshmi on his left lap in a tight embrace and gazes at her lovely face through 'liquor-addled eyes.' The sensuality of this verse is stunning.

The theory linked to this story was that Purushottama became Jagannatha and the other two idols were added later.

But these are just a few of the legends linked to Jagannatha. There is the story of the Kanchi conquest that is depicted to this day in Odissi dance. There are tribal folk tales and mythic symbols, all of which, like the juggernaut gather steam in a devotee's imagination.

When I left Puri, my mind was in a whirl. Here was a god whose creation story was linked to Jainism, Buddhism, and many arms of Hinduism including the Shakti and Vaishnava cults. What a magnificent God this Jagannatha was. No wonder Bengalis and Odias view him with unmatchable fervour.

Takeaway

Jagannath stayed with me for many months after I returned from Puri. I remained fascinated by his legends. But more than anything else, I started to obsess about faith and the 'flow' state. The singing that I had seen at the Govind Devji temple and the blissful trance-like dancing that I had seen in all the photographs of Chaitanya Mahaprabhu that adorned many a space in Puri made me want to experience this bliss. If religion could make you forgetful yourself, if faith could induce a flow state, if surrendering to God made your heart less weary and your mind strong, then what was wrong in embracing faith? And why was I hesitating so much? On the one hand, I wanted to 'lose' my mind in that I wanted to experience the ego-less expansion that I saw in the devotees. On the other hand, I was afraid that I would lose my mind.

Here was the problem. I had to choose. I couldn't be a non-believing believer. I couldn't be a somewhat faithful devotee. I had to go whole hog. And you know what? After a lifetime of being rational and sceptical, I was ready to take the plunge.

Perhaps it was the energy of the temples that I visited, perhaps it was the people I encountered or perhaps it was the subtle influence of the sacred food that I was eating. Whatever the cause, I knew that I had changed in ways that I couldn't articulate but could certainly feel.

Was there a way to embrace the beauty, music, art, poetry and rituals that came with faith without becoming small-minded? The answer would come to me in Haridwar in the form of a guru.

12

Kumbh Mela: The Largest Human Gathering in the World

THE ROYAL RELIGIOUS PROCESSION, *Jamat Peshwayi*, begins in Jwalapur, a dusty town an hour outside Haridwar, where some two million Hindu saints, ascetics, healers, mystics and saffron-clad monks have camped out overnight.

On the morning of the fifth royal bath, the *shahi snan* or ritual immersion into the Ganga is taking place. This royal bath coincides with the auspicious Shivaratri, or Night of Shiva, in this mammoth celebration and spectacle, which occurs once in twelve years (the ardh-kumbh or half-kumbh happens once in six years) and brings forth a confluence of Hindu mystics to this riverine town.

I'm standing in the crowd along with millions of people on the road to Haridwar to watch the saints go marching by. The crowd and procession is orderly, thanks to a large police presence, but the religious fervour is palpable. With me are Hindu men and women offering sweets, water, fruit and flowers to the saints: guavas, melons, dry fruits and water. They mutter prayers and prostrate themselves on the road, clasping their hands in a fervent 'namaste'. Countless camera-toting Indian and foreign tourists squeeze through for better vantage points, their faces delirious, as if they cannot believe they are actually here.

Occasionally, burqa-clad ladies emerge from within homes to throw flowers at the saints. 'The Kumbh Mela is a symbol of our secular democracy in action,' says Swami Avdeshananda, whose sprawling ashram is in the old Kankhal neighbourhood of Haridwar. 'For example, most of the Hindu religious offerings used in the Kumbh are packaged by Muslim craftsmen, and the music bands have Muslim and Christian performers.'

The music bands walk along with the saints, but even their spirited drums and trumpets cannot drown out the chants of *'Bum Bum Bole'* and *'Har Har Mahadev'*, both of which refer to Lord Shiva, from whose matted locks, legend has it, the river Ganga sprang forth.

The fountainhead of faith

The origin of the Kumbh—which means a rounded pot in Sanskrit—dates back to the Vedic period, from 1500 BC to 500 BC. According to Hindu mythology, the gods and demons churned the ocean of milk for the nectar of immortality. When the *kumbh* bearing this *amrit* or nectar of immortality arrived, one of the gods took it and ran away from the asuras who gave chase. The four places that the god rested the kumbh were Haridwar, Allahabad, Ujjain and Nasik, and it is in these four places that the Kumbh Mela is held. Another version of the tales says that four drops of this amrit fell in four places on earth before the gods spirited it away into the heavens. It is at these places that the kumbh mela is held. As legends go, it is a pretty good one.

The dates of the Kumbh Mela in each of these four towns are decided based on astronomical and astrological calculations: the position of the sun, the planet Jupiter, and the constellation Aries. The Haridwar Kumbh is held when Jupiter is in Aquarius and the Sun is in Aries, in March–April, the month of Chaitra in the lunar calendar. The Allahabad Kumbh occurs in January–February, or the month of Magha, when Jupiter is in Aries (or sometimes Taurus) and the Sun is in Capricorn. The Nasik Kumbh occurs in August–September, the month of Bhadrapada in the lunar calendar, when both the sun and Jupiter are in Leo. The Ujjain Kumbh happens in Vaishaka or April–May, when the sun is in Aries and Jupiter is in Leo, or when all three are in Libra. Some say that the twelve zodiac signs or *rashiyan* will appear in a circle during this confluence.

The Maha Kumbh Mela occurs once every twelve years. Some call it the world's largest religious gathering, with a daily footfall of nearly 5–6 million, and an estimated 100 million people attending the Kumbh Mela over the course of four months. On the most auspicious day in the Kumbh Mela, which occurs on a specific full moon day, over 80 million people take a ritual bath in the waters of the Ganga. This human congregation is visible from space.

Devotees believe that bathing in the river during the Kumbh Mela can remove all sins. For a Hindu, it symbolizes many things: the triumph of good over evil, a glimpse of immortality and being in the presence of countless revered saints. In that sense, the kumbh is a process, a meeting place and a fair (which is what the word *mela* means).

Said Mark Twain in 1895 after attending the Kumbh:

'It is wonderful, the power of a faith like that, that can make multitudes upon multitudes of the old and weak and the young and frail enter without hesitation or complaint upon such incredible journeys and endure the resultant miseries without repining. It is done in love, or it is done in fear; I do not know which it is. No matter what the impulse is, the act born of it is beyond imagination, marvellous to our kind of people, the cold whites.'

The largest human gathering in the world?

The Kumbh Mela has grown in strength year after year, not so much in the number of people it attracts, but in terms of how it is organized. Usually, a separate budget is kept aside to set up a sprawling campsite for the visiting saints and feed them over the four months of the mela; there is a media centre, and a special officer in charge of the entire event. In a sense, the Kumbh Mela is a symbol of mythology and mysticism married to modern-day organization and technology.

During this time, millions of Hindu ascetics, called *Naga Babas* (Baba means saint), who spend their lifetimes sans clothes, desire, food and drink, converge at the Kumbh Mela to engage in religious discourse and catch up with each other. Although they live in makeshift campsites during these four months, they take holy dips in the Ganga on ten bathing dates.

Since the number of saints who want to bathe on these days is large, there is a queue system, or in this case, a procession. First in line are the *mahants* or seers, who are at the top of this hierarchy. They go by on grand golden chariots. We throw yellow flowers at them. After the mahants come the heads of the various religious orders or *akharas*, Swami Avdeshananda amongst them. He rides by along with many of the religious heads, whose faces are plastered on billboards all over Haridwar. There is Pilot Baba, so called because he used to be military pilot. There is Somnath Baba, riding along with some Western women, drawing stares from the crowd. 'What is he doing with these foreign women?' people mutter. Then come the senior saints, riding by on horses, elephants and camels. Finally, the younger ones come walking by, and the true spectacle begins. Save for a few, all the walking Naga saints are sans clothes, their matted locks coiled on top of their heads. Gray ash is smeared all over their bodies. Some are fat, but most of them are lean and lithe.

As the atmosphere gets charged up, many of these Naga Babas engage in feats of skill and strength—stick and sword fighting, pulling chariots with bare hands, lifting other saints on their shoulders. All these displays are to prove to the waiting populace that these Naga saints can and will protect Hinduism, which, as it turns out, is their declared purpose.

The seven centres of Advaita spirituality

In the eighth century, an influential philosopher and saint called Swami Shankaracharya (yes, the same Shankara of Kalady) traversed India on foot and established seven akharas or groups of saints. They were named Juna (the largest group), Niranjani, Ananda, Agni and others. The word akhara literally means a wrestling arena, but is used in this context to refer to a group of warrior ascetics. 'We are religious warriors,' says Harihar Puri, a loincloth-clad ascetic who belongs to the Niranjani Akhara, while resting at his campsite before the procession. 'Our goal is to protect Hindu dharma (values).'

To show that they still have the strength, the Nagas demonstrate their strength and skills to the adoring crowd all the way to the river, where, in a final act of purification, they immerse themselves en masse into its chilly depths.

As I witnessed in Kashi, it would be hard to overstate the importance of the river Ganga in the Hindu Indian's psyche. For my mother, who accompanied me to the Kumbh, the highpoint of the visit was not the parade, prayers or blessings from the saints. It was immersing herself into the Ganga every morning while chanting *'Ganga Mata Pavitra hai'* ('Mother Ganga is pure.').

Although my mother had visited Haridwar before, it was her first time at the Kumbh, which somehow made the Ganga more sacred in her mind. Like many older Hindus, my parents had made the prescribed pilgrimage to sacred Hindu towns like Varanasi, Allahabad, Rishikesh and Gaya to pay homage to their departed ancestors. The Kumbh Mela is another matter altogether.

Most Hindus I know, particularly those who live in South India, far away from the spots where the Kumbh is held, rarely attend the Kumbh, even though there is a hunger and longing to go. They are intimidated by the crowds and the accompanying inconveniences— lack of good hotel rooms for one.

Communal feeding by a grateful community

Food is plentiful at the Kumbh in countless ashrams and in *bhandaras*, which are makeshift tents or shamianas erected so that sponsors can feed the pilgrims. Even amongst the *bhandaras*, there are many types: some only feed sadhus, while others are like *langars*, feeding anyone who wants to eat. Most places have people sit on the ground and eat from palm leaf plates. The food is simple but

tasty. Some serve khichdi and a samosa. Others are more elaborate
with excellent hot puris served to what looks like 500 people, along
with a potato sabji, some chole in a separate bowl and a hot jilebi to
round things off.

Late one night, I join a line of people walking into a *bhandara*.
There are wooden partitions that herd us through, somewhat like
an airport security line. At the end of our zigzagging journey is a
long table with hundreds of plates. Each plate has a roti, chole or
chickpeas sabji, some raw onion and tomato salad and some sweet
boondi. 'Jai Shri Ram,' shouts the man standing at one end, serving
each person a plate.

As I walk out, I ask one of the organizers, 'Why are you not
saying "Bam Bam Bhole" like in the other shamianas?'

'The sponsor of this is a Ram-bhakt,' he replies. 'So we say Ram's
name. But really, aren't they all the same?' he asks with a smile.

I nod and carry out my filled plate. Outside the night is cool. I sit
alongside several others under a banyan tree and eat the Lord's food.

The young and playful Ganga

When I returned home after the Kumbh Mela, I got dozens of phone
calls from elderly aunts, uncles, relatives and friends, all of whom
were thrilled and envious that I had attended the Kumbh Mela.
They wanted photos, detailed descriptions, links to the article I was
writing. They wanted the Kumbh experience even though they were
afraid to make the actual trek.

The Ganga, however, particularly in Haridwar, where she is a
'young' river just downhill from the Himalayas, is not intimidating.
Many Hindus come to Haridwar frequently. My own parents have
been here twice, mostly to take a dip in the Ganga.

'Make me pure too,' my mother whispered to the river just before she immersed herself while facing the sunrise. This timeless scene of staring at the sun, muttering prayers, while standing waist-deep in the Ganga is repeated all along the river's course by countless devotees.

The Ganga in Haridwar is fast-flowing and playful, just like the long-haired tempestuous maiden she is depicted to be. She is always freezing cold. As the sun rises and the glaciers melt, the Ganga gets colder, which is why the faithful bath in the Ganga before sunrise.

Over breakfast at the Haveli Hari Ganga, Haridwar's best hotel, where I am staying, a British couple tell me that they had come with the same qualms. 'But it is so clean!' exclaims the retired gentleman called Tony. His wife, Claire, adds, 'When I immersed myself in the Ganga, I began crying. I don't know why. I mean, we aren't Hindu or anything. But the course of miracles that we took makes us more open, I suppose. And when I saw the faith of the people here, I suppose some of it rubbed off.'

Har ki Pauri is considered the most sacred place in Haridwar, and this is where the procession ends. It is more like a water tank really with a strip of the Ganga meshed between two concrete platforms interlinked by bridges. It is at this spot that Saint Bhagiratha is said to have sat and meditated for eons to have the river Ganga come down from the heavens to purify the souls of his dead ancestors lying in the underworld.

Immersing yourself in a river en masse

By late afternoon, I am positioned on a wooden platform that has been erected for press photographers. People are squeezed together as far as my eye can see. Finally, the first batch of saints arrive for their holy dip. With smiling faces, they run down the steps of the bathing ghat and jump into the Ganga.

I had expected pandemonium, masses of people running helter-skelter down the steps. I feared stampedes. It isn't an orderly march, but it isn't a stampede either. The Naga Babas come lithely down the steps and immerse themselves into the Ganga to the reverberating chant of 'Ganga mata pavitra hai'. Cameras click furiously all around me. After the requisite three auspicious dips, the saints climb out of the river and make their way back up in a streaming U that never seemed to stop.

The riverbank at Har ki Pauri is a condensed space bordered by temples on either side (one to the river Ganga and the other to Shiva). Strange and wonderful things happen during the ritual immersion. One yogi stands in a corner, dancing in sheer delight. He demonstrates a series of virtuoso yoga poses—the headstand, the scorpion and several others—before melting back into the crowd. Somnath Baba—he who rode with white women—appears wearing a fire-engine-red loincloth. 'Must be a present from his foreign devotees,' titters someone, and we all laugh. People wait in serpentine queues to pour milk on the Shivling in the temple. Monks with begging bowls march past, collecting donations from the waiting masses. As the sun sets, the lines of saints kept coming. Having had my fill of the mass immersion, I too melt into the crowds and walk by the Ganga to my hotel's private bathing ghat.

The Haveli Hari Ganga and its two sister properties have prime locations along the river, each with private access to the Ganga. As I wade into the Ganga's chilling depths, I think of this river of India. What mysterious and majestic sights has she seen on her way to the sea?

Haridwar and Hinduism: in sync

As I take my first dip into the sacred river, the temple bells begin clanging. Is it a sign? Actually, it is merely the beginning of the daily evening aarti or lamp-lighting. Soon, tiny flower-boats made of leaves and flowers come floating down, each carrying a little twinkling oil-lamp. Devotees send these oil lamps down the river to make their wishes come true. *So many wishes*, I think. So much pollution.

Swami Avdeshananda thinks that devotees shouldn't throw a single thing into the Ganga. 'I just dip my flower into its waters and bring it back,' he says. It is a progressive thought for someone steeped in ancient Hindu principles, but then, Haridwar is a special place. Indeed, for a devout Hindu, it is perhaps a paradise, for it follows a lot of Hindu tenets for a sattvic or spiritual life. The entire city is vegetarian. Drinking is not allowed, and the police can throw people into jail if they are caught with alcohol.

But Haridwar too, like Hinduism, makes allowances. The Naga Babas eat and drink little beyond tea, but in their campsites they all smoke hashish and pot.

At my hotel, some eighty yogis from Europe and America have descended for ten days in Haridwar. I speak to a handsome Swedish Swami called Kapilananda who is clad in saffron but has short, platinum-blonde hair. He tells me that his group constitutes teachers of the Sivananda yoga method, and they are in Haridwar to attend the Kumbh.

They plan to spend their mornings learning scriptures from a visiting guru who speaks English, and the afternoon visiting the campsites and talking to the saints. Some of them plan to stay for a week when the next big procession and royal bath will take place.

The day after the procession, I wake up early and take a walk along the Ganga. As always, men and women are already immersing themselves into its waters. Temple bells are clanging. Roadside carts are selling tasty hot samosas, kachoris and jalebis. Saffron-robed saints are walking the streets. It's just another day in the holy city.

The secret to life and longevity

Swami Somnath Puri is explaining the secrets of longevity to a motley group sitting around his campfire in Haridwar: French tourists, Israeli backpackers, saffron-clad American yogis, elderly Indian women and the occasional slum youth with dirt-streaked hair.

Longevity is all about breath control, says the Swami in Hindi. The moment you are born, Brahma, the Hindu god of creation, writes down exactly how many breaths or *svaasa* you will take in your lifetime. When the count runs out, you die. The trick is to elongate every breath you take so that each inhalation lasts about two minutes, and similarly with the exhalation.

The swami rises, and immediately the group does that looking-without-looking eye-roll that men do when confronted with cleavage. Save for the yellow chrysanthemum garland around his neck, Swami Somath Puri is naked.

The swami disappears into his tent and reappears with a terracotta cone—about half the size of a normal ice cream cone. He stuffs it with dried green grass—handmade hashish called *charas*—stokes the fire, lights the cone and begins sucking from the bottom. This is why we Naga Babas live long, he says from within a cloud of smoke. Our bare bodies aren't protected from the elements, we don't sleep, we don't eat…'

'Yeah, all you do is smoke grass,' mutters someone irreverently from the back of the group. A few people chuckle.

The swami chuckles good-humouredly too as he looks up through bloodshot eyes at the group. 'Come on. Sit down. Have some chai,' he invites.

The group squeezes itself around the campfire. The charas pipe gets passed around. The French woman with matted hair inhales deeply and appreciatively before passing it on to her companion. The Indian grandmother who was standing with her palms clasped together in a respectful 'Namaste' looks mildly outraged, then disgusted. She walks away, as does the disapproving American yogi. Swami Somnath Puri reaches into the fire and smears some more ash on his already grey body. He puffs a few more times and settles down to pontificate on truth, war and breath control.

Swami Somnath Puri is a Naga—a warrior saint belonging to the Juna Akhara. He has camped out in Haridwar for the Kumbh Mela, which this time is from 15 January to 28 April. For these four months, Naga saints come out of their Himalayan caves and tropical jungles to converge in one place. They cease their itinerant wanderings and stay put at sprawling makeshift campsites, talking to visitors, engaging in feats of strength (like pulling a chariot with a penis) and smoking pipes.

Meeting a spiritual guru

'Hinduism is a very diverse religion with many paths to God: puja, meditation, yoga, pranayama, pilgrimages, fasts, chanting and *satsang*,' says Swami Avdeshananda. 'The Kumbh is where all this diversity comes together.'

Swami Avdeshananda is the *mahamandaleshwar* or the head of the Juna Akhara, the largest of the Naga clans that arrive at the

Kumbh. His serene face adorns numerous billboards in Haridwar. He has a TV show, speaking engagements, a magazine and a devout army of volunteers, one of whom (an architect) has designed his sprawling leafy Harihar Ashram in the old Kankhal neighbourhood of Haridwar. Inside, there is an auditorium, temple, meditation and prayer halls, a cafeteria, cottages where visiting followers can stay, a shop selling gemstones and books, and a large courtyard where the Swamiji receives visitors every morning at 9.30 a.m.

The gun-toting policemen spring to action and mutter into their walkie-talkies as soon as the tall, saffron-clad figure emerges from his living quarters. In person, the Swami is smiling and animated, marrying discipline with charm. He is a handsome, youthful man, more Barack Obama than Baba Ramdev, who holds court upriver in Rishikesh. Surrounded by a posse of assistants, public relations officers (PROs), schedulers and junior ashramites, the Swami cuts an imposing figure as he strides to the sacred peepul tree on the premises. Amidst loud chanting, he waters it, pours milk on its roots, throws flowers, hugs the tree and rests his forehead prayerfully on its trunk before smearing the truck with sandalwood paste and vermilion powder. The same routine follows for the sacred Rudraksha tree (Elaeocarpus ganitrus), the oldest such tree in the state of Uttarakhand, according to volunteers. 'When you pray with milk, flowers, water and leaves, your body becomes sensitive to nature and its vibrations,' Swami Avdeshananda says. 'How can you harm the earth after praying to it?'

Nature worship and nirvana

A long queue of devotees and followers snakes all over the central courtyard. Swamiji delves into the crowd like a politician. He holds hands, kisses babies, poses for the camera with families, teases jeans-clad young men who seek his blessing and smiles reassuringly at countless supplicant faces that look to him as a saviour who will make things happen: jobs, babies, promotions, cures and money. Twenty saffron-clad monks appear. 'You people are my wealth, my lifeline, my strength,' the Swami exclaims as they fall at his feet. Someone hands him a pair of sunglasses. He puts them on and hams for the camera. Another group of saints arrive, bearing gifts. Flowery language flows. 'It is thanks to my past life's merits that I have been able to see a mahant (religious leader) like you!' exclaims the leader of the delegation.

'*Arre*,' Swamiji waves away the praise. 'I am just a simple man. You are the great mahant.'

He invites the entire group to breakfast.

The last in line is a well-dressed, prosperous-looking woman. 'Swamiji, I want to see Shiva,' she says.

Swamiji stares at her as he digests the intensity of her desire. Finally, he says, 'God is everywhere. God will be with you.'

The answer seems to satisfy the woman who smiles gratefully.

Across town, a long line of Naga Babas make their way to the Ganga to seek salvation in her depths. *Bhikshus* arrive bearing begging bowls. Saffron-clad American swamis dole out cash. Tourists click away with their cameras. Gypsy women squat on the street outside Birla House selling chains and Rudraksh beads. (Fun fact: Real Rudraksh beads, being seeds of the fruit of the tree, sink in water. Those made of wood or plastic float. Easy hack to test the real ones.)

Visitors breakfast on kachoris, samosas, jalebis or lassi. I try them all and pray that I get reborn as a Haridwar-vaasi (resident). You see, if I had to pick a last meal on earth, I would choose the breakfast that I had in Haridwar. If I had to pick one dish, I would pick the

samosa. Triangular, deep-fried, with a savoury filling, samosas are
sublime. They came to India from Arabia and are the opposite of
what constitutes 'health food' today. But samosas, like much of the
food in Haridwar, are soul food.

A good samosa ought to contain a few ingredients (mostly
potatoes) with restrained spices – cumin, salt, and maybe a dash
of fresh ginger – all encased in a thin shell of dough. No fancy puff
pastry; no fudging with carrots or celery; and, above all, no messing
with the shape.

Samosa, I may love, but the other chaat dishes found all over
Haridwar could give my favourite a run for its money. The aloo
kaddu kachori, the golgappas which explode in your mouth with
juices tinged with mint, chilies and cumin—the food in Haridwar
is glorious and indeed sacred, touched by soul and spirit.

Before every meal, be it a humble if delicious naan khatai
baked on the spot in homemade ovens or a dal tadka with just a
few ingredients, I saw vendors begin with a bow and prayer to the
makeshift altar in a corner of their shops. In Haridwar food is not
far away from gods, even if the gods inhabited corners of food carts,
tiny chaat stalls and humble restaurants.

On the day I leave, I drive past lines of people partaking of the
food before they go for prayers.

Holy Haridwar is strutting its stuff, and the Kumbh is in full
swing. Till the next Kumbh twelve years later.

Takeaway

I grew up in a house where doing puja was part of the daily routine.
Perhaps as a result, I wasn't very much for doing pujas. I didn't light
the lamp in our house—my husband did it every morning. For him,
puja was a pause, a way to take a breath.

Rituals are so much a part of Hinduism. They were quite beautiful and gave the devotee peace and joy. It bothered me that I didn't see the point.

Well, in Haridwar, I saw the point. After visiting Swami Avdeshananda's ashram and listening to his explanation about puja as a way of connecting to nature, I took slow and small steps towards adopting the practices that were so much a part of my childhood. And so today, this is how I do puja at home. By giving thanks to nature and its bounty. By using fallen flowers, leaves and shells that I have collected. By seeing the universe in a grain of sand and God in a single rock.

13

Kerala: Ambalapuzha's
Paal Payasam

PERHAPS IT IS THE fish they eat. Or perhaps is the *kudam puli* (pot tamarind) or Malabar tamarind—with its musical botanical name, Garcinia gummi-gutta—that they ingest in vast quantities, along with shrimp, duck eggs and coconut oil— brain benefactors all. Whatever the reason, Malayalis possess an astonishing amount of intelligence, displayed and, you could argue, wasted in organizing protests, reading Karl Marx, engaging in quick repartee replete with stinging wit and withering sarcasm, and figuring out where to go and what to do. The Gulf is the current favourite destination.

Their entrepreneurial zeal is legendary—witness the number of jokes about the Malayali opening a tea shop wherever there is a flat plateau in the Himalayas. In Bengaluru, where I live, all the small provision shops I frequent are run by Moplah Muslims from the Calicut area: Family Supermarket, Safe Medicals, Lake View Vegetable Mart—all of them run by Malayalis.

My driver in Kerala, Vinodh, is a typical specimen. With his starched white shirt and matching pants, his broad forehead smeared with sandalwood paste, he exudes the Malayali concept of *vritthi* or cleanliness, so abundant in this verdant luscious state, with flora and fauna practically falling out of the earth. He is neat, punctual, crafty in his approach towards cutting through traffic and disdainful of rules ('rules are for lazy minds,' he told me). He arrives at 6 a.m. to take me to Ambalapuzha temple, famed for its paal payasam or milk pudding.

The word *ambalam* means temple in Malayalam; *puzha* refers to river. Ambalapuzha literally means river by the temple, or temple town. The Krishna temple here is famous—world famous, if you believe the administrative officer, Hari Kumar—for its *paal payasam,* or what North Indians call kheer. Milk pudding is a poor translation. 'People come from all over the world to drink this *neivedhyam* (sacred food offering),' says the genial Hari Kumar, who sits behind a desk in the temple office, counting wads of cash, directing the rituals and the 100-odd employees and volunteers who work at the temple.

Wrapped in a simple white cloth to approach God

Every field has a dress code. The dress code for Kerala temples is that the men wear a simple white *veshti* or dhoti and pretty much nothing else. The idea is to approach the deity in your simplest and purest attire. Certainly, the men who work at the temple are dressed this way.

As far as Kerala temples go, this one is typical, with wooden pillars instead of the carved stone or marble ones elsewhere. It does not have the majestic scale, the multiple *praharams* or sanctums of the Tamil Nadu temples. It is compact, clean and strict about rules. Men have to remove their shirts and appear topless in the inner sanctum, which is fine if you are wearing a dhoti, as most men used to. Today, men in pants awkwardly wear their shirts loosely on one sleeve in compliance.

Women are mostly in saris. Here too, there are changes over the years. Gone are the pristine white handloom saris, known variously as *kasavu* saris or *set mundu*, if the woman is wearing a dhoti-like bottom combined with a half-sari-like top. Instead, Kerala women have embraced multicoloured sarees. Thankfully, the long, dark, curly hair nourished by massaging and imbibing gargantuan quantities of coconut oil over a lifetime remain.

The first person I meet is Pran Kumar, who has been deputed to take me around the temple. Pran manages the storeroom—behind a locked red door—and is a singer. He sings to welcome the Lord in the evening. When I ask for a demonstration, he smilingly refuses, saying that he cannot call the Lord at midday for the evening worship.

Funny how you remember certain things about childhood. The one thing I remember from travelling up and down Kerala by bus during my childhood is that the men in Kerala have pink gums. So it is with Pran when he smiles, which he does, quite a lot.

Of paddy, rice and huffy Brahmins

Like most Hindu temples, Ambalapuzha's origins too are the stuff of legend. Historian Ambalapuzha Gopakumar gives me a rundown of the most popular one. The legend goes like this. Eons ago, the local king borrowed a huge loan of paddy from a brahmin. Years passed, and suddenly one day, the brahmin appeared demanding the reimbursement of his loan, else he would not allow the king to worship at the temple. In a quandary, the king asked his minister to take care of the problem, and in those days, ministers would.

The minister asked all the citizens to donate some paddy, and soon, the entire central hall of the temple was filled with paddy. The minister then ordered the brahmin to clear the paddy before the noon worship. Turns out that no person would help the brahmin remove the paddy. In frustration that quickly turned to piety, the brahmin donated the paddy to the temple with the instruction that it should be used to feed visiting pilgrims. And so it came to be that Ambalapuzha paal payasam was cooked to feed the devotees. This particular legend is somewhat circuitous and really doesn't make sense, because this particular payasam is made not with paddy, but with rice—although that can be explained away by stating that the money that came from the paddy is used to make rice payasam.

The other legend is more interesting and will please those who are mathematically inclined. In it, Lord Krishna, disguised as a sage, appears at the court of the local king and challenges him to a game of *chaturanga*... Chaturanga, some claim, is inspired from chess, while some say it inspired chess. It is a similar game, though not quite chess.

The king is a good player, but he loses. Naturally, as kings do, he masks his failure by offering a gift to the sage. The sage asks for a few grains of rice in a particular order. The first square of the chessboard would have one grain of rice; the second square would have two; the third square would have four; the fourth square, eight; the fifth square, sixteen. The king immediately—and foolishly as those in the know about geometric progression would realize—agreed. The number of grains rapidly increases to the point where the king could not fulfil his promise.

As an unknown math buff has explained on Wikipedia, the total amount of rice required to fill a sixty-four-square chess board is 2^{64}–1 (1 being the first grain in the first square). It comes to a total of 1,84,46,74,40,73,70,95,51,615 grains or 18 billion billion grains of rice. This amount of rice would weigh about 460×1012 kg, or 460 pentagrams, or 460 billion tonnes, assuming that 1,000 grains of rice weigh about 25 g. This amount of rice would also cover the surface of India 2 meters deep. No king could have paid a price so great to a sage who had defeated him in Chaturanga. Naturally, the king fell at the feet of the sage, who then, in typical *Amar Chitra Katha* fashion, revealed himself to be Lord Krishna and magnanimously agreed to take the rice in future installments in the form of paal payasam to devotees.

Reducing milk till it turns golden in colour

Ambalapuzha paal payasam—now famous enough to be a well-recognized phrase, at least in Kerala—is made by reducing milk for about six hours, says C.P. Arun, a junior priest in the temple. He is known as *keezh shanthi*, while the main priest is called *mel shanthi*. There are several junior priests, but only one main priest.

Kerala priests usually have the honorific '*thirumeni*', and so Arun is referred to as *Arun thirumeni*. His day begins bright and early at 2.30 a.m. when he arrives at the temple for a dip at the special temple tank used by priests. At 3 a.m., the temple opens, and so begins the cooking of the payasam. The ratio is one part milk to three parts water. The water is taken from two temple wells. The milk comes from the resident cows at the *gaushala* (cowshed) affiliated to the temple.

On the day I visit, 100 litres of milk mixed with 300 litres of water is boiling in the large brass *uruli*, but the quantity depends on the orders that have been received for that day. On this particular day, 8 kg of pounded rice is added to this mixture. 'Rice, sugar and milk: that's it,' says Arun casually.

Of course, it is a little more complicated than that. Just as Chennai folk claim that the taste in their coffee comes from local milk and water, the taste of Ambalapuzha's payasam comes from the well water, the local milk, the pounded red rice of Kerala, the smell of the metal uruli and, if you like, the stirring with the long wooden spoon. Most of all, the taste comes from the slow reduction of this mixture, which goes from 400 litres to 90 litres between 5 a.m. and noon, give or take half an hour.

While waiting for the payasam to reduce, I pay a visit to a distant relative whom I have never met in my life. This is how religious tourism works in India. Most temple towns don't have hotels. Certainly, the sole hostelry, Vrindavan Lodge in Ambalapuzha, doesn't inspire confidence.

When I travelled with my grandparents to temples, elaborate arrangements would be made for food and lodging. My grandfather had a memory for connections that would make a political lobbyist envious. Before we went on pilgrimages, the wheels in his head would begin turning. He would phone relatives and friends who had some connection to the remote temple town that we were visiting, to make arrangements for our stay and food. This tradition continues.

Through a distant relative in Chennai, I hear about his relative who has a home in Ambalapuzha. While waiting for the payasam to reduce, I decide to pay this stranger family a visit.

An eighty-six-year-old lady named Saraswati welcomes me, and we immediately engage in the pleasant if pointless exercise of figuring out how we are related to each other. This is typical. No matter where we go, this cross-referencing of family trees is what we Indians do.

Most South Indian names are long, relative to our North Indian counterparts. This is because a name isn't just a name for a South Indian; it is a geo-mapping system that places individuals in the context of their genealogy, genetics, community, village, caste, and family lineage. It is like a resume that can be furnished for matrimonial and professional purposes; except that instead of printing out a piece of paper you could merely recite your long name.

My father's name, for example—and fair warning here, it is very long—is Vaidhyanathapuram Ramaswamy Narayanaswamy Iyer. The first word is the name of his village, the second word is his father's name, the third word is his name; and the last word is the name of the caste he belongs to. This is typically how names were constructed for Tamil Brahmins, which is the caste I belong to. When my father left his village, he tried to simplify his name by using initials. Thus, he became V.R. Narayanaswamy. My father ditched his caste identity – Iyer, when he left his village. When he went for a fellowship at Leeds University, he discovered that even his simplified name was hard for Englishmen to wrap their tongues around. So he shortened it some more. He became V.R.N. Swamy.

Migration from village to city

When people migrated from their villages, they needed new cross-references. Turns out that the company they worked for was a great vector for this purpose. It gave strangers and accessible contact point for reference checks and possible information about salary and housing allowances. Spencers Sundaram is an uncle of mine who worked for the British company, Spencers, and was called this long after he retired. Railway Raju is a cousin who works for the Indian Railways. Singer Bombay Jayashri follows the diaspora nomenclature. I have heard of a man called Jackpot Sundar, so named because he won the 1977 Derby in Bombay.

The Matunga area of Mumbai is full of South Indians, particularly TamBrahms who have reconstituted their identities in a new land. They left southern villages with long, syllable-laden names and returned as posh Mumbaikars. Suryanarayanan became Suri; Ananthapadmanabhan became Padi; Balasubramanian became Balan.

These early South Indians who migrated to Mumbai didn't forget their roots. Rather, they transformed their love and longing for their ancestral homeland by duplicating its ecosystem in their new home.

Certain areas of Mumbai, like Chembur and Matunga, were dominated by Palghat Iyers. These were people who could trace their roots to the Palghat pass between Tamil Nadu and Kerala. Palghat Iyers or Pattars as they were called, were TamBrahms who migrated from Tamil Nadu to Kerala, and felt equally at home speaking Malayalam and Tamil. My father is one.

We are better than you

Palghat Iyers believe (as does pretty much every Indian caste and community) that we are better than our neighbours. Our women are beautiful and accomplished; our men are fair and charming. We take pride in our food, our character and culture. We drop names in select circles to prove our superiority. This is why India is united —not because we are tolerant, but because we haven't been able to prove, definitively and without doubt, that we are better than our neighbours.

As Palghat Iyers, my family only cared about proving their superiority to Iyers from Thanjavur, or those pesky Iyengars. If you were a Bengali or Punjabi, we didn't have a quarrel with you. You may as well have been an Albino Mexican or an Armenian Jew for all we cared. We would accord you the courtesy of a guest, but you were as foreign as the man from the moon. Our petty hierarchies and feuding quarrels were limited to the neighbours who occupied our land.

One way in which Palghat Iyers claimed superiority was through music. The line list of musicians who hailed from Palghat is long. The other was a belief in the curative powers of coconut oil. We douse everything—our body, our hair and our food—with this oil. A third was the belief that immigrating to a new land made us mentally nimble.

'You know why the Jews are like Palghat Brahmins?' asked my grandfather. 'We both left our homelands and made our fortune in foreign shores. It is why we are mentally superior.'

My grandfather believed that moving far from our native village forced us to square away different, and sometimes opposing, constructs. It forced us to think creatively and be entrepreneurial.

It taught us how to settle in a new home but leave our stamp on it. Most importantly, it taught us how to preserve culture and identity while adapting to foreign conditions.

Shooting the breeze with a relative and stranger

The stranger in front of me has had an opposite life-path. She is 86 and has never left Kerala. We exchange names and places. Turns out that she knows my father's cousins. What follows is a typical recitation of our family tree, and a check on how various cousins are doing.

'Do you know Rajagopalan?' she asks. 'He is my grandmother's elder sister's brother-in-law-by-marriage's sister's son.'

'Yes, he is my father's cousin brother,' I reply.

'Didn't he marry his elder sister's daughter? The one who had polio?'

And so it goes, while she makes me dosas, serving one after another, ignoring my pleas of 'enough', while determinedly reciting our mutual connections. She is agile and active. When I ask her how she spends her days, she points to the four cows tied in the backyard. 'I cook, I garden, I milk the cows, take care of my grandchildren,' she says simply.

Healthy living for a healthy life, I am tempted to add, even though it sounds like an advertising slogan.

She wears a simple purple cotton sari with a temple border. I covet it and try my best to get her to offer it to me.

'You know, I love these old saris, such as the one you are wearing,' I say, fingering her sari. 'In fact, when I meet my elder aunts, I tell them not to buy me new saris. I just want their old saris. Yours is beautiful.'

To no avail. She doesn't get my hints. Nobody asks for old saris in India, except the *raddi-wallah* (the recycler), and he too only wants the *zari* border.

Dancing and calling the Lord

Fully fed, I walk back to the temple, worried that the payasam will be ready. I have been told that the final mixing of the sugar is ceremonial. A man will shout *'Vasudeva!'* and invoke the god before mixing the sugar. I don't want to miss this bit of pomp and circumstance. Thankfully, the milk is still boiling.

In the intervening time, the ever-smiling (except when posing for the camera) and obliging Pran shows me the 'cultural hall' where poet Kunjan Nambiar developed *ottam-thullal*, a type of dance.

Ottam-thullal is perfect for Kerala, given that its people are adept at satire and sarcasm. The lyrics are in Malayalam, not Sanskrit, and make fun of politicians, businessmen, teachers and people in power. A typical sequence goes like this. The actor on stage is playing Hanuman who has been captured in Ravana's court. He sings about all the stupid ministers that are sitting in Ravana's court, but his hands point to the actual true-life ministers that are sitting in the first row of the audience. The backbenchers naturally hoot with laughter. The discomfited Kerala ministers who have been pointed at get up and walk out en masse.

Like kathakali, this dance form too uses kabuki-like face paint, and drums as the sole accompanying instrument. In fact, the first copper drum that Kunjan Nambiar used is still displayed in the temple.

The architecture of Kerala temples

Ambalapuzha was known for its cultural activities. Dance and music performances were regularly held at the theatre adjoining the temple. Like the famous Padmanabhapuram palace, much of Kerala architecture is made with wood covered by a red-tiled roof. The wooden beams are connected to each other using an interlocking system that eschews the use of nails. The idea is that these precise joints and alignments would allow for play during the monsoon when the rains would cause the wood to become flaccid and later shrink in the summer heat. Today, these *nallu-kettu* (four pillars) or *ettu-kettu* (eight pillars) homes are dismantled and moved from place to place by builders and developers who service rich clients longing for their past.

The community theatre too has long beams that are connected to the pillars without nails. One stunning example shows a twisted wooden circular beam that is deftly inserted into a square peg. It is here that the evening performance will be held, says Pran. In this season (April–May), the performance is called *velakali*. *Kali* means 'game' in Malayalam. Velakali has male dancers who hold a rattan sword in one hand and a shield in the other. They walk through the village, displaying martial arts movements, and end up at the temple tank. They stand on one side and sway gracefully so that their shadows ripple in the water in time to their—hopefully—rippling muscles. Across the tank, on the other side, stands a caparisoned elephant with the bronze idol on top, to witness the performance. Velakali's movements are reminiscent of Kerala's martial past in which soldiers fought each other on the banks of rivers and lakes.

The temple tank is quite beautiful, as these tanks tend to be. I don't dare step in and swim in the water but see many people taking a dip before entering the temple.

Temple murals on the wall

Temples, much like medieval churches, were the places where arts flourished, and so it is with Ambalapuzha temple. The walls of the sanctum sanctorum have beautiful Kerala murals painted on them. Even though I didn't grow up in an obviously artistic family, I must have imbibed this aesthetic: the round faces of the gods, the earthy colours—vermilion, mustard yellow, dark green—and the distinct way of depiction. I find myself inordinately attracted to these and wonder if aesthetic beauty—what type of art resonates with you—has to do with personal history. My Marwari friends, for instance, are drawn to images of Nathdwara as depicted in the Pichwai paintings.

Although most people don't realize it, the performing arts are vibrant in Kerala. Always have been. The sound of Kerala, you could argue, is the sound of the *chenda* drums, most resplendently displayed during the Trichur Pooram festival, when caparisoned and decorated elephants stand in a long line and receive (or endure, depending on whether you are an animal rights activist) this drumming display. Thousands of people watch and are reduced to a daze because of the rhythms.

Ambalapuzha temple has its in-house singers and drummers. Pran is one of three singers. 'There used to be nine of us,' he says, 'but with budget cuts, we are now only three singers.' As we walk through the office, the sound of drums draws us to a small room. Inside, we see a young drummer practising for the evening's performance.

Walking around the temple works up quite an appetite, and we return in time for the ceremonial adding of sugar into the milk payasam.

Just as with restaurants, the point of cooking prasadam is consistency: recipes are handed down through the generations and the cooking technique is unwavering. This must be boring for the regulars, and indeed, the young girl—Saraswati's granddaughter—who takes me through the temple tells me that she is tired of drinking Ambalapuzha's famous payasam.

Sometime between 11.30 p.m. and 12 noon, the temple cooks determine that the payasam has reached the right consistency and its typical pinkish colour. This is when sugar is added: a ritual that begins when one of the cooks comes to the door and shouts, 'Vasudeva!' as if calling out to the Lord to arrive.

Mixing sugar with milk and rice

On the day I visit, 30 kg of sugar are added and stirred just before removing the payasam from the stove. During festivals, that amount triples or even quadruples, which takes longer to cook. 'The midday puja commences only after the payasam is done,' says Arun, defining the priority in this temple.

Nobody is allowed to cross the priests as they carry the milk payasam into the sanctum sanctorum: direct and first access is given to the deity in residence. A woman in an orange sari sprinkles water in the passageway between the cooking area and the sanctum sanctorum, a way of purifying the passage. Observers stand on either side and watch the main event: the carrying of the cooked payasam into the sanctum sanctorum. There are multiple large containers filled with frothy hot payasam.

Most religions incorporate sound into their prayers. Christians (and Hindus) ring bells at specific times, Muslims sing to the Lord and some Hindu temples use the conch as a way to remind, call and register their presence with the Almighty. Blowing a conch is no mean feat; I have tried. The man who performs this duty at Ambalapuzha does so with insouciance. He blows the conch several times as two priests carry large vessels filled with the sweet liquid as offering.

Right after the payasam is offered to the God comes the distribution to the long line of people who have been waiting to carry home 1-litre containers of sweet payasam. It costs ₹100 for a plastic container filled with payasam.

As for the payasam itself, it is the most delicious payasam/kheer that I have ever tasted. It is not thick but has girth, if that makes sense. It is rich but not gooey. It is condensed milk, but made the old-fashioned way, not by adding a tin of condensed milk, which is my shortcut for rich payasam. This milk is condensed through fire and evaporation. The proportion of rice to milk is perfect. There is enough rice for body, but it doesn't overpower the milk. And it has that implacable aura—difficult to articulate—that makes a dish sing.

Takeaway

A lot of Hindu ritual involves the imagination or *bhavana*. When you call out to Krishna to come and eat payasam, it is bhavana. It plays on the believer's mind and allows it to soften. It shapes consciousness in a way that is only now being understood by science.

Why does Michael Phelps visualize all his moves before a championship? Why do athletes mentally imagine the steps to victory? And why do we dismiss it as superstition when believers call out 'Vasudeva' to an errant god?

Ambalapuzha's lesson had to do with the acceptance that faith is in large part about the imagination. Visualizing Lord Krishna as an infant in Udupi and as an aesthete who likes the arts (and good payasam) in Ambalapuzha are part of this mental training.

Prayer as a route to unlocking the imagination? Why not?
Prayer as a route to creativity? Yes, indeed.

After all, some of the world's greatest art was created by the faithful as we see in temples and churches everywhere.

Ambalapuzha's paal payasam was about sacred food, yes. But more than that, it was about visualizing a god who would come at the appointed time and keep his promise.

14

Patan: In Search of the Sky-Dancer Goddess

I AM IN PATAN, Nepal to find a goddess named Dakini. I didn't plan on looking for her, didn't know she existed even. Yet, here I am, through a confluence of coincidences at this picturesque UNESCO World Heritage Site, obsessed by a female Buddhist deity who is both muse and mystic.

When the seeker is ready, the seer will show up. This is a phrase I have grown up with. The phrase applies to a teacher—when the student is ready, the guru appears (or a dakini in my case).

The Srividya cult

My mother is part of an ancient Hindu lineage that is linked to goddess worship. The worship is called 'Sri Vidya,' and is visually and aesthetically very beautiful—with flowers, incense, oil lamps, hand gestures called mudras, sacred drawings called mandalas or yantras, and the chanting of mantras. Mudra, mandala and mantra—the triumvirate as it were is at the root of this goddess cult.

One of the most powerful Sanskrit texts in this lineage is called the *Lalita Sahasranamam* or the thousand names of the playful goddess, Lalita. It includes a phrase that talks about the goddess as a dakini, someone who leads you to wisdom. I have chanted this 1,000-passage text countless times by rote. The phrase 'dakini roopa dharini' is a mantra that I have glazed over without paying heed. But what is a dakini?

'Dakini represents the feminine energy in Buddhism,' says Dzongsar Jamyang Khyentse Rinpoche, 57. 'It is a raw naked cognizance, like a baby: unaltered, uncontrived, unfabricated, uneducated.'

It is a broad statement, so broad as to be quite meaningless to me. In this age of #MeToo, what is the role of 'feminine energy', even one that is about 5,000 years old and lauded, quite contradictorily as one of Buddhism's most fundamental yet subtle truths?

Tall and erect, in monk-red robes and quick gait, Rinpoche is a Buddhist Lama (akin to guru, meaning high priest or teacher). Born in Bhutan, he currently lives in India and travels the world giving lectures and teaching students. He is the author of two books and has shot four award-winning films that have been screened at Cannes, Venice, Locarno, Tribeca, Busan and other film festivals. His latest film *Looking for a Lady with Fangs and Mustache* is about a sceptic seeking a dakini who will literally grant him life, which is why the Rinpoche and 168 members of a global crew are in Patan.

The abode of she who plays

The ancient name for Patan is Lalita-pura: the abode of the goddess Lalita. The *Padma-purana*, a Hindu text says, 'Having passed beyond the worlds, she plays; hence she is called Lalita.' Separated from Kathmandu by the holy, and hugely polluted river, Bagmati, Patan is the third of the three kingdoms in Kathmandu Valley: the other two are Kathmandu and Bhaktapur.

In Patan, goddesses are everywhere. Like an addict obsessed with crack or a musician who hears drumbeats, I see them everywhere. There is Chinnamasta: the goddess of contradictions, who severs her head and dances nude on a copulating couple. There are yoginis and mahavidyas: goddesses who offer knowledge. Tiny shrines on streets have pyramid-like mounds with serpent like hoods: the coiled kundalini rising through the chakras. People pause to pray. They offer flowers and bow down in solitude. They take red kumkum powder and smear it on their forehead. They channel the dakini perhaps.

What is a dakini?

Dakinis are female goddesses, forest nymphs, spirits, and witch-like deities. This I know. They go by many names Kali, Durga, Tara, Vajrayogini, Vajravarahi, all of which conjure up an image of a powerful, fierce, sensual, naked dancing goddess—a sky dancer as lore says—a 'thunderbolt sow', to translate the Sanskrit name: Vajra Varahi. She wears a skull garland, drinks blood, carries a spear on her shoulder, has a female pig's ear behind her head, and sports in cremation grounds.

The Patan Museum has exhibits—bronze sculptures—of her in coital embrace with her male counterpart, Heruka or Chakra

Samhara: a wrathful god who breaks through the tenets of time and leads the faithful towards wisdom.

Whimsical, moody, magnanimous, the dakini is muse and mother, lover and loner, terrifying and sensuous, epitomizing the paradoxes that suffuse the goddess cult in India and Nepal. The Shaktas, as the goddess worshippers are called embrace what Carl Jung calls the "shadow," the darker sides of personality. Nepal is a hotbed of this lineage. The two faiths that percolate this mountainous land— Hinduism and Buddhism—exchange ideas and concepts seamlessly. The dakini is one such example: a feisty flirty flighty fierce goddess who lays claim on Kathmandu valley.

This notion of the dakini as muse is easy to intuit but hard to articulate. It is also one of Vajrayana or Tantric Buddhism's most esoteric ideas, tightly held amongst its secrets. Dakini worship revels in dreams and contradictions, and eschews the rational for the emotional, all of which, as it turns out are part of the Jungian psychology I studied in university.

'One of the messages of my movie is that you should not become a slave to reasoning alone,' says Rinpoche. 'Because there are so many things in the world that have no reason, that are so magical. That is the real life. The moment reasoning creeps in, your life will become square, like a Starbucks coffee. That's it. Then it is franchised.'

Tantra and its traditions

Religion began in this liminal space of magic realism. Ancient faiths had shamans and healers who looked at the stars, drew out horoscopes, took clues from omens, engaged people's superstitions, tried to game chance (using books such as the I Ching or Tarot cards) and healed through magic. The Dalai Lama once told me that he makes decisions based on many factors 'including divination'.

Eastern faiths, primarily Hinduism and Buddhism, continue these practices, mostly in the tantric sect.

'Tantra is so tricky and so mean sometimes,' says Rinpoche. 'Anything that is the worst is the best. Things seem close yet so far. That is why the tantric lineage is called the left-handed path because left hand is the lower hand.'

Like many Indians, I grew up hearing the word tantra all the time. It had many meanings. The temple priests in Kerala were called tantris and philosophic concepts were called tantra. My mother belongs to the Shakta faith: people who worship the Shakti—the female principle. She is also a guru who initiates students to specific mantras that take you up through multiple levels till you reach what Buddhists call 'the pure land', where you break free of the sufferings of 'samsara' or mortal life and become akin to a child. Goddess worship in both Hinduism and Buddhism involves visualization. You visualize your body as being the home of the Vajrayogini, your surroundings as being the 'mandalas' of the goddess and the world as being the pure land of the dakini.

Entire books are devoted to practices that initiates can use to discover or rekindle their inner dakini. 'The compassion of a master is key,' says Rinpoche. 'It is like a destitute beggar sleeping on top of a gold mine. He is right on top but missing it all the time. So you need a master to shift your focus. We (masters) need to have lots of tricks to help students.'

Offer gifts with grace

One shortcut that Rinpoche suggests is offering gifts to women or anyone who has the feminine energy 'even dogs and other animals.' This involves a certain kind of openness of course, difficult for those of us who peer into smartphones as we walk the streets. In order to give a gift to someone with feminine energy, you have to see her first. Or take a chance.

Rinpoche's suggestion is very specific: 'Go offer a gift to a stranger woman and say "You are my queen for ever and ever." That takes guts and not many people are willing to do that in this age of inhibition.'

As luck would have it, I get a chance to do just this. One afternoon, I am conscripted as an extra for a shot. I have to sit in a coffee shop with another extra—a Nepali woman and drink coffee while the hero of the film walks by, peering into the coffee shop as he searches for his dakini. Over the course of 15 takes and retakes, I chat desultorily with the woman. Her name, I learn, is Babita and she is a shopkeeper. After the shot, she invites me down to her shop with her. On an impulse—a little nervously—I unclasp the bead bracelet that I am wearing and clasp it on her wrist. 'A gift for you,' I say in explanation. I am unable to call her 'my queen for ever and ever,' like the Rinpoche instructed. That would be too cheesy. Babita however, puts a different reason for my gesture: Dasain, the annual festival that celebrates the goddess.

Celebrated all over the subcontinent—as Dusshera in India and Dasain in Nepal, the festival celebrates the goddess's victory over evil. Women go to each other's homes and receive gifts. Bangles and bracelets are as popular as chocolates and flowers in the West—perhaps the reason why Babita accepted my gift as a matter of course.

You never know where you will find her

In Buddhist legend, a dakini reveals herself in the most innocuous and surprising of places. Since you don't know where you can find her, you try different things till you become sensitized to her clues. Through a variety of practices including worshipping the elements of water and fire, through mantras and rituals, an evolved practitioner can make a connection with a dakini. Her grace can make things happen in a jiffy. Most scholars say that dakini worship is the shortest path to spiritual evolution.

The Kumari is not a dakini, although she could be. The three erstwhile kingdoms of Nepal each have a kumari or young goddess. One morning, I decided to visit Patan's Kumari. One of the film crew's extras knows the family and walks me to her house. It is traditional to take gifts for the Kumari so we stop by and buy some Horlicks, a drink.

The Kumari's home is large and rambling in the centre of town. We are ushered into an anteroom where we sit cross-legged and wait. The Kumari's father carries her in and seats her on the throne. She is five years old. I offer her my gift. For a few seconds, the Kumari is preoccupied with opening the lid of the bottle. She plays with it, turning it up and down. I bend and prostrate—touching the ground with my forehead as Hindus are wont to do at temples. On cue, the Kumari puts some vermilion powder on my forehead. Manoj, the man who brought me, also bows to her, offers her some cash and leans forward as she applies powder on his forehead. He prostrates himself before her again and she sits still, with dignity, accepting our reverence as a matter of course.

I am told that in order for a girl to be chosen as a kumari, she has to have certain facial features and marks; that she should exhibit composure in large crowds and have a certain 'feminine energy' in her. There it is again: this phrase. Unexplainable perhaps, but easily felt. I feel it in the Kumari's presence. Am I getting sensitized—getting better at spotting a dakini?

The dance of the Durgas

That night, the whole town gathers near Durbar square for the Nava Durga dance: the nine forms of the goddess. At 7:30, a long line of dancers wearing robes and masks come dancing down the streets. Predictably, given that these are ancient rituals, the dancing goddesses are all men. Somehow, in spite of the fact that I am a feminist who strongly supports the #metoo movement, this channelling of female energy by men pleases me. It feels less like a man taking away a woman's job and more like a man trying to worship and channel the divine feminine.

A crowd gathers to propitiate the goddesses. They walk down the long line of colourful masked figures, offering cash, fruits and flowers; touching their palms together in reverence. On impulse, I do the same. I walk up to each masked goddess, offer some cash like the others, and say 'You are my queen for ever and ever.' The goddess doesn't blink. Emboldened, I try to say it with feeling. I try to keep an open mind to feel the feminine energy swirling around me. I cannot spot a dakini but at least I know that she is there.

Seeing God in a grain of sand

Suddenly, Babita appears within the crowd. And then it dawns on me. I have seen her twice in two days in the most innocuous of places. I have been searching all over from a stranger with good feminine energy. Babita has been in front of me all along. Is she a dakini? Is she my dakini? What does this mean? Will she guide me to a better place?

Babita says in Hindi that she wants to take me to a special temple. Mute and obedient, I follow her. We walk silently through the dark streets. The sound of hammer beating metal follows us.

Patan is the place where bronze statues of all the Buddhist icons: Tara, Buddha, Avalokiteswara, all get made and shipped to temples across the world. There are rows of shops selling singing bowls, prayer beads and golden bronze statues. After praying at a shrine, we return to her shop. It is a wooden stall spread out on the lane behind Durbar Square. On impulse, I tell Babita that I want to buy as many goddess statues that I can get. She rummages through a black garbage bag underneath the wooden bench and pulls out small statues of yoginis, Kali, Durga, and to my shock and delight— a dakini in coital embrace with Heruka—just like at the Patan museum. They are small and cost 1,500 Nepali Rupees. Babita sells me 24 small idols and says that she wants to offer me one for free.

I pick the dakini who comes home with me.

Takeaway

Several books by Buddhists scholars talk about the "pure land of the dakini" and the "dakini's warm breath." These pure lands are not neccessarily literal but metaphorical and spiritual advances achieved through meditation, visualization and practice.

The book *The New Guide to Dakini Land: The Highest Yoga Tantra Practice of Vajrayogini* by Geshe Kelsang Gyato says, for instance, that there are different pure lands associated with different Buddhist goddesses such as Sukhavati and Tushita. But it is only in dakini's pure land that 'beings can receive teachings on the highest Yoga Tantra and put them into practice.'

One of the 'tricks' described in Gyato's book suggests that people can try to 'see' dakini by using the left side of their body a lot more than they do. This left-handed lineage can be practiced quite literally, by forcing yourself to use your left gaze, left hand and left leg.

I try to do this more often. I believe that it opens the right brain which is the emotional, imaginative, creative and intuitive side. It allows us to see and feel things that are linked to soul and spirit. If nothing else, it makes us ambidextrous, always a good thing.

15

Mathura: Dance of the Peacock

MY MOTHER AND MOTHER-IN-LAW are in a cycle-rickshaw together, trundling through the narrow, dusty, dirt-addled streets of Mathura. Beyond family weddings and pilgrimages, they rarely travel. Offer them a trip to Ananda in the Himalayas and they will raise a ruckus about its exorbitant prices. The Maldives and other beach resorts hold no appeal to them. Tell them to accompany you on a ten-day cruise through the Mediterranean and they will politely pass. Invite them for an all-expenses-paid trip to South Africa and they will enquire about vegetarian meals. Yet, here they are in Mathura to see a Yadav cowherd who held up Mount Govardhan with his little finger.

Mount Govardhan is a modest hill, not a mountain. And even if you charitably assume that all mythology originated in reality, there is nothing about this particular hill that exudes the kind of drama that it was part of. The story goes like this: when Indra, the king of the gods, unleashed his fury on this community through incessant rain, thunder and lightning, Krishna, the young cowherd, lifted Mount Govardhan on his finger and invited his entire clan to stand under the mountain to gain shelter. I stare at the mountain, trying to imagine the scene. Barring a few cows wandering amidst its rocky cliffs and bushes, there is nothing vaguely resembling a levitating mountain. Would have been cool if there were some sort of a sign, I think to myself, as proof that it was lifted by a little boy. Perhaps it could have been off-centre, dislodged a bit when Krishna set it back down. But there it sits, squat and rocky, a symbol of what is really a fantastic tale worthy of J.K. Rowling.

Then again, Krishna was the original Indian Harry Potter, except that he was 'way cooler' to use the current term. Where Harry was tentative, Krishna was bold—jumping on serpents, charming cows, dominating the animal kingdom, while dancing with beautiful women on moonlit nights. Barring perhaps Shiva, Krishna is the most charismatic god in Hinduism. Certainly, the 500 or so people thronging into the Banke Bihari temple in Vrindavan seem to think so.

The purveyor of joy

The term *Banke* (bent) Bihari (enjoyer) comes from the famous *tribangha* (or bent in three locations) pose that is often held by Krishna: in sculptures and paintings. Certainly, the idol standing in front of us has a gentle S-shape that Odissi dance and Indian aesthetics view as the height of beauty and sensuality. It isn't easy to hold—I tried. The temple is located in Vrindavan.

Legend has it that the image of Radha and Krishna (as a couple) was too beautiful to behold so Lord Krishna was asked to merge into one, 'like clouds with thunder and lightning', to use the words of Swami Haridas who consecrated the temple. So it is that only one idol stands in the temple, and even this one is shown to devotees for short spans of time. 'If you stare at the image for too long, you will fall unconscious,' says one worshipper to me, not following his own advice as he stands on tiptoe staring at the Lord.

To look at an idol and see divinity requires humility, subjugation of the ego and imagination—bhavana, as I said before. I am not there yet. I see merely a marble statue of the flute-playing Krishna that is not that different from all the other idols that I have seen in other temples. The call of this land is another matter. Mathura is one of the seven sacred lands or *kshetra*s where a cosmic connection with the heavens guarantees mere mortals moksha or release from human bondage. The others are Ayodhya, Haridwar, Kashi, Kanchipuram, Ujjain, Puri and Dwaraka. Mathura is special because it is associated with Krishna's youth: places where he was born, grew up and came of age. Together they epitomize a pastoral form of Hinduism, beloved to the people of this area.

Ram or Krishna?

Hinduism is ostentatious, flamboyant and glitzy, with a focus on food, family and feel-good stories. It is open, public, rambunctious, full of festivals and free of guilt. For many, it is above all a religion grounded in stories.

For those unfamiliar with the Hindu pantheon of gods, the triumvirate of Brahma the creator, Vishnu the protector and Shiva the destroyer of evil are probably a good place to start. Each of these gods has a consort. Brahma's is Saraswati, the goddess of learning, who also happens to be his daughter, but that is another story altogether. Vishnu's spouse is Lakshmi, the goddess of wealth. And Shiva is married to Parvati, also called Uma.

Under this broad umbrella are the other gods. Ganesh and Muruga are sons of Shiva and Parvati. The ever-popular Rama and Krishna are considered Vishnu's avatars. Some believe that Shakti, the goddess, exists above all the gods as the supreme power. Shakti takes many forms—the dark Kali, a favourite of tantrics, and the fierce Durga, who rides a tiger.

Vishnu the protector is said to have taken nine of the ten incarnations or avatars to save the world, the tenth being the one that will appear to end Kali Yuga. One of my favourites is Krishna—the blue-hued god who plays the flute, charms the women and steals the butter he loves so much. Another is the ever-dutiful prince, Rama, who renounced his kingdom to preserve his father's honour. According to Hindus, Vishnu's last avatar will be that of a horseman (Kalki) who will appear on a white horse signifying the end of the world as we know it. Hindus are still waiting for the Kalki avatar (incarnation) to appear. Climate change may well induce this pralayam or watery end to all species.

It is easy to descend into the parlour game of who is better—Rama or Krishna. Rama commands extraordinary loyalty—from his wife, siblings and an army of monkeys per mythology, and human devotees in the current day. Mahatma Gandhi died uttering the name of Rama, and in North India, a common greeting is to say 'Ram Ram' instead of 'Hello'. Of course, it is equally common to say, 'Radhe Radhe' or 'Jai Shree Krishna,' so perhaps I am asking the wrong question. Whether you like Rama or Krishna depends on you, your emotions, proclivities and stage of life.

I have to say, I find Rama a bit too perfect for my taste. I much prefer Krishna, who seems far more human. Krishna's boyhood pranks are fodder for many a bedtime story. My grandmother used to tell me how Krishna used to gang up with his friends and hide the clothes of the *gopika*s while they bathed in the river, about how he and his friends used to form a human pyramid to climb aloft and take the butter pots stored high up in the kitchen and about how Krishna used to play sweet music on his flute and enthral everyone who heard, young and old.

Krishna's flute, believed to have been blessed by Goddess Saraswati herself, is the epitome of divine transcendent music that touched all animals and humans.

Krishna killed tons of bad guys with his bare hands, yes. He also loved and married several women—Radha, his first love, Rukmini, his wife, and Satyabhama, the one who helped him defeat the demon Narakasura. All of this happened on this very land that I am treading: Braj Bhoomi, it is called. The land where Krishna grew up and played in.

Braj or Vraj refers to pastures, and Braj Bhasha is a softer form of Hindi. Krishna roamed these pastures, bathing in the 1,000 or so *kunds* or water wells, and dancing in the 137 forests and glens that dot this area of 3,800 square kilometres spanning three states: Uttar Pradesh, Rajasthan and Haryana. The land of Krishna is pastoral, or used to be. Its people are closely linked to nature or used to be. They have a zest for life, as seen in the different festivals that are celebrated with gusto here. Each district is known for a particular sweet: Mathura's peda, Agra's petha, Kasganj's soan papdi, Nauhjheel's malpua, Raya's soan halwa, Iglas's chamcham, and a variety of milk sweets. I sample them all as I visit the dozens of temples in the area.

Bringing God to arm's length

The Keshav Dev temple stands on the exact spot where Krishna was born—in an underground prison, according to legend. The Yamuna river is a stone's throw away. The original temple is ancient, but was destroyed by a series of Muslim rulers, including, in the end, Aurangzeb. The current temple was built in only 1965. We climb up dozens of steps to a rather kitschy exhibit of Krishna's birth. Each room has a section of the story, which culminates in Vasudev, the father, carrying his infant across the Yamuna river to save his son's life.

We leave the temple complex to drive to Gokul. Unlike Krishna, we cannot cross the river Yamuna, which is deep and severely polluted. Instead, we take the long route, which takes half an hour. Magnificent humped cattle that belong to the Bos indicus species dot the roads and fields all along the way.

The temple in Gokul feels new. Inside, a shrewd priest offers us a variety of 'packages' to help us gain good fortune through prayer. This then is the big contradiction: holy men who barter and negotiate with devotees to route the God's blessings for the highest price. We refused his offer and simply pray to the now-familiar image of Lord Krishna and Radha. Deprived of his commission, the priest proceeds to tell us stories about Krishna's life in the area.

These Hindu myths serve one powerful purpose—they make the gods accessible by portraying them with 'human' flaws and foibles. Krishna's mischief, Ganesha's fondness for food, Shiva's anger, Brahma's arrogance, Sita's forbearance and Parvati's strong maternal instinct weren't just storytelling devices made up by the ancient saints to hold their audiences. They brought the gods down to earth and into the hearts of the devout. Any schoolchild can

relate to Krishna's penchant for stealing butter. Any mother can
relate to Parvati's dilemma when her son runs away from home in
a fit of anger. Any gourmand can relate to Ganesha who ate his fill
at a feast and then packed a few snacks for the road. The modern-
day metrosexual man can certainly relate to Krishna's fondness for
grooming, his sandal-paste massages, golden robes, glittering jewels
and fragrant garlands.

Acceptance of extremities

For me, Hindu gods and deities serve as a wonderful illustration of
the fact that the divine can coexist with the mundane. Anger can
coexist with serenity as it does in Shiva; maternal love can coexist
with maternal wrath as it does in Parvati. The same person can be
both playful and profound as is exemplified by Krishna.

Perhaps Krishna's most significant role is that of the charioteer
who revealed the Gita to the warrior Arjuna as he mulled over a
dilemma on the battlefield. The Bhagavad Gita is a virtual treatise
on yoga, and in my mind, one of the most important books a yoga
student can read and digest. There are eighteen chapters covering
the four types of yoga—bhakti yoga, raja yoga, gnana yoga and
karma yoga. In my limited understanding of the Gita, what I
find fascinating is how relevant it is to my modern-day daily life.
It answers many of the questions that vex me today. How can we
deal with the grief that assaults us when something bad happens
to a loved one? What is a good way to prevent being disappointed
and depressed when you don't achieve what you aspire to? The Gita
answers these and many other questions.

Be like a lotus leaf

The Gita is both specific and poetic about detachment. Lord Krishna tells Arjuna: 'Therefore, without attachment do you always perform the action that should be done, for by performing action without attachment does man reach the Supreme.' Fair enough. But how? And then the Gita gets poetic. It urges us to be like a lotus leaf, which shrugs off the water that falls on it and remains unaffected—*padma patrami vambhasa*.

Hinduism, in that sense, is like a spicy concoction. There is the masala made up of tangential ideas, each one layered to embrace mundane, minutiae, materialistic aspirations as well as profound spiritual goals. Hindus go on pilgrimages to heal themselves from life-threatening cancers, they attach makeshift red cradles on holy trees to conceive a child and they also visit temples for transactional goals: to win some money, to get a promotion or for an American visa. Elastic and flexible, Hinduism was an easy religion to grow up in. No guilt for one thing. Very little fear. And the opportunity to negotiate with God. During exams, for instance, countless school children have a devout if business-like relationship with God. I used to do this. Before important exams, I would go to the temple and engage in some serious bargaining. Good grades, and I would circle the temple 101 times. Medium grades, and it would be less effort: maybe I would break a coconut. For stretch goals, I offered to go on a pilgrimage.

In that sense, Hinduism is anything but holier than thou. It doesn't make you guilty or afraid. It offers options from a host of forgiving and accepting gods.

Beads, flowers and food

The business of worship at any temple begins before sunrise. Here in Mathura, priests go to the river, Yamuna—ravaged by sewage as it is—to collect holy water. By sunrise, bustling processions of devotees make their way to the dozen or so temples that dot this landscape. They carry flowers and incense, milk and honey, butter and pedas—Krishna's favourite sweet. Inside the temple, the tools of the trade are cleaned and readied. There are lamps, ritual water containers, prayer beads, trays containing flowers, fruits and sacred food. Bells are rung, inducing fevered piety amongst the thronging crowds.

Explaining Hinduism in a sequential, logical fashion is nearly impossible. It is rambling, tangential and sometimes contradictory: more like a montage of images rather than a hierarchical or a linear story. The esoteric philosophies of tantra, vedanta and yoga contrast with simple and beautiful daily rituals that make sense even to a child. The religion is not congregational, even though people come together in temples—sometimes visiting the same temple multiple times a day. To paraphrase Walt Whitman, Hinduism is large; it contains multitudes.

It is evenfall when we begin the drive back to Delhi. We have missed seeing Vrindavan's famed widows. Some 10,000 of them live in the city and gain succour and sustenance through songs in praise of Krishna. We haven't even visited all of Krishna's temples. But we have met countless *Braj Vasis* (residents) who are convinced that they live in the blue god's homeland. We have visited the places that are in Indian history and mythology books. We have eaten well and visited a number of Krishna temples.

For now, this is enough.

Takeaway

Mathura influenced me in an interesting way. I started reading the Ramayana after visiting it. Like I said, I was in two minds about Rama. He seemed too perfect. He was the obedient son, willing to forgo his kingdom to preserve his father's word. When his stepmother, Kaikeyi, made his father banish him to the forest for fourteen years, he had only kind words for her. Although he was a superlative archer and swordsman, he wasn't slave to the passions of a warrior. Rama was a just king, loyal husband, dutiful son, kind brother, generous friend ... I mean, the man could do no wrong.

After returning to Mathura, I picked up the Ramayana yet again. This time, perhaps because I had experienced an overdose of Krishna, I began to feel more sympathetic towards Rama. I began to understand why Lord Rama struck a chord with so many people. I learned his flaws. I could identify with his humanity.

Rama was balancing many constituencies: his subjects, his family, his conscience. His moral struggles mirrored my conflicts: choosing between duty and obligation, between people's perceptions and own desires. As a woman, I do this every day.

Mathura gave me another unexpected benefit—it made me fall in love with cows all over again. After writing about cows (in my previous book), it was amazing to say magnificent native breeds of cows in Mathura and Vrindavan. They occupied the streets and the minds of people.

They occupied my mind and dreams long after I left Mathura–Vrindavan.

16

Conclusion

WHEN I BEGAN THIS journey, it seemed like a simple, fairly obvious exercise: travel to temples, eat good food, make peace with your faith. Repeat.

What I hadn't bargained for was how my faith would touch me, the questions it would raise and answer. Hinduism is a vast, magnificent religion—deep and mysterious, compassionate and complex. This pilgrimage reintroduced me to my faith and offered me beneficial practices that I adopted into my daily life.

Religion is an inheritance and a choice. I was born Hindu and I like the religion enough not to choose another. But being a proud Hindu is something that I wriggle away from. In Goa, a Hindu Member of Parliament told me that he was a 'proud Hindu within the confines of [his] home, but outside, [he was] an Indian first and a Hindu last'. That sounds about right to me.

When I travelled across India, I discovered the power of faith and also its prejudices. Religion is one measure of identity, but it cannot be the only one, especially in a land where several of the world's major religions thrive. No matter what our faith, we need to reach beyond religious divides and embrace our common humanity. To me, that is the hope and pleasure of living in a multicultural pluralistic society like India.

The cantonment area of Bengaluru, where I live, is populated by Hindus, Muslims and Christians. Family Supermarket, where I get my groceries, is run by Moplah Muslims from Malabar. They are pious—closing shop at 4 p.m. every Friday. Equally, they are friendly, efficient, and they don't differentiate between the Hindu and Muslim households that they service.

Kerala, a state that I love, is full of Christians, whose families resemble my own: the link between generations, the unsparing gossip about scandals, all passed around with a tinge of self-righteousness at weddings, the obsession with food, the code of honouring your word.

We may pray to Jesus, Rama or Allah, but at the end of the day, we are all children of God. We each have many identities. Religion is one, but there are others. We are each of us son/daughter, spouse, sibling, friend and professional. I tend to identify myself through my work, and I would suspect that most of my readers are the same way.

I am attracted to the beauty of Hindu rituals, to its pujas, pomp and circumstance. At the same time, I like Christian gospel music, Buddhist philosophy, Sufi poetry, Jewish literature, Sikh generosity,

Parsi identity. In India, we are lucky enough to be able to experience
them all, enjoy them all.

So yes, I am Hindu. I like my faith. But please, that's not all I am.

And now if you'll excuse me, I have a frig-full of prasadams
(sacred food) that I need to eat.

Index

Padma-purana, 250

Palani Temple. *See* Arulmigu
    Dhandayuthapani Temple

Palani, the oldest Jam in the
    world, 81–103

palayan thodan, 183

Palghat Iyers, 239, 240–41

Paltrow, Gwyneth, 13

Panchamritham (or five nectars),
    98–102

Parasurama, 119

Parfitt, Tudor, 112, 129–30

Pasquale, 30

Patan, Nepal, 248–57

Patanjali, 38, 101

Perunthachan, 184

Pichwai paintings, 244

pilgrimages (*tirtha yatra*), 17,
    179, 265

Pilot Baba, 220

Plato, 38

Poets of the Fall, 165

politics of religion, 180–81

pollution and purity, 31–32

prasadam, 1–2, 12, 17–18, 56,
    98, 111, 135, 138, 140,
    152–53, 168–69, 194, 200,
    204, 244

Puranas, 24, 97

Puri, Harihar, 220

Puri, Odisha, 194–215

Puri, Somnath (Somnath Baba),
    220, 224, 226–27

Purushottama, 207, 213–14

Qandozi, Sheikh Ibrahim, 75

Raas Lila, 161

rabdi, 169

Radha Damodar temple, Jaipur,
    168, 169

Radha Krishna cult, 160–61

Radha Vinodhi Lal temple,
    Jaipur, 168

Raghava Bhatta, 214

Raghunandana, *Prayaschitta
    Tattva*, 32–33

Rahabi, David, 125

Rajaraja, Ganga king, 212

Raktabeeja, 25

Ram Das, Guru, 189

Ram Dass (Richard Alpert), 108

Rama, 136, 183, 261–62, 267

Ramakrishna, 46

Ramananda, 52

Ramanattam, 183

Ramanuja, 38, 67, 212, 213

Ramayana, 267

Ramen Girl, The, 198

Rameswaram, 195

Rath Yatra, 201–02

rational and spiritual, divide, 29

Ratner, Chana, 130

Ravi Varma, Raja, 25

Ravidas, 161

Rayalu, Jagannatha Panditha;
    Ganga Lahiri, 52–53

religion, religious belief, 29–30,
    71, 76

    hypocrisies and double
        standards, 178–79

    and identity, 128, 269

Acknowledgements

FOR THEIR SENSE AND sensibility about everything Indian, for opening doors all over India, and for ideas and contacts throughout the project, I wish to thank the following people:

Puri: Nitin Pai; Aditya Dash; Jay Panda. Mr Panda's office, particularly Jyoti Ghose, connected me to Suresh Chandra Mohapatra and Sudip Chatterjee at the Jagannath Puri temple. Anyone interested in Odisha should read the excellent *Cultural Heritage of Orissa* series published by the State Level Vyasakabi Fakir Mohan Smruti Sansad, Bhubaneshwar. I found the 1,000-page special volume on Puri engrossing.

Madurai: K.S. Bharath and his mother gave me insights into the culture of Madurai; Selva helped me with local arrangements.

Ananth and Ramya Nageshwaran of Singapore for the temple trip through Tamil Nadu with a Tamil scholar So. So. Me. Sundaram (which is how he says and spells it—in the Tamil fashion).

Amritsar: Amuleek Singh, Gagan Kaur and Rasil Ahuja.

Kashi: Rudra Chatterjee; Edward Oakley; Rajesh Kumar of Obeetee Carpets; Deepa Krishnan of Magic India Tours; Shashank Singh of Hotel Ganges View.

Ajmer: Manish Sabharwal and Shailendra Agarwal.

Kerala: My in-laws, Padma and (late) V. Ramachandran, were (and are) the road to everything Kerala.

Mumbai: Deepa Krishnan; Yael and Ralphy Jhirad; Hanna Shahpurkar; Nissim Moses of Tel Aviv; Naresh Fernandes; Vikram Doctor; Kishore Mariwala.

Goa: The late great Wendell Rodricks and his vast network of contacts in this beautiful state.

This book sprung from a series I wrote for *Mint*. I wish to thank R. Sukumar, the editor of *HT Media*, for his support, and Sidin Vadukut for his editing expertise.

I am blessed to have a great group of friends who serve as my sounding board and generator of ideas: Namma Adda, Salon, Ivory, BIC PC, TWC, BWC, N&N, MHC... all are real (not WhatsApp) groups who inspire and engage me. To all these friends, I say, thank you.

My mother, Padma Narayanaswamy, has been the biggest influence on this book. She took her somewhat reluctant family—my father, brother and me—to countless temples, the strength of her faith sailing through our sullen mutterings. This continues to this day.

Shyam, Priya, Harsha and Chakku—for those trips to Kollur, Kerala and beyond. Family, faith and food—always.

This book is dedicated to my sister-in-law, Lakshmi, and my brother-in-law, Krishnan. They along with their children—Nithya and Arvind—are our fellow travellers through life, food and faith. When Nithya brought her new husband, Ryan, to India, we took him—of course—to Hindu temples. We fed the newlyweds prasadams and conducted Hindu rituals for their happy married life. So yes, food and faith are intertwined in our family. This book is a tribute to those many pilgrimages that we took together, but also to who they are. All five are compassionate physicians who epitomize the best of their profession. Their job is their religion and they practice it with devotion. It gives them strength and succor, which they in turn, pass along to a vast and ever-expanding group of family and friends.

But in the end, this book is for Siddhartha and all the children who come after him in the family.

Ranju and Malu: this will sound corny, but love, light and faith always—and yes, I think you will discover faith sometime in your life. Thanks to the people in this family, if nothing else.

For R, who dislikes public displays of affection, let me just say, I could not have done this (or pretty much anything else) without you.

My agent, Michelle Tessler, took the book and steered it through to its current state. For that, I am grateful.

This book landed in the hands of Ananya Borgohain at HarperCollins. She asked the right questions, made appropriate suggestions and vastly improved the book. I also wish to thank the following people at HarperCollins: Mriga Maithel and Shreya Lall who edited and proofread the manuscript with meticulousness, care and sensitivity. Thank you, Krishan Chopra, for publishing the book.